IMAGES
of America

MILLBURY

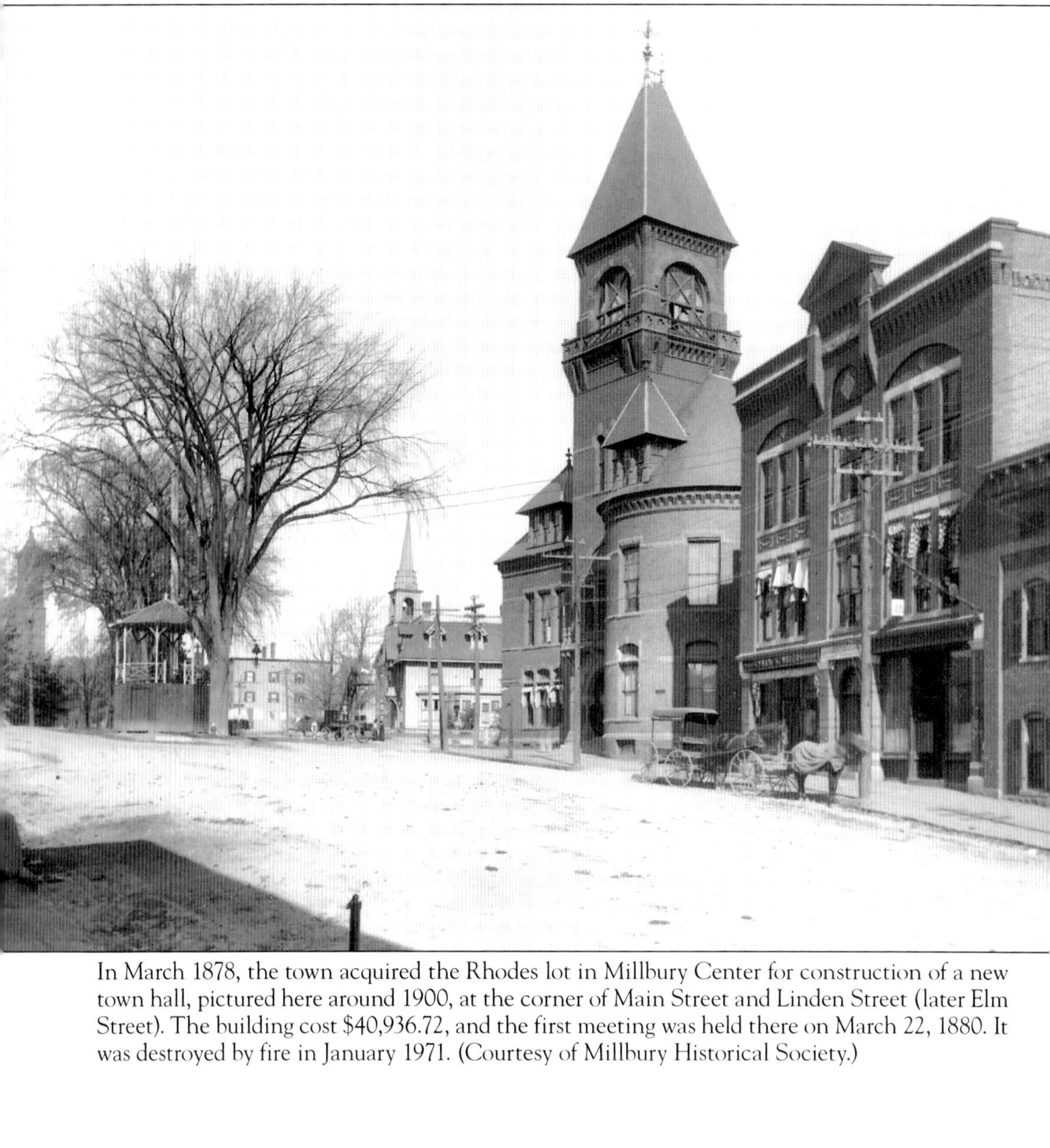

In March 1878, the town acquired the Rhodes lot in Millbury Center for construction of a new town hall, pictured here around 1900, at the corner of Main Street and Linden Street (later Elm Street). The building cost $40,936.72, and the first meeting was held there on March 22, 1880. It was destroyed by fire in January 1971. (Courtesy of Millbury Historical Society.)

On the Cover: Workers at the Watson-Williams Company are shown in the company's manufacturing facility on River Street in this c. 1913 photograph. Founded by Hudson Warren Hakes in 1879, the company manufactured shuttles and heddles for the weaving industry. In 1909, the business acquired the assets of the J.H. Williams Manufacturing Company of Utica, New York, and within a few years, had the second-largest payroll in Millbury. Today, the historic mill along the Blackstone River houses a variety of small businesses. (Courtesy of Millbury Historical Society.)

IMAGES
of America

MILLBURY

Chris Sinacola

ARCADIA
PUBLISHING

ISBN 978-0-7385-9266-4

Published by Arcadia Publishing
Charleston, South Carolina

Printed in the United States of America

Library of Congress Control Number: 2012930668

For all general information, please contact Arcadia Publishing:
Telephone 843-853-2070
Fax 843-853-0044
E-mail sales@arcadiapublishing.com
For customer service and orders:
Toll-Free 1-888-313-2665

Visit us on the Internet at www.arcadiapublishing.com

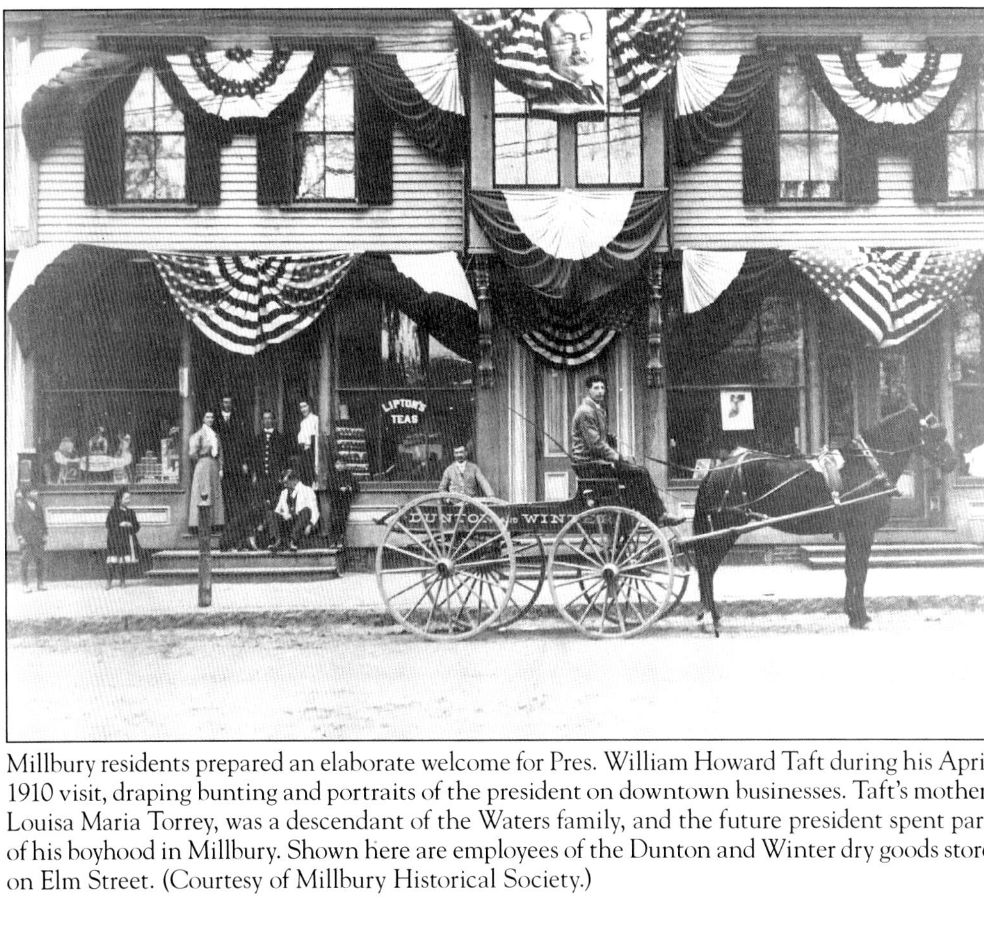

Millbury residents prepared an elaborate welcome for Pres. William Howard Taft during his April 1910 visit, draping bunting and portraits of the president on downtown businesses. Taft's mother, Louisa Maria Torrey, was a descendant of the Waters family, and the future president spent part of his boyhood in Millbury. Shown here are employees of the Dunton and Winter dry goods store on Elm Street. (Courtesy of Millbury Historical Society.)

Contents

ACKNOWLEDGMENTS

Every project that illuminates the past depends upon a long chain of contributors, many whose names cannot be reclaimed from the pages of any history. Millbury is doubly fortunate to have been born from Sutton, which has a long history of carefully preserving its past, and to have had residents who established an extraordinary portrait of the town a century ago with publication of the *Centennial History of the Town of Millbury*.

The 1905 town meeting named George F. Chase, John C. Crane, Ira N. Goddard, George W. Mallalieu, and the Rev. George A. Putnam to a committee to organize a centennial celebration. Later members included Henry W. Carter, Henry A. Phillips, and Henry W. Aiken. These men oversaw efforts by many others, who compiled vital statistics and genealogies, committed family and business histories to paper, and captured extraordinary images of the townspeople and landmarks of 1913. To these men and women of a century ago, Millbury residents owe a debt that can only be repaid by chronicling our times for the benefit of those a century hence. Happily, the Millbury Historical Society—and in particular its president, Frank Gagliardi—has continued the effort to preserve the town's past. Many of the photographs in this volume come from the society's archives.

Since 2008, the Millbury Bicentennial Committee has overseen planning for the town's 200th birthday. This book would not have happened without them, especially the leadership of William Kane Sr. and Roger Desrosiers and the technical advice of Paul Raffa. Other contributors include Rich Hamilton, Mary Lou Mulhane, Robert and Barbara Pearson, Roland and Kay Lachance, Richard and Nancy Hagstrom, Carol Vegnone Vulter, Paula Beauregard, Janice Fortin, and Jerilyn Stead. Special thanks go to Judy O'Connor, who provided photographs from the late Harold C. Kilmer; to Gerald K. Sortor, general manager at Buck Brothers; and to the librarians at the *Worcester Telegram & Gazette*, whose patient labors over decades proved an invaluable resource for the history behind many of these photographs.

Finally, thanks go to my wife, Nancy, and my children, for their advice, counsel, and patience throughout this project.

INTRODUCTION

In a simple burial ground at the eastern foot of Grass Hill, surrounded by meadows, orchards, and streams, stand the monuments to many of those who, two centuries ago, gave new identity to a growing industrial community known as Millbury. Here lie many of the farmers, soldiers, clerks, manufacturers, and shopkeepers who, as members of Sutton's North Parish, had long petitioned for a town of their own, a wish that was granted on June 11, 1813. By then, families with names as elemental as the landscape itself—Waters and Wood, Marble and Stockwell—had been farming the fertile soils of central Massachusetts for a half-century and more.

And, by 1813, the men of Sutton's North Parish had done more than their share in establishing American independence. Col. Jonathan Holman, Lt. Asa Waters, and many others—carrying weapons fashioned by the Waters family in Armory Village—had answered the alarms at Lexington and Concord in April 1775. They had served through the long years of war, until King George's redcoats had withdrawn from the new nation.

Much as they had tamed the British, these men and their families now turned their attention to harnessing the natural resources of a town truly their own. Gen. Caleb Burbank, a leading citizen of the new town, suggested the name Millbury, one as unassuming as the residents themselves. Like the West Millbury Cemetery, Millbury itself occupied a middle ground in 1813. It shared history with bucolic highlands of Sutton and Oxford to its south and west and resembled in some measure the growing industrial powerhouse of Worcester to the north.

But Millbury was its own town now and pursued an independent course. Yankee ingenuity, immigrant labor, and the blessings of waterpower and central location meant a leading role in the industrialization of the Blackstone Valley and the building of America. Irish canal workers opened the Blackstone Canal in 1828, helping the town get its products more quickly to markets in Worcester, Providence, and beyond. Railroads supplanted the canal a decade later, offering faster service and expanding opportunities for residents and workers.

Mills and workshops on the Ramshorn and Singletary Streams had for decades turned out shoes, shingles, and paper. The Waters family armories supplied the young American Army with weapons. As the town's industries and population grew throughout the 19th century, Millbury became dominated by mills, which turned out countless quantities of fabric, shuttles, thread, and machine tools.

Lured by the favorable location and a ready supply of labor, brothers John, Charles, and Richard Buck moved their business from Worcester to Millbury during the Civil War. They located on the Dorothy Stream and produced the finest chisels in the nation—recognized with blue ribbons at the World's Columbian Exposition in Chicago in 1893.

On Tainter Hill, Moses D. Garfield, who never joined the Army or took up arms, did his part for the Union by perfecting a technique for domestic production of porcelain shuttle eyes critical to the weaving industry. Garfield's work enabled the mills of the North to keep the Union Army properly clothed during the war—in a sense helping to stitch the fabric of the nation back together.

As Millbury grew, it took advantage of the world's labor, welcoming newcomers from Canada and Europe. Roman Catholic parishes were formed for Irish and French Canadian communities. The public schools grew.

As Millbury neared its centennial, the children and grandchildren of those first families took care to mark their progress with four days of celebrations, including historical exhibitions, children's games, concerts, and a parade. On Tuesday evening, June 10, a massive bonfire was ignited on Burbank Hill. The next day, Wednesday, June 11, 1913, which was 100 years to the day since the town's founding, former president William Howard Taft, a descendant of the Waters and Torrey families, delivered a speech from the steps of town hall.

But the residents of Millbury a century ago left something more—a remarkable town chronicle that summarized the works and days since the town's founding. They captured, in words and photographs, the richness of Millbury's history. Thanks to such efforts, Millbury residents today know about Josiah Holbrook, a Connecticut native who, in 1826, delivered scientific lectures to farmers and merchants in Millbury, marking the start of the American lyceum movement. They know of Ira Goddard, who served 62 years as Millbury's town clerk, among the longest such tenures in the nation's history. And they can piece together the meteoric rise of Charles B. Atwood, who rose to architectural fame in New York and Chicago and died all too young. Today's residents also know much about the lives of the many thousands of less prominent citizens, the ones whose blue-collar occupations did so much to feed and clothe the nation in times of peace and supply its weapons in times of war.

The present volume builds on that foundation from a century ago, as supported by the efforts of local historians in the decades since. The families and individuals who have taken the time to preserve their stories and images have helped shape this work, although these pages can only reflect a small portion of the history that endures today in archives, scrapbooks, libraries, and vaults. By drawing upon printed histories, maps, and newspapers, it has been possible to further illuminate many of the images in this volume. It has been a pleasurable puzzle to establish the location of long-disappeared homes and mills and to offer readers views of landscapes and villages that have been rendered unrecognizable by decades of progress. Perhaps future historians will be inspired to continue the stories outlined here.

The departed of West Millbury Cemetery and the other resting places of Millbury include some who fell in battle, too many who did not survive the hazards of childbirth, epidemics, or the often harsh life of a farmhand or mill worker; and the many more fortunate ones, who lived long, full, and satisfying lives, enjoying the comforts of family and the fruits of their decades of labor. One cannot help but wonder what those past generations of Millbury residents would think could they see their town today. Surely, they would be shocked by a major shopping mall atop Woodchuck Hill, where Indian pathways once ran. At the same time, they would likely be comforted to see the Cunningham, Barrow, and Armsby Buildings downtown, still standing and still busy.

But it is in the mills that the generations who have called Millbury home would come together most surely. For, remarkably, against all economic odds, some of those mills are still spinning their wares. While some have disappeared or fallen silent, still others have successfully adapted themselves to new uses in the diversified and globalized economy of the early 21st century.

Those mill workers of 1913, hardworking men and women of modest means, would recognize themselves in the workers, blue-collar and white-collar alike, who carry on their legacy. A century ago, those workers paused from their labors just long enough to stare into the camera's lens and make a bit of history. They little realized that we a century later would be staring back, connecting their lives and labors to our own.

One

A New England Town

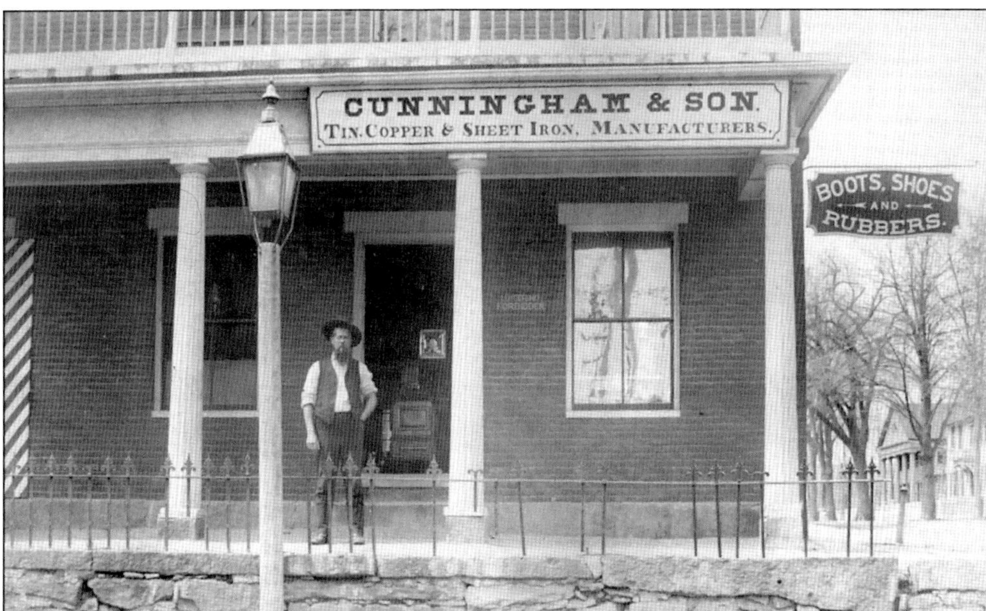

Winthrop R. Cunningham of Spencer came to Millbury in 1837 and ran a hardware store in the Randall Block in Millbury Center. His son R. Clark Cunningham is shown at the business in the early 1890s. This building burned in 1894, and after the elder Cunningham's death, his son carried on the business in the new Cunningham Block on the same site. (Courtesy of Robert and Barbara Pearson.)

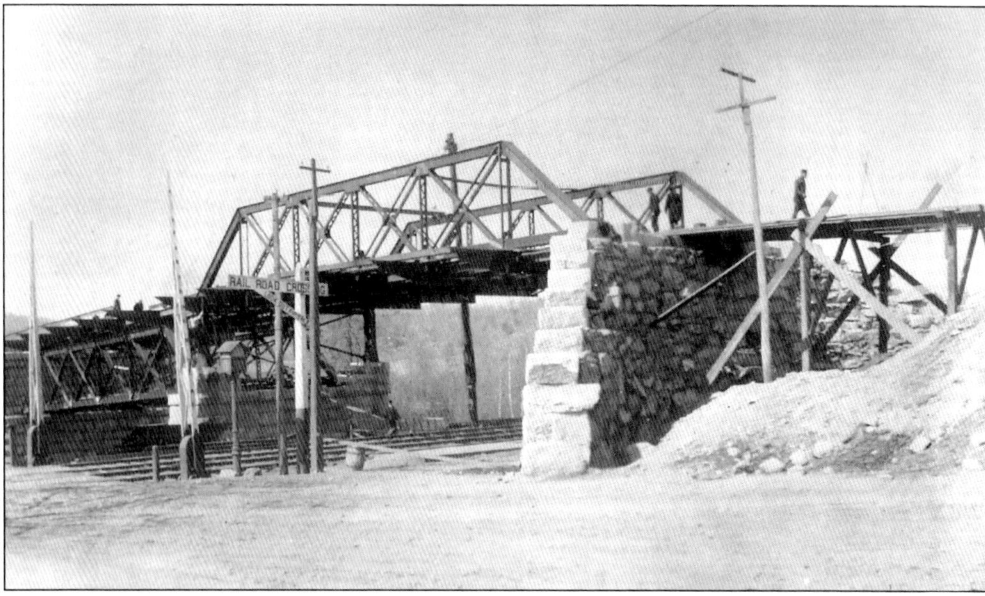

The Benjamin Gowing Bridge is the main crossing of the Blackstone River and railroad line near Millbury Center. Originally a grade-level crossing, it was named for a local man among the 3,000 British troops, who, in 1755, sailed to Nova Scotia and wrested that province from the French. In 1895, the span was replaced by the McGowan Bridge, shown under construction in the photograph above. The new structure spanned river and rails. Equipped with steel plates, it "sang" under traffic and served for nearly a century. The 1896 photograph below looks west toward Elm Court and shows the completed bridge. Dorothy Park, age 3, is in the left foreground. In 1983, the bridge was rebuilt, and selectmen voted unanimously to return to the Gowing name. (Both, courtesy of Millbury Historical Society.)

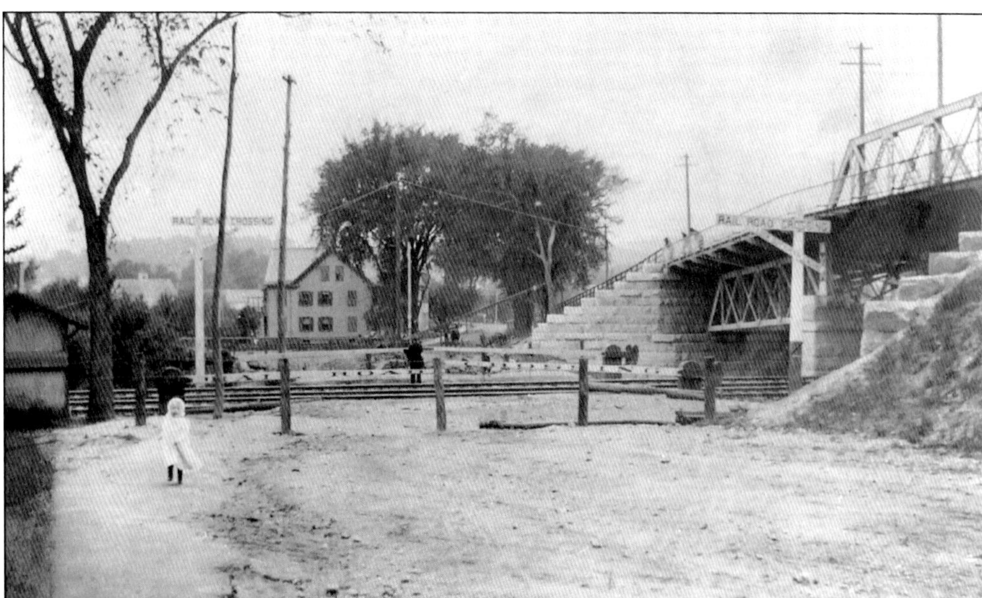

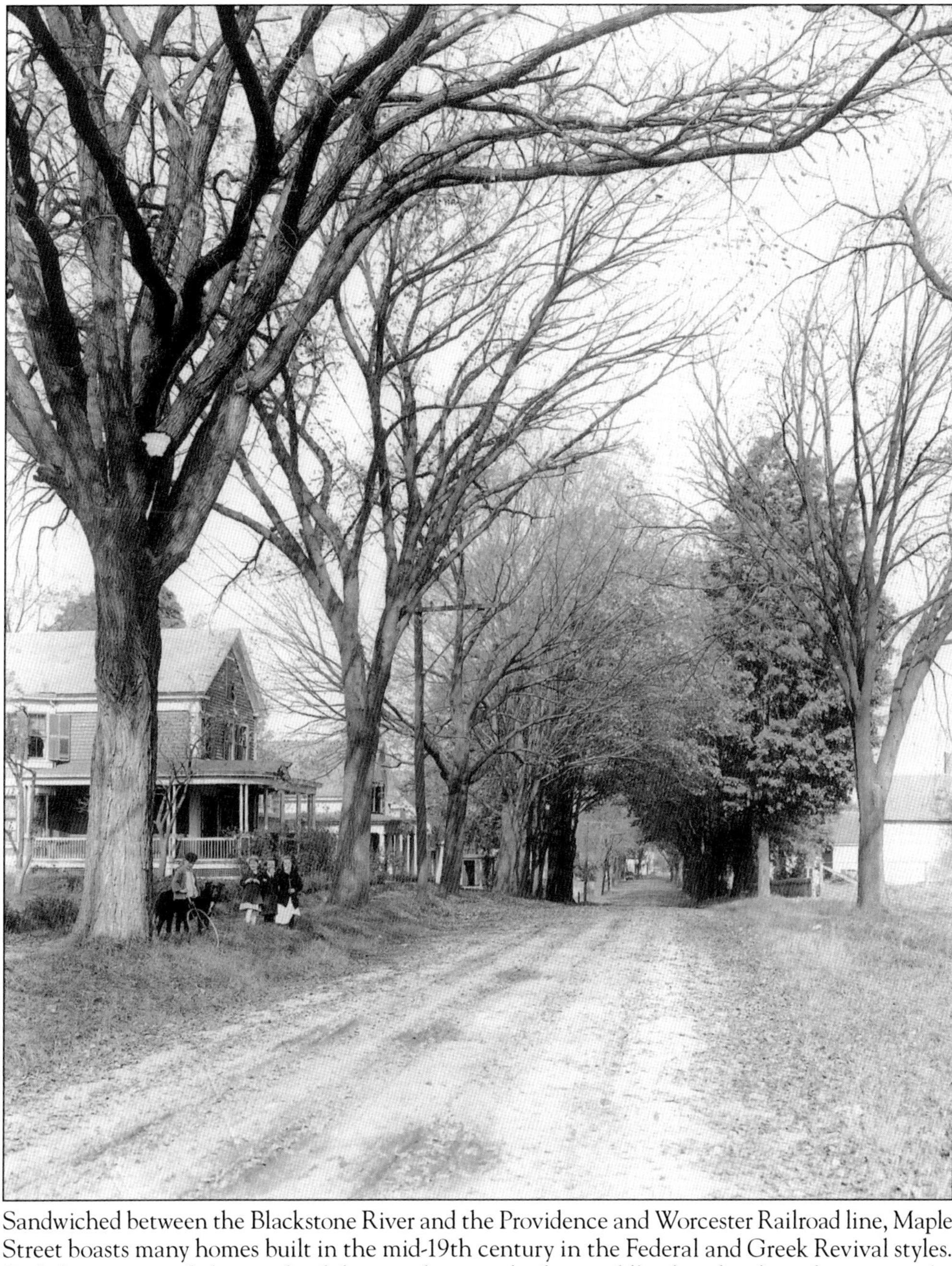

Sandwiched between the Blackstone River and the Providence and Worcester Railroad line, Maple Street boasts many homes built in the mid-19th century in the Federal and Greek Revival styles. Such homes served the needs of the merchant and other middle-class families who occupied a middle ground between the row houses that housed many mill workers and the luxurious mansions that belonged to mill owners. These homes were within easy walking distance of downtown mills, shops, and trolley and train lines. In March 1913, the town voted to allot $2,250 for the publication of a town history to mark its centennial, a project that included a great number of photographs of homes, mills, street scenes, and panoramas. In this scene, looking northeast along Maple Street, these children, with a bicycle and a dog, look on with curiosity as the photographer captures them for posterity. (Courtesy of Millbury Historical Society.)

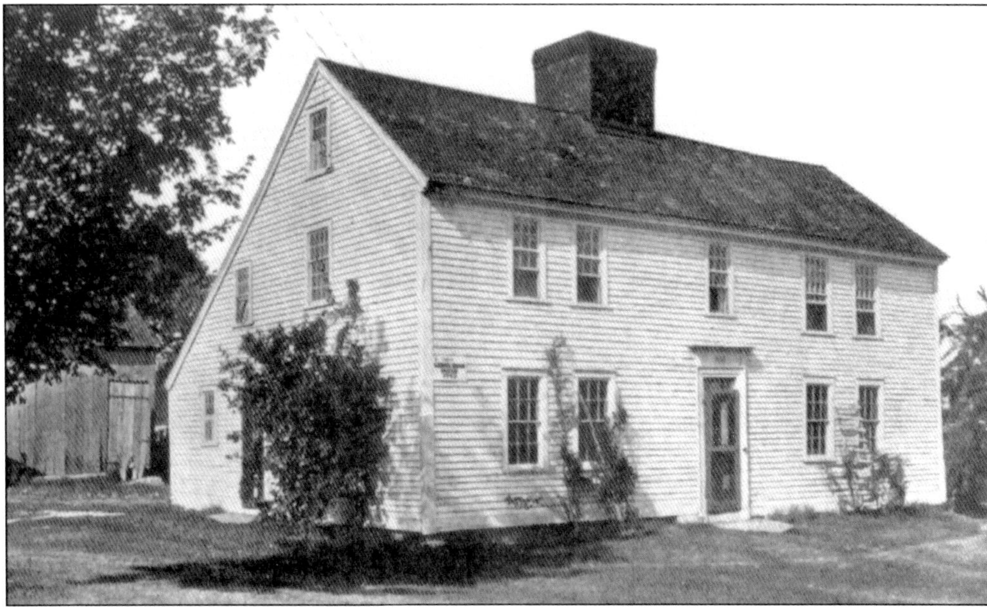

The Fuller-Trask-Davidson house was built about 1743, when Millbury was still part of Sutton. Owner Jonathan Fuller sold the house and 48 acres to Capt. Samuel Trask, a minuteman in the Revolutionary War. Located on West Main Street in West Millbury, it was, at the time this photograph was taken in 1913, the oldest surviving house in town. (Courtesy of the Hagstrom family.)

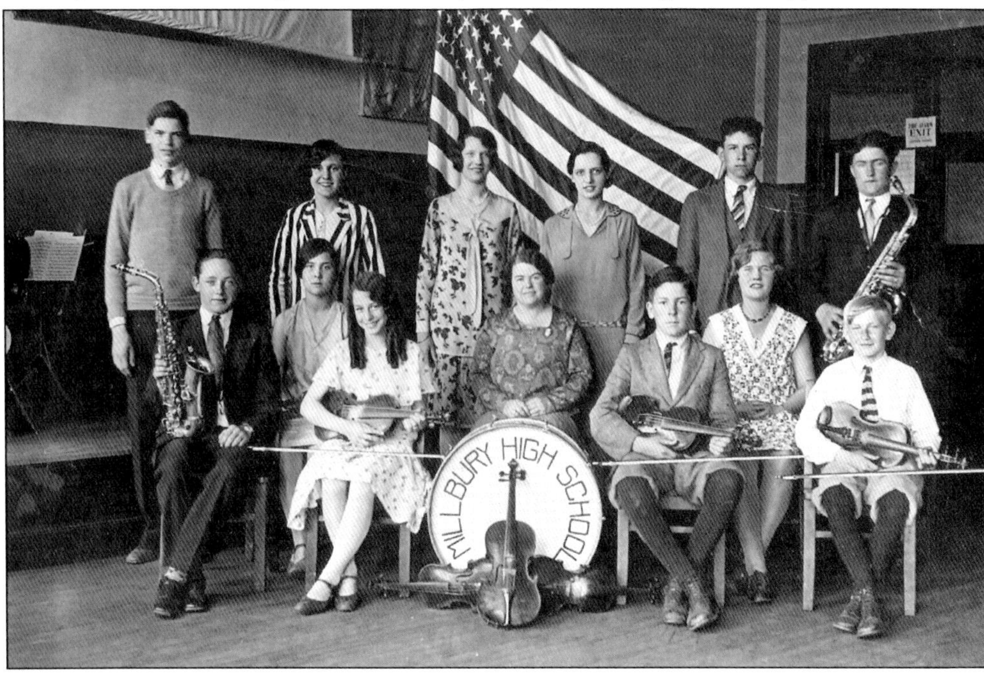

Millbury High School's first orchestra was formed in 1928. Seated in the first row on the far left is Ernest "Jack" Lachapelle, with his saxophone. Teacher and music instructor Bridget E. Connor is seated in the front row at center, behind the drum. In the back row, at the far left, is Robert White, and Elizabeth White is standing in the back row, fourth from the left. (Courtesy of Millbury Historical Society.)

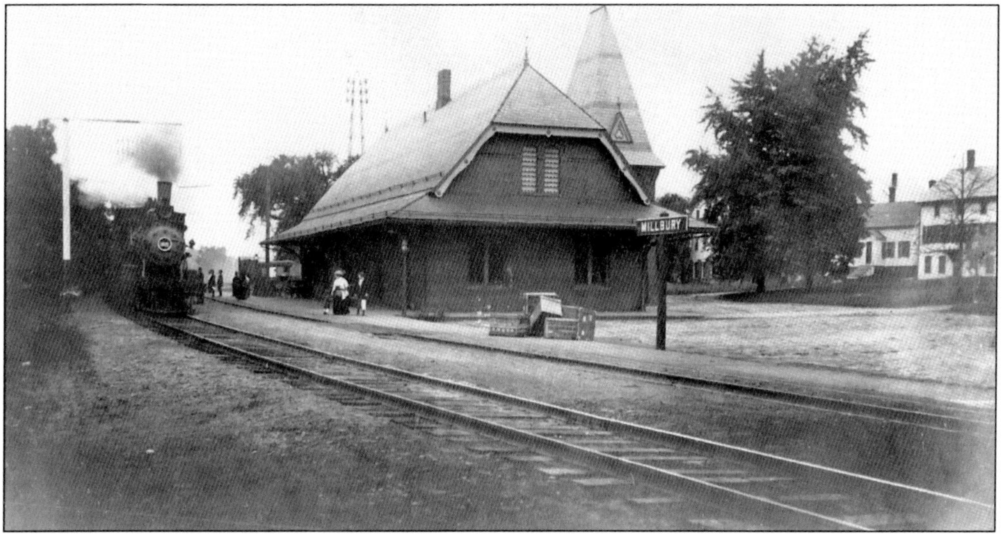

A family waits to meet the 4:20 p.m. train at the Providence and Worcester Railroad station near Millbury Center in this 1902 postcard view. The depot was located near one of the Crane & Waters mills, along what would later become River Street. The town's Senior Center, built to resemble a train depot, now stands on this site. (Courtesy of Millbury Historical Society.)

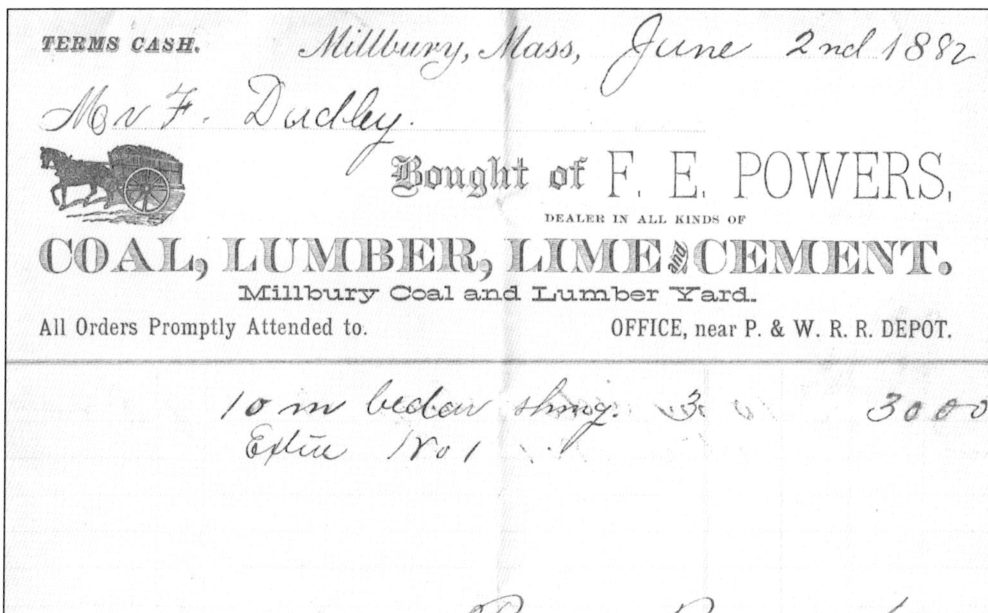

TERMS CASH. Millbury, Mass, June 2nd 1882

Mr F. Dudley.

Bought of F. E. POWERS,

DEALER IN ALL KINDS OF

COAL, LUMBER, LIME and CEMENT.

Millbury Coal and Lumber Yard.

All Orders Promptly Attended to. OFFICE, near P. & W. R. R. DEPOT.

10 m Cedar shing. 3 30 00

Extra No 1

Rec'd Payment

F. E. Powers.

5 m delivered.

Location has always been a key factor for businesses. Proprietor Frank E. Powers set up his coal and lumberyard near the Providence and Worcester depot for easy rail access. He served on the board of directors for the Millbury National Bank and was married to Laura Bell Lincoln on June 15, 1882, two weeks after concluding this sale to a Mr. Dudley. (Courtesy of Chris Sinacola.)

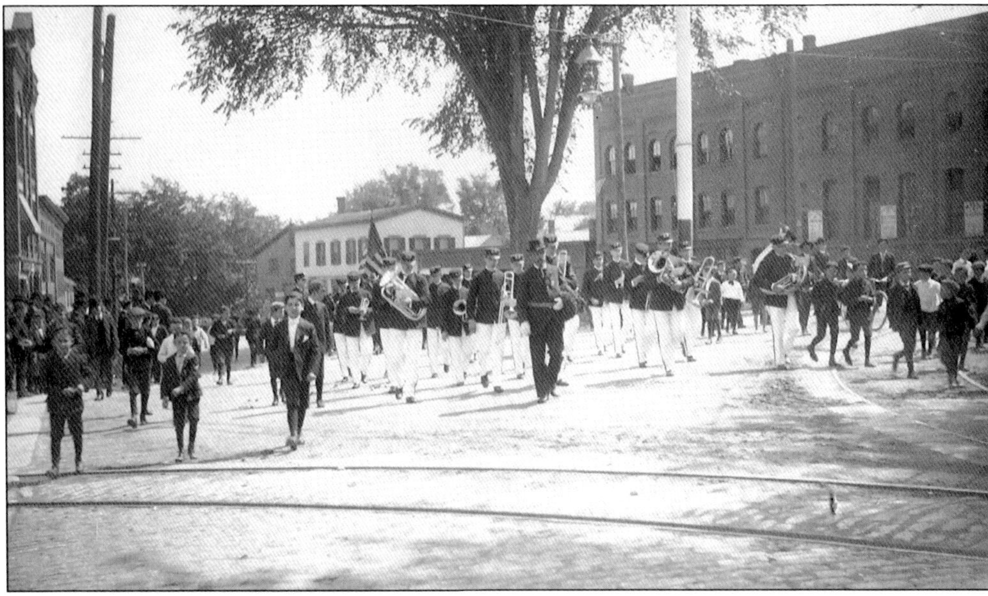

A marching band is shown in Millbury Center, at Main and Elm Streets, about 1900. To the right, the new Cunningham Block was built in 1895 to replace the Randall Block that had been destroyed by fire the year before. A stately elm tree dominates the scene. (Courtesy of Millbury Historical Society.)

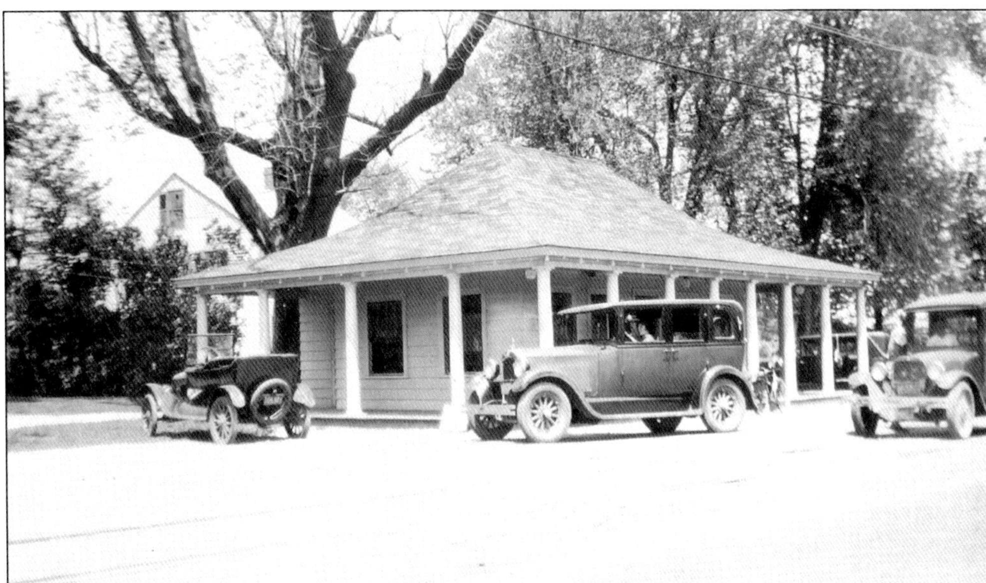

Shown in the late 1920s, this building on Canal Street was for many years an ice cream parlor run by Daniel F. Donovan Jr. Donovan was a 1940 graduate of the College of the Holy Cross in Worcester and, following his service in the Army Air Forces during World War II, came home and ran his ice cream business for 40 years. (Courtesy of Millbury Historical Society.)

On June 10, 1913, residents enjoyed an exhibit at town hall for Millbury's centennial celebration. Blanchard Hall was filled with portraits of town founders, family heirlooms, an old-fashioned kitchen, and the replica of the eccentric lathe shown here. This lathe, perfected by Thomas Blanchard, was used in the Millbury Armory and US Armory at Springfield, Massachusetts, for making gunstocks. (Courtesy of Chris Sinacola, from the *Centennial History of the Town of Millbury.*)

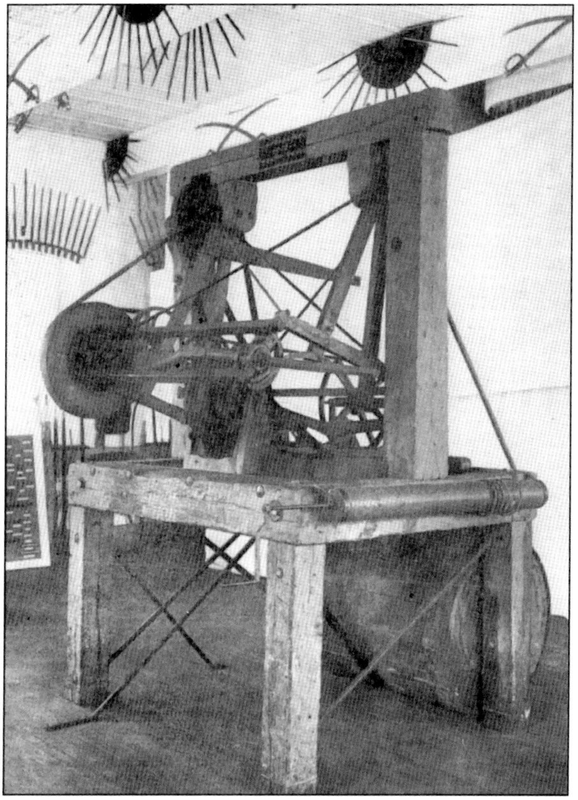

The Cordis Mill dam impounded the waters of the Blackstone River at Millbury Center for many years. The water was taken by a diversion channel under Canal Street to power the mill, located north of the river. The dam, shown in 1913, was removed after the floods of 1955, although heavy rains can still occasionally cause flooding along this stretch of the river. (Courtesy of Millbury Historical Society.)

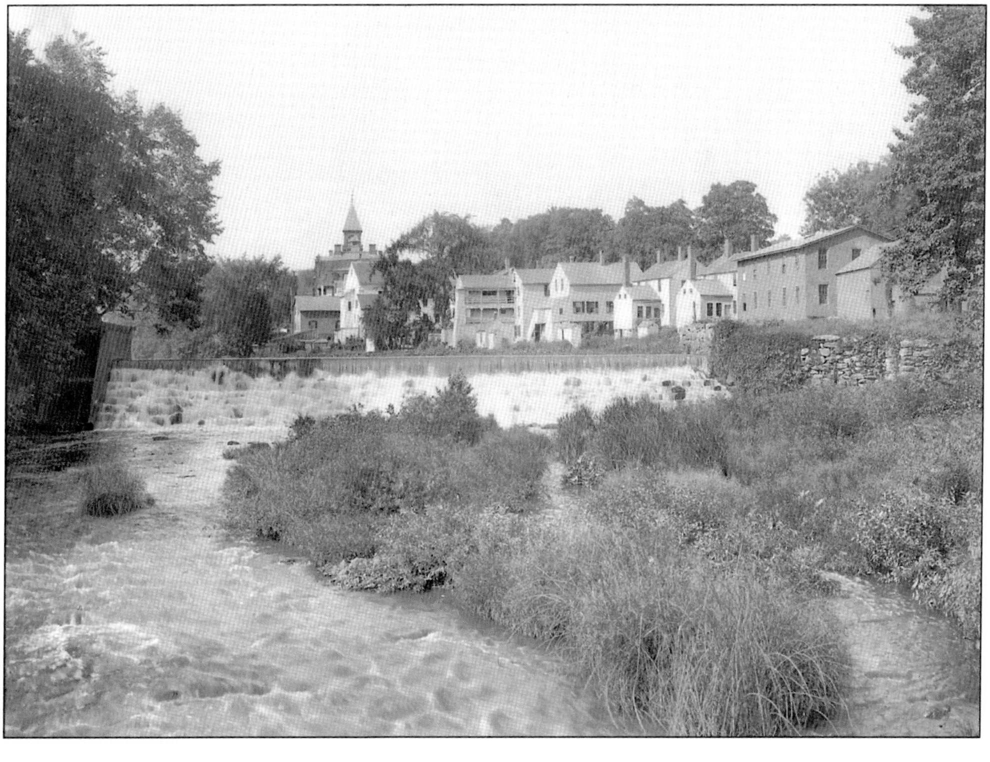

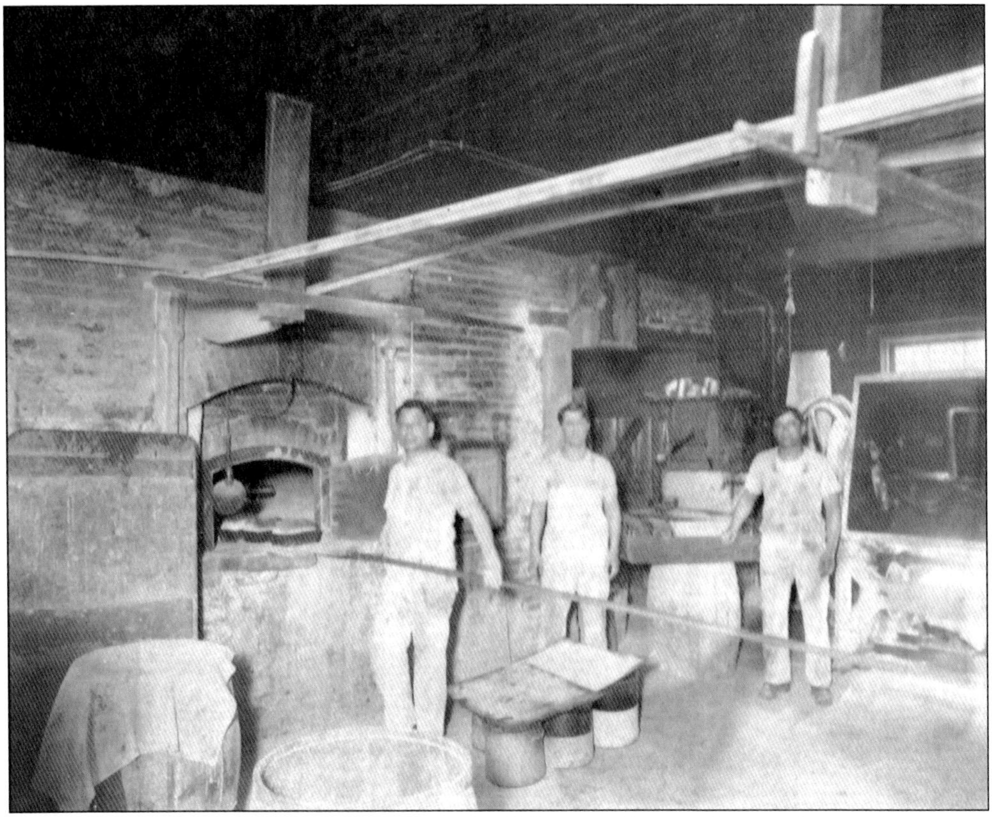

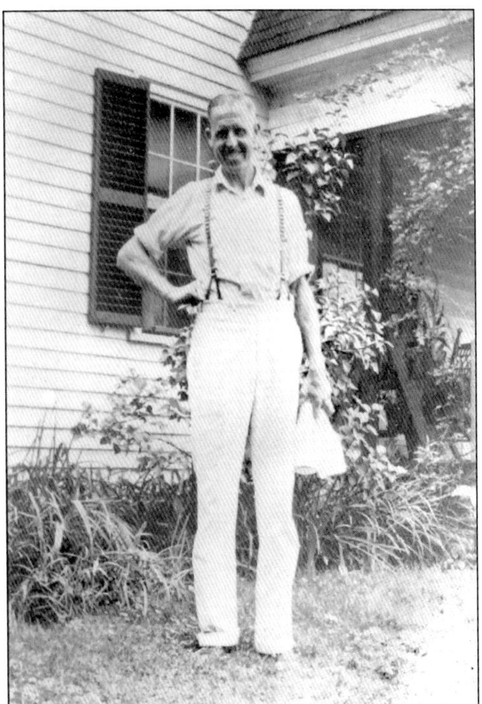

Whatever their profession, the people of Millbury were hard workers. This view from 1913 shows the interior of the Thibeault family bakery, located at Cherry and Summer Streets and later purchased by the Cofske family. In those days, brick-oven cooking was not a rustic throwback, but the industry standard. (Courtesy of Millbury Historical Society.)

Oscar Pearson and his wife, Esther, continued the dairy farm and milk business in West Millbury begun by her family in 1908. They began home delivery of milk in 1934. Their son Robert and his family have carried on the business, Pearson's Elmhurst Dairy, one of only a handful of local dairies in Worcester County that continue to deliver milk to customers' doors. (Courtesy of Robert and Barbara Pearson.)

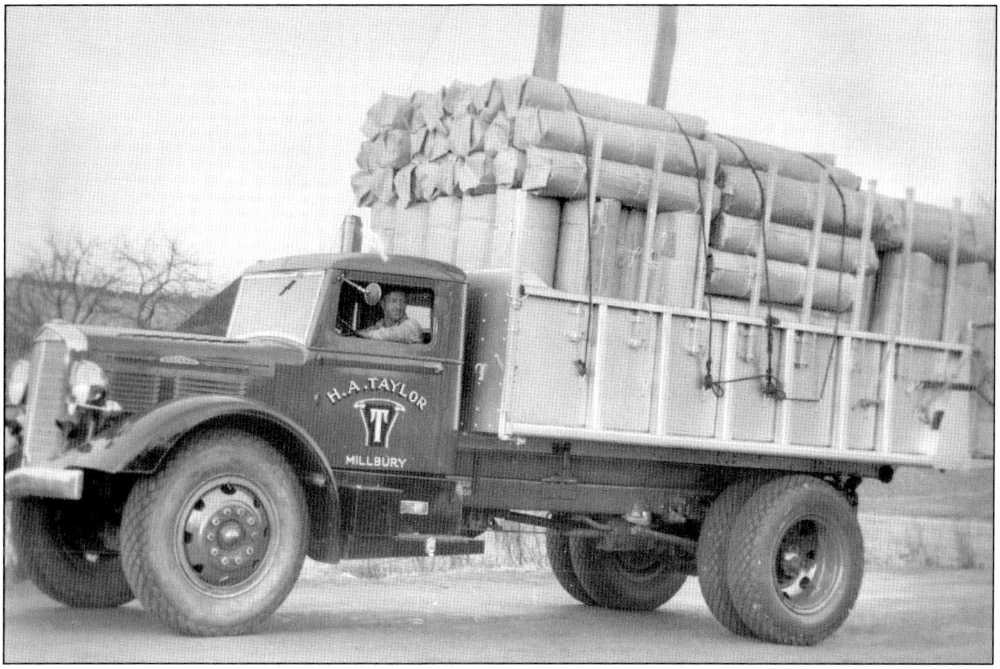

Millbury's blue-collar industries offered abundant opportunities for small businesses, such as H.A. Taylor trucking, shown here during the 1940s with a load of what is probably woolen materials from one of the town's many mills. The truck is a Brockway, from the Brockway Motor Company, a Cortland, New York, maker of heavy-duty trucks from 1912 to 1977. (Courtesy of Millbury Historical Society.)

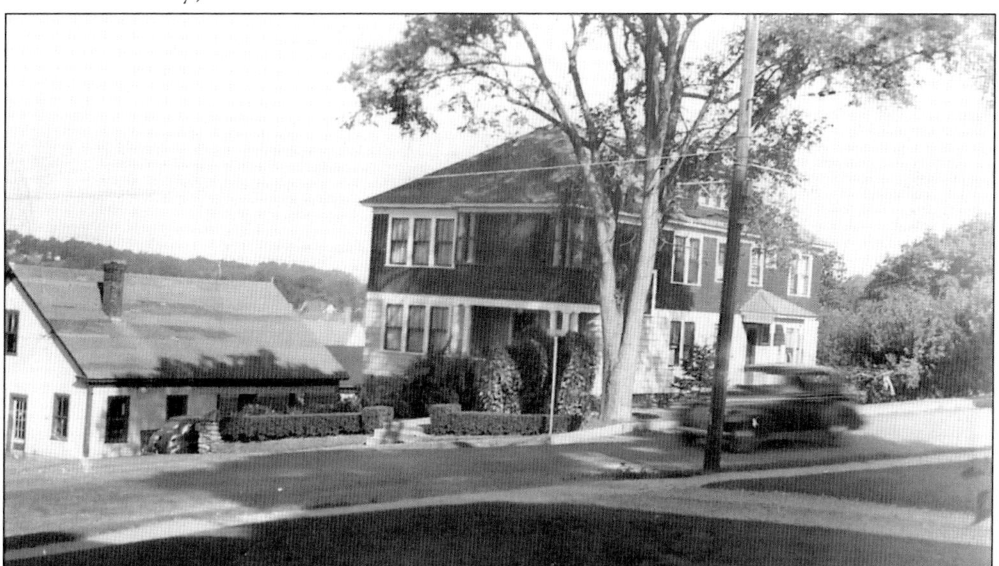

Highland Dairy, run by the Matson family, was one of several working dairies found within the town. The business, located at Highland and Prospect streets, is today a private home. Millbury's dairying tradition continues with Pearson's Elmhurst Dairy in West Millbury and IBA Inc., a family-owned business that has served the needs of dairy farmers for half a century. (Courtesy of Millbury Historical Society.)

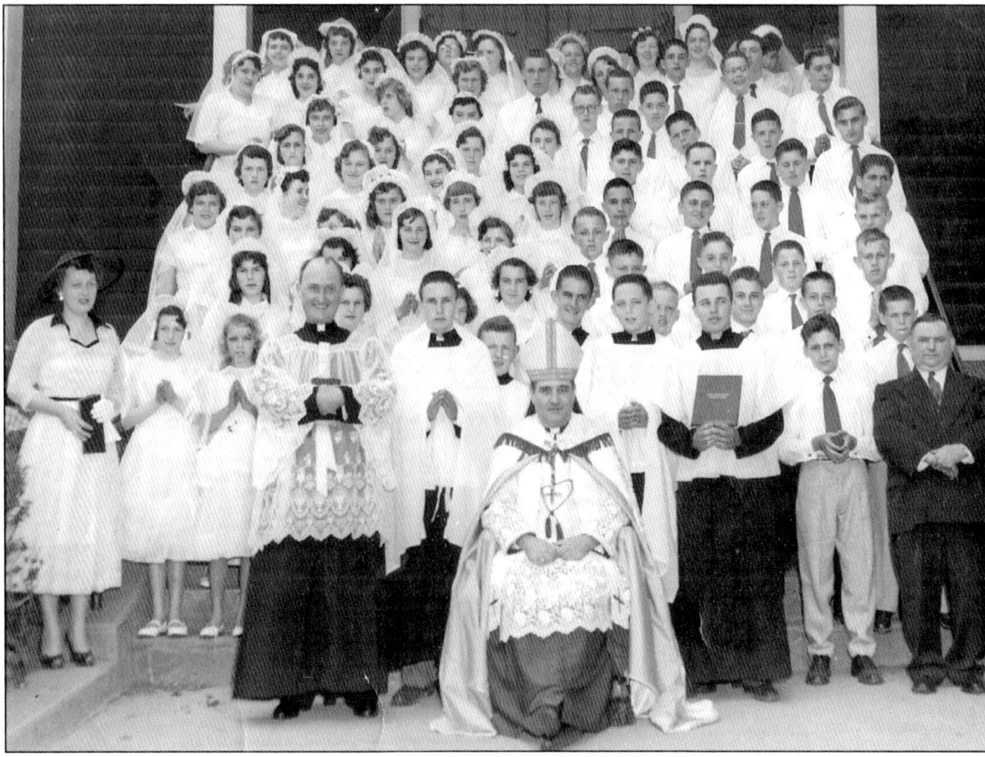

A confirmation class is shown at Our Lady of Lourdes Roman Catholic Church in East Millbury during the mid-1950s. Bishop John J. Wright, seated in the center to the front, later became a cardinal. He was the first bishop of the Diocese of Worcester, which was established in 1950 from the Diocese of Springfield. Our Lady of Lourdes Parish later built a new church to the north, in Worcester. (Courtesy of Millbury Historical Society.)

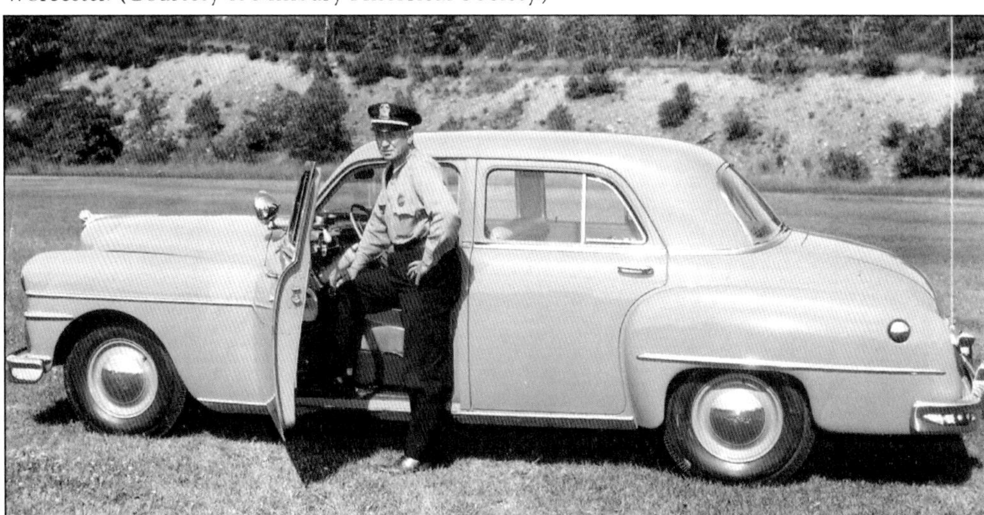

Born in Virginia in 1896, Frederick H. "Joe" Vulter came to Millbury as a young man. He served in France during World War I and was a selectman and member of the fire and police departments, serving as police chief from 1938 until his retirement in 1961. He is shown here with the town's first police cruiser during the 1940s. (Courtesy of Millbury Historical Society.)

The incident at Roswell, New Mexico, was hardly the only alleged sighting of flying saucers in mid-20th-century America. Many Americans reported seeing flying discs at one time or another, but few could sink their teeth into a flying saucer burger as Millbury residents did by visiting this classic burger joint on the Millbury-Worcester line. (Courtesy of Paula Beauregard.)

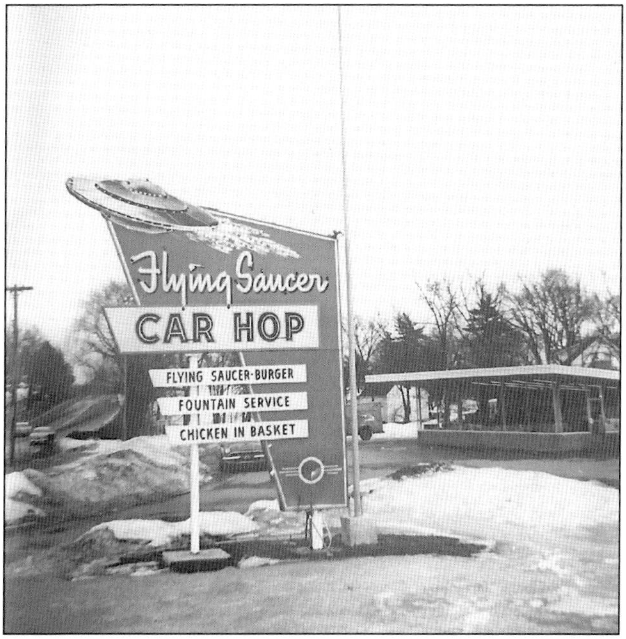

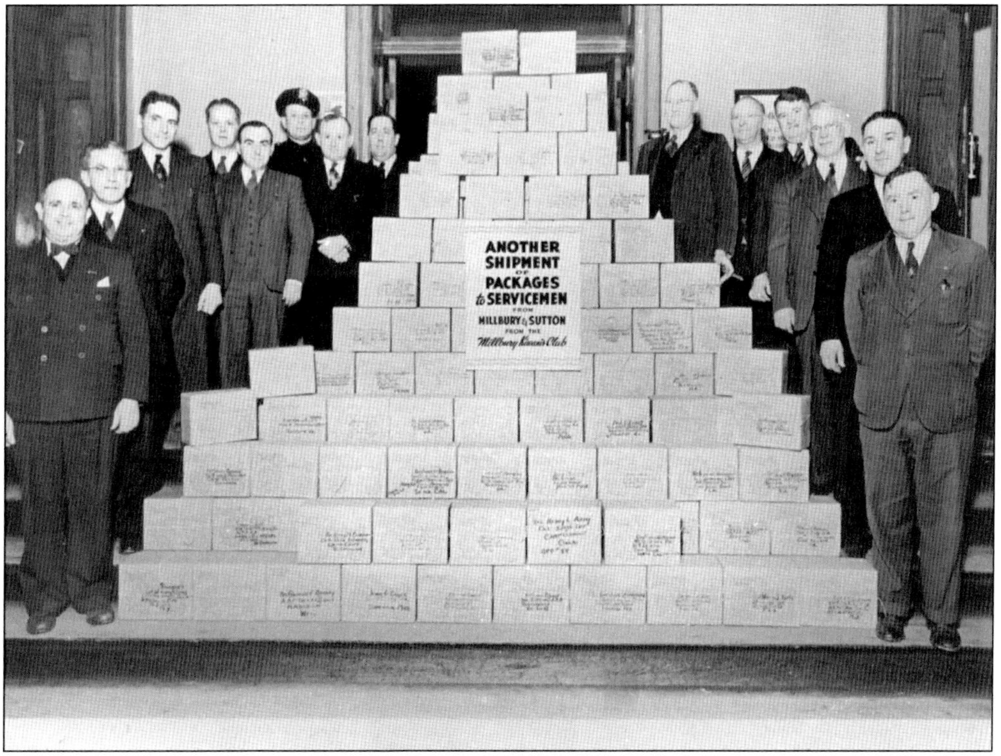

Dozens of men and women from Millbury and Sutton served their nation during World War II, and members of the former Millbury Kiwanis Club were ready to help families from both towns support their loved ones with care packages during their training. These are addressed to local soldiers in camps throughout the nation, including Virginia, Wisconsin, Florida, Oklahoma, and North Carolina. (Courtesy of Millbury Historical Society.)

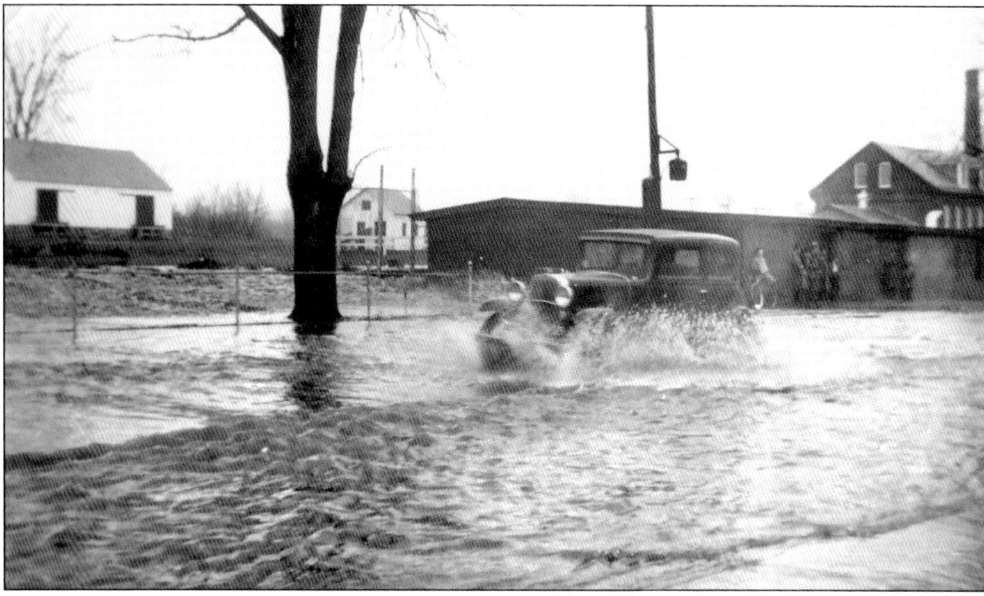

On March 9, 1936, a warm front stalled over New England, leading to more than a week of rains that, in combination with melting snowpacks, caused destructive flooding throughout the region. Above, a motorist braves floodwaters along Canal Street in downtown Millbury. The smokestack and buildings belonging to the Cordis Mill can be seen in the background. In the photograph below, the raging waters of the Blackstone River can be seen at the World War I–era bridge on Providence Street. The floods of March 1936 caused more than 150 deaths and more than $300 million in damages throughout New England. (Both, courtesy of Millbury Historical Society.)

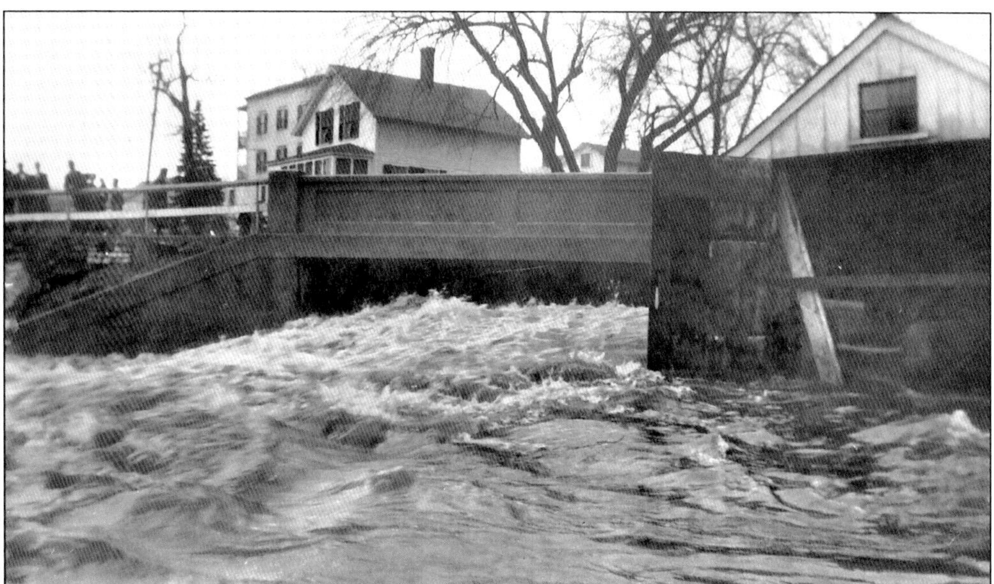

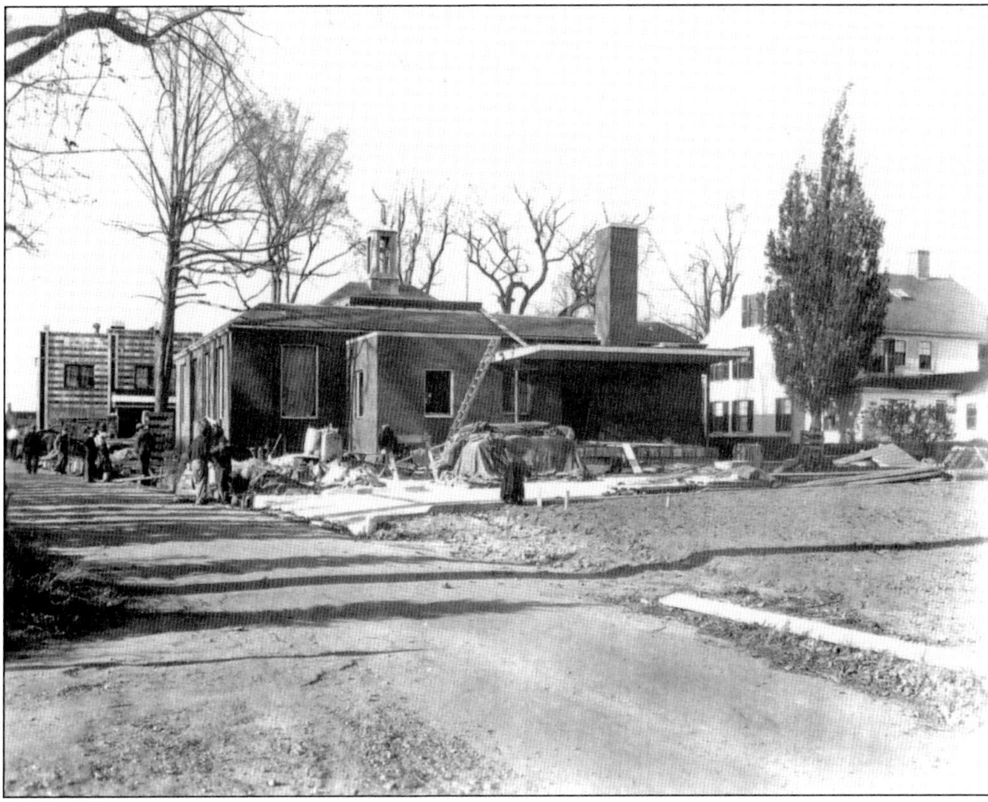

The Millbury Post Office is shown under construction in 1940. The building's lobby features a New Deal–era mural painted in 1941 by Joe Lasker; it shows a stylized scene from King Philip's War. On the left in the background is the Paradise Theater, across Elm Street. (Courtesy of Millbury Historical Society.)

In 1900, Msgr. Thomas Griffin of Worcester, along with other Roman Catholic clergy and laymen, purchased a site on Park Hill and opened Mount Saint Joseph's Industrial School to provide Catholic boys who were homeless or in need of direction a place for shelter and education. The school was run by the Xaverian Christian Brothers until 1915. (Courtesy of Chris Sinacola, from *Centennial History of the Town of Millbury*.)

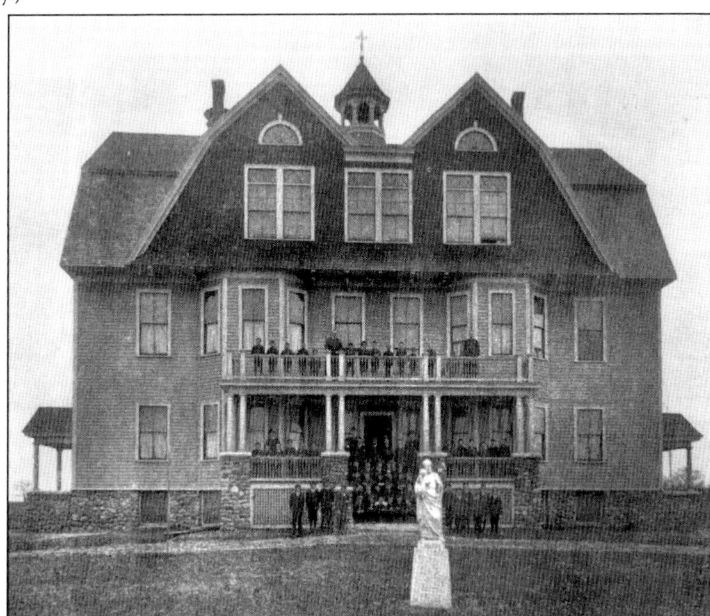

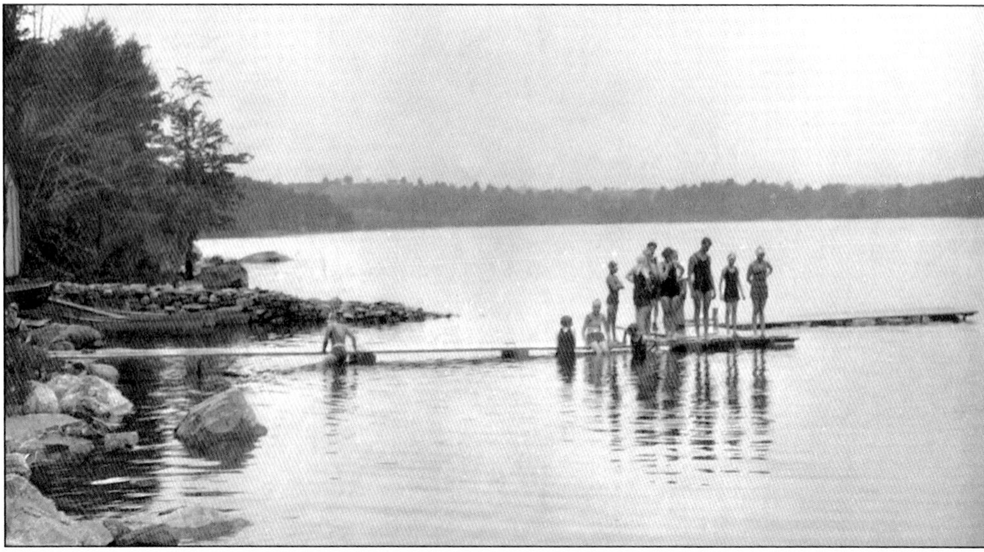

Bathers enjoy a dip in Dorothy Pond in East Millbury in 1931. The *Centennial History of the Town of Millbury* asserts that the earliest name was South Pond, although the name Dorothy also appears, but how that name came about is unknown. Maps and records over the years have recorded many variations on the spelling, Dority being one of the most popular alternatives. (Courtesy of Millbury Historical Society.)

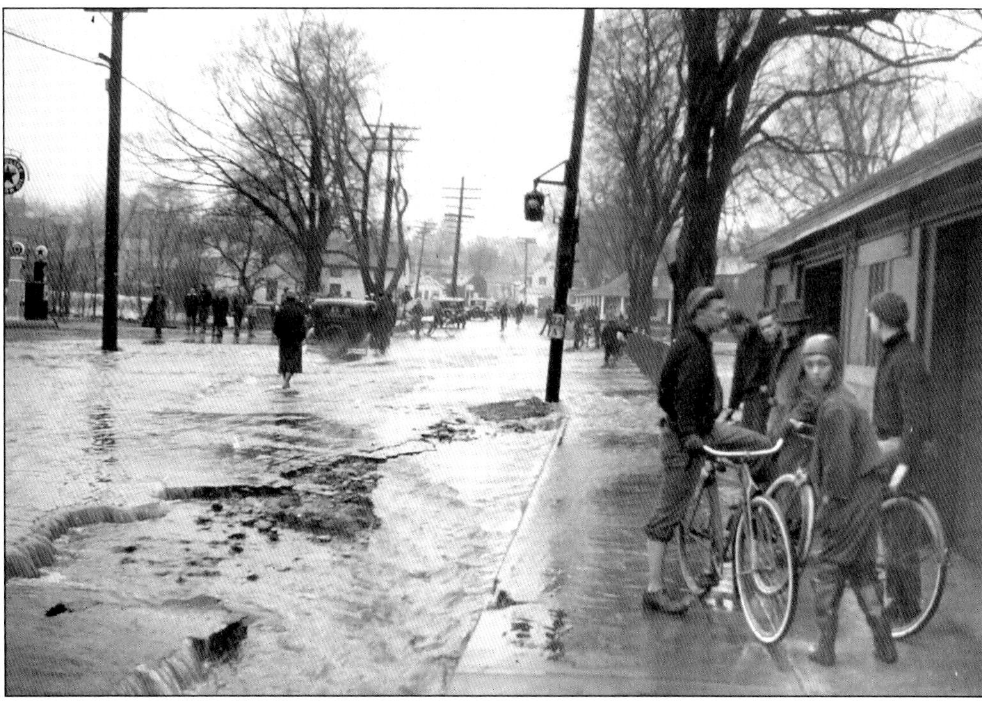

Nothing draws a crowd like natural disasters, and the flooding of March 1936—some of the worst in Millbury's history—brought many residents into the streets. Here, onlookers are shown along Canal Street. The Blackstone River is to the left of the photograph. The Blackstone Canal, which operated from 1828 to 1848, ran just to the north of this street. (Courtesy of Millbury Historical Society.)

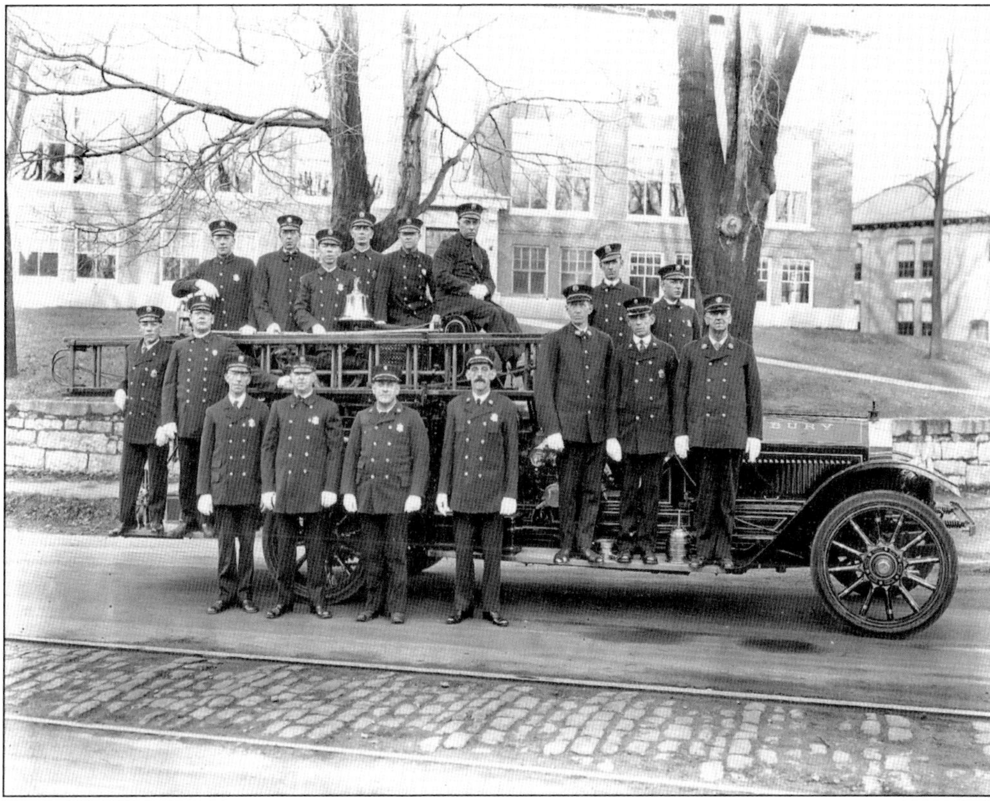

Millbury has long enjoyed an outstanding volunteer fire department. Members have gathered for this group photograph in 1927. They are, from left to right, (first row) C. Army, W. Welsh, E. Burstoff, M. Shaw, H. Flagg, R. Army, Fire Chief William Horne, J. Army, R. Whitehead; (second row) F. Horne, A. Horne, P. Gabree, F. Paine, W. May, P. Gibson, H. Horne, P. Army. (Courtesy of Millbury Historical Society.)

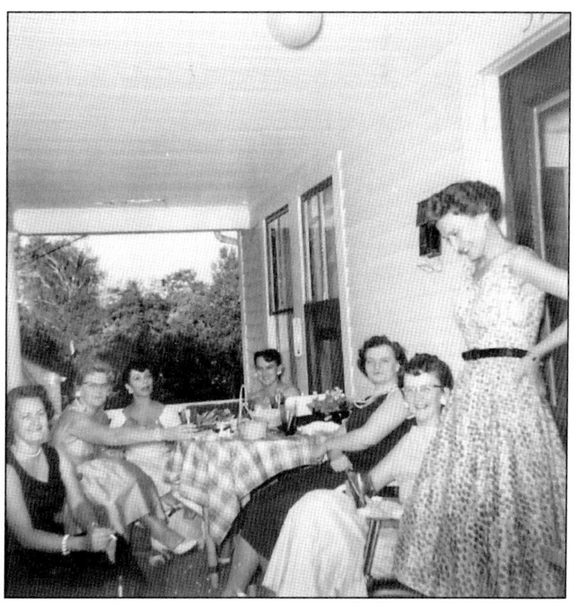

Joy Putnam Young (far right), shown here with friends at her home on Elmwood Street, was director of sales promotion at Worcester Mutual Fire Insurance Company. In December 1963, as part of an effort to boost morale after corporate mergers, she initiated "Operation Smile," made a rough sketch, and hired commercial artist Harvey Ball, who developed her idea into the "Smiley" famous around the world. (Courtesy of Chris Sinacola.)

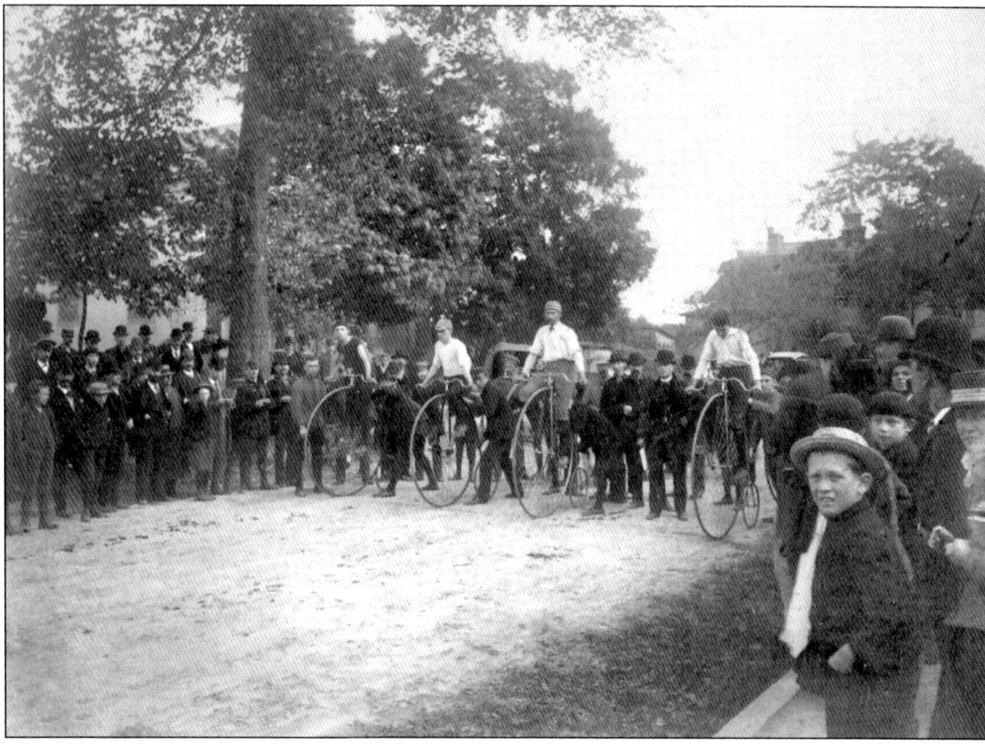

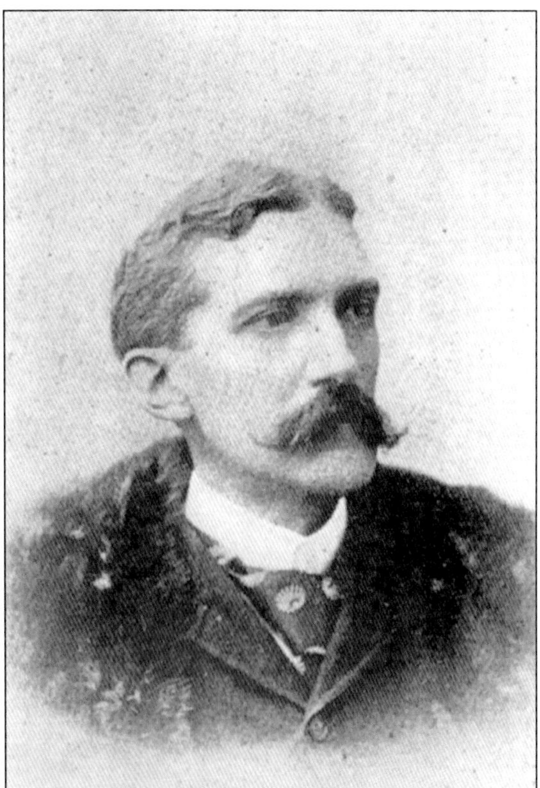

In this undated photograph, probably taken between 1880 and 1900, several contestants perched atop their high-wheel bicycles prepare for a race in Millbury Center. These bicycles were developed in England and later dubbed penny-farthings, given their resemblance to those two British coins laid side by side; they were popular throughout the United States after 1880. (Courtesy of Millbury Historical Society.)

Born in 1849, Charles Bowler Atwood grew up in Millbury and trained at architectural firms in Worcester and Boston before building his career in New York. In 1891, he joined Daniel Burnham in Chicago to help design the 1893 World's Columbian Exposition. Among his works was the masterful Palace of Fine Arts, which later became the Field Museum of Natural History. He died in 1895 and is buried in Millbury's Central Cemetery. (Courtesy of Chris Sinacola, from *Centennial History of the Town of Millbury*.)

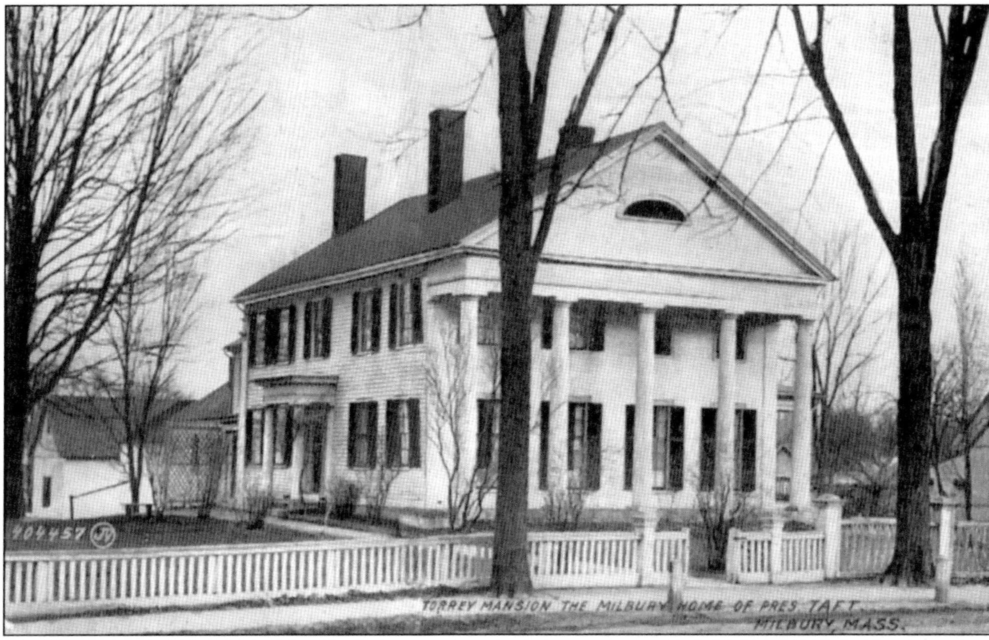

The Torrey Mansion on Elm Street was home to Samuel Torrey and his family. Born in Mendon in 1789, Torrey lived in Millbury for nearly 50 years. In 1824, he married Susan Holman Waters, daughter of Asa Waters Jr. Their five children included Delia Chapin Torrey, named for her father's first wife, and Louisa Maria Torrey, who was the mother of Pres. William Howard Taft. (Courtesy of Chris Sinacola.)

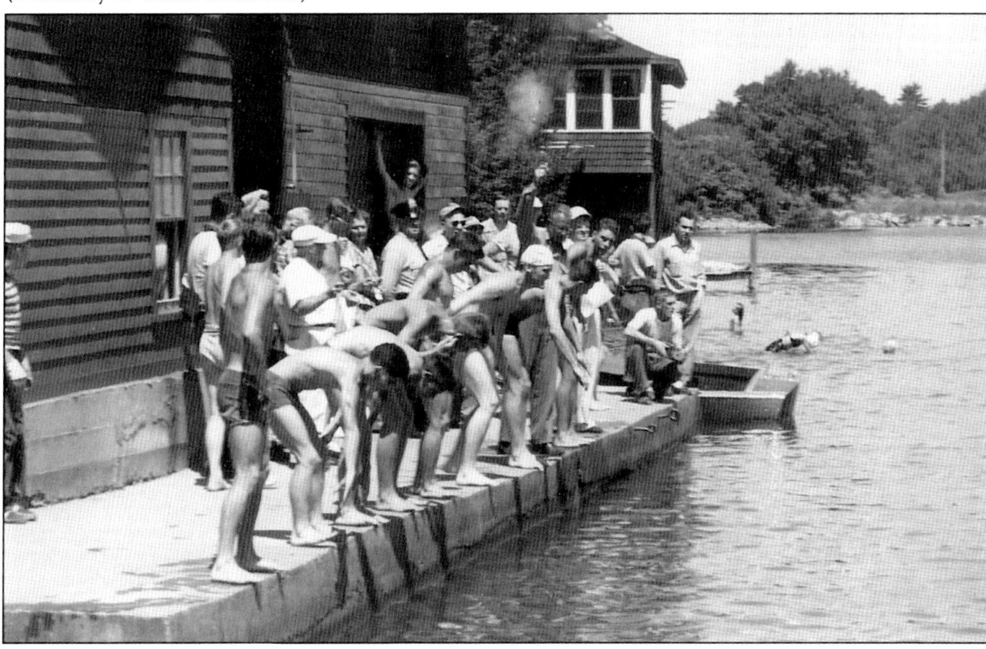

Generations of Millbury youth socialized and learned to swim at Singletary Nook, located on the Millbury shore of Singletary Lake, a 365-acre "great pond" that lies in both Sutton and Millbury. This scene from the 1950s captures the moment just after the starter's gun has given a group of boys the signal to begin a race. (Courtesy of Millbury Historical Society.)

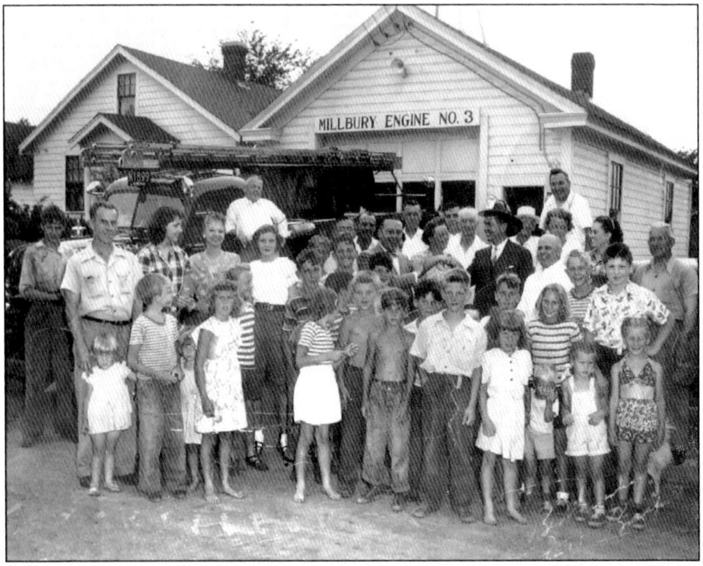

When East Millbury received a new fire truck one day in 1948, children and neighbors gathered at the station to meet Gov. Robert F. Bradford, who is standing at right center in this photograph and wearing a fire hat. Selectman Warren Harris, wearing glasses and bow tie, is at center, and Bob Swift, known as the "Mayor of East Millbury" is smiling broadly and standing immediately to Bradford's left. (Courtesy of Carol Vulter.)

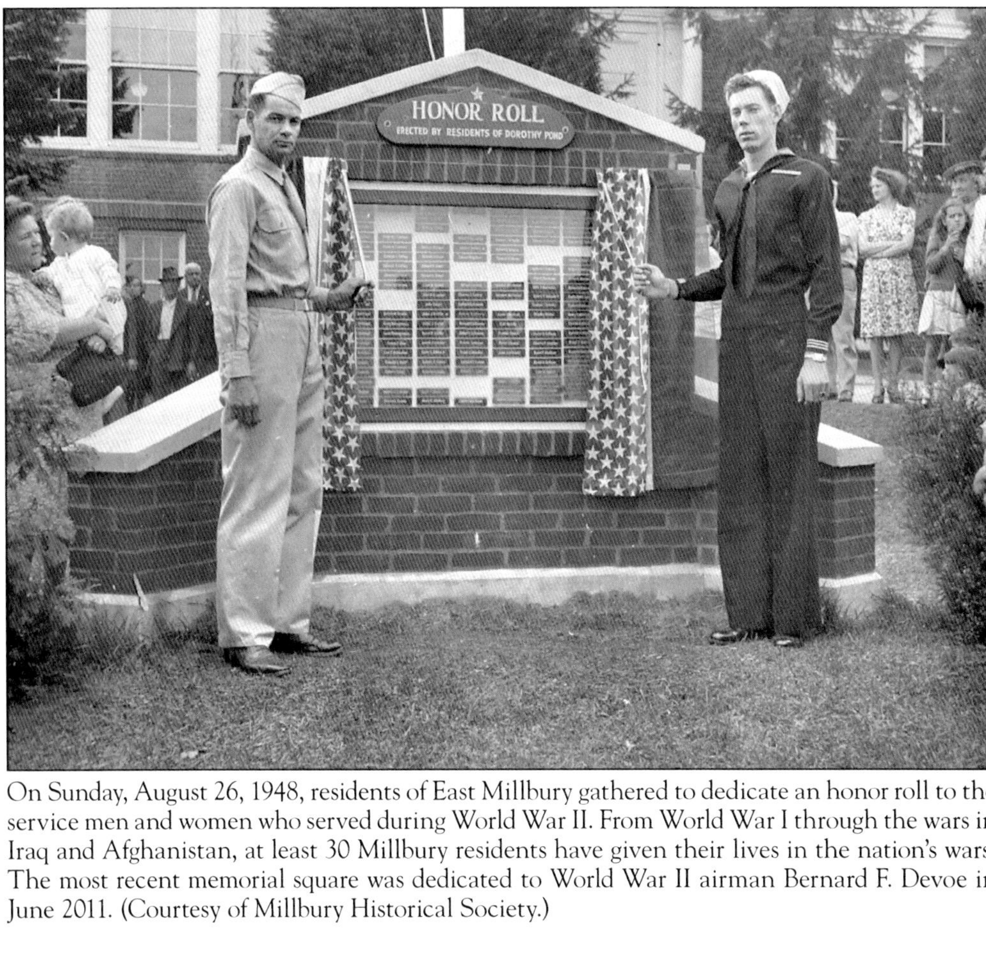

On Sunday, August 26, 1948, residents of East Millbury gathered to dedicate an honor roll to the service men and women who served during World War II. From World War I through the wars in Iraq and Afghanistan, at least 30 Millbury residents have given their lives in the nation's wars. The most recent memorial square was dedicated to World War II airman Bernard F. Devoe in June 2011. (Courtesy of Millbury Historical Society.)

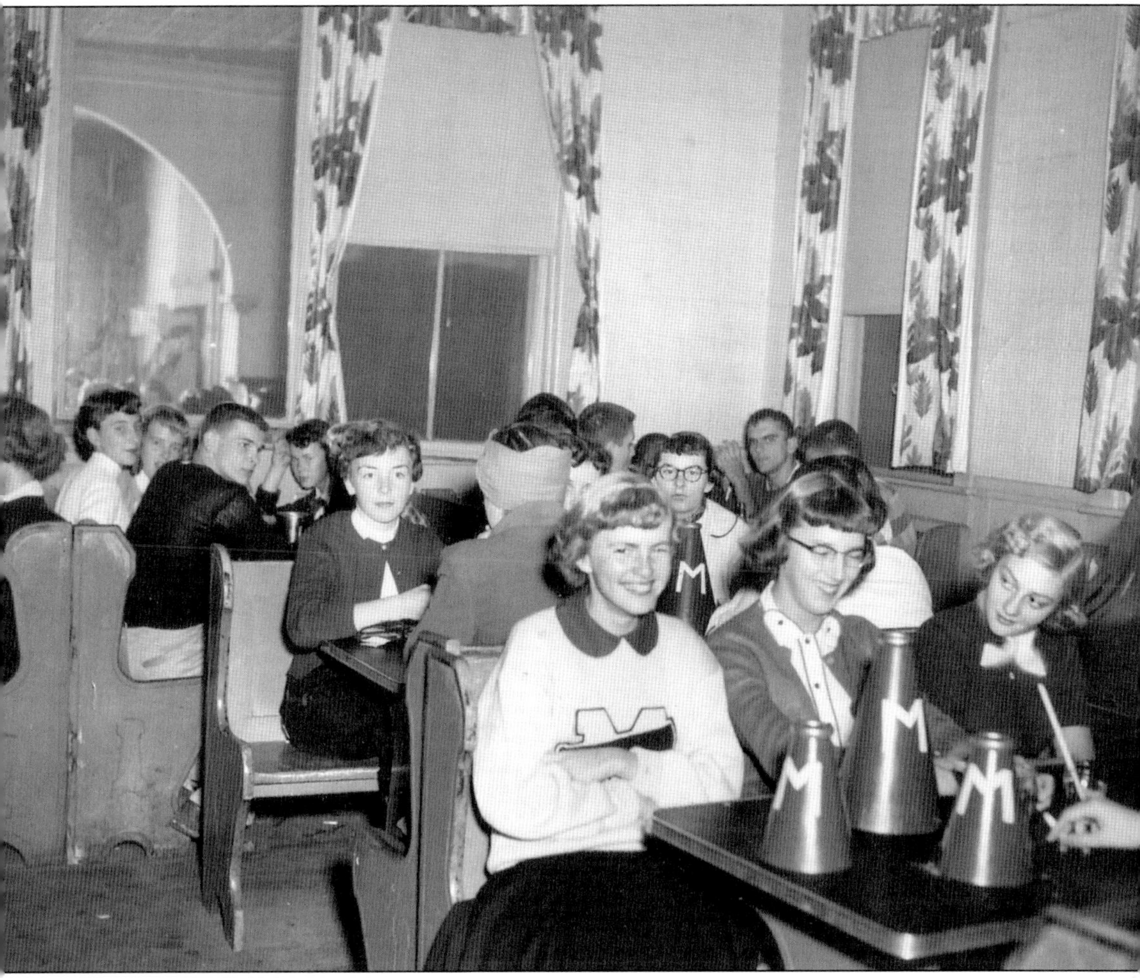

Although the sign outside read Donovan's Spa, Millbury residents from the 1950s through the 1970s knew it simply as "Chick's," run by the popular Charles "Chick" Riley. Riley took a job at Donovan's in the early 1920s and stayed for more than 50 years, assuming ownership of the business after Daniel Donovan's death in 1950. In its early days, the spa was a popular place for politicians and the scene of many backroom deals that launched political careers. By the 1950s, Riley, always wearing a bow tie and a smile, was running the place to be for Millbury youth, with Chick's offering penny candy, fast food, a jukebox, plenty of booths, and all the time a teen could want to hang out and gossip. The downtown spa was sandwiched between the old town hall and the Barrow Block. Sitting in the first booth are, from left to right, Gail Webber, Virginia Matthew, and Ann Briddon. Seated in the second booth are Sheila Murray and Eleanor Sheehan, wearing glasses. (Courtesy of Millbury Historical Society.)

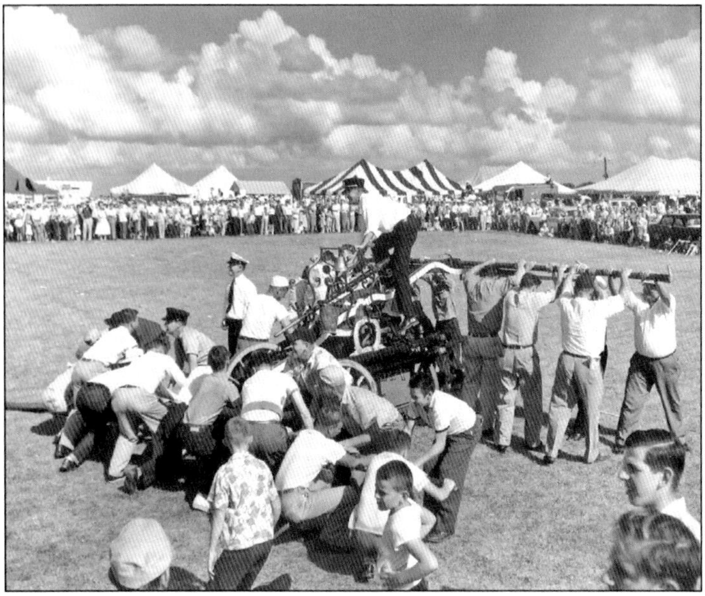

In 1955 and 1956, the farmers of Worcester County held their annual field days at Windle Airport in West Millbury, with events from water dowsing and sheep dog demonstrations to beekeeping, crop dusting, and a chainsaw contest. Members of the Millbury Fire Department are shown here at the 1955 event, preparing to show their prowess handling antique pumping equipment. (Courtesy of Robert and Barbara Pearson.)

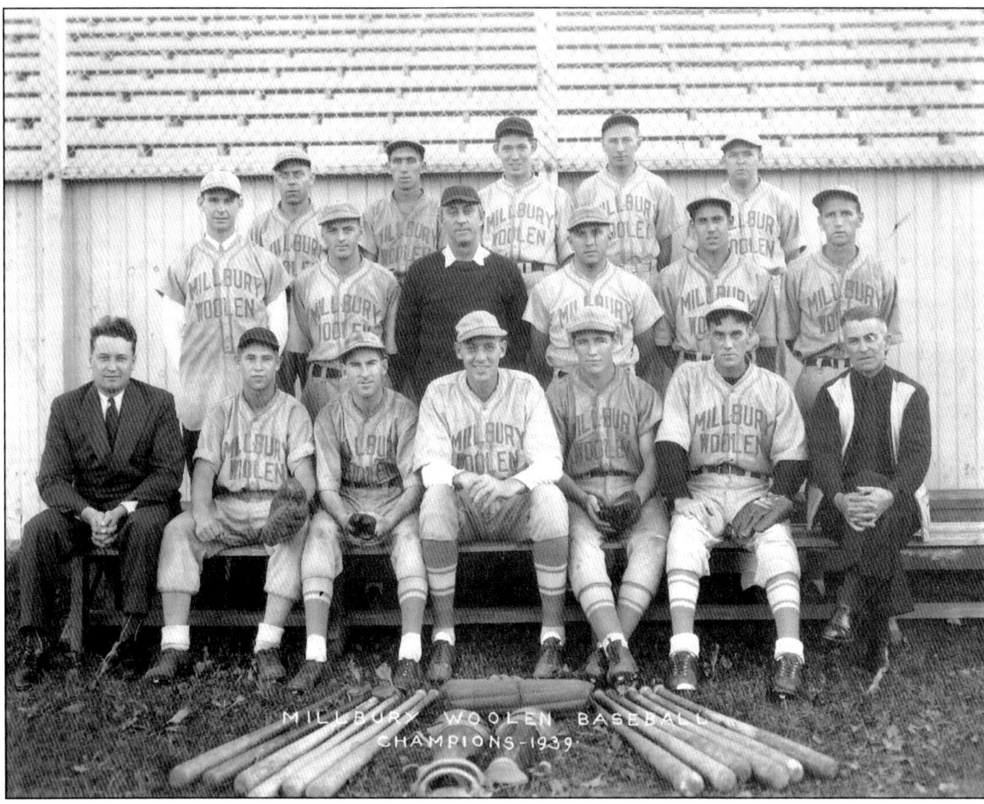

The mill towns of the Blackstone Valley were dominated for decades by large industrial firms that provided employment, housing, and recreation for generations of workers. The Blackstone Valley League was founded in 1924 and grew to include baseball teams from Whitinsville, Rockdale, Hopedale, Uxbridge, Grafton, and Millbury. In 1939, Millbury Woolen Company won the league championship. (Courtesy of Millbury Historical Society.)

Two

A Century Ago

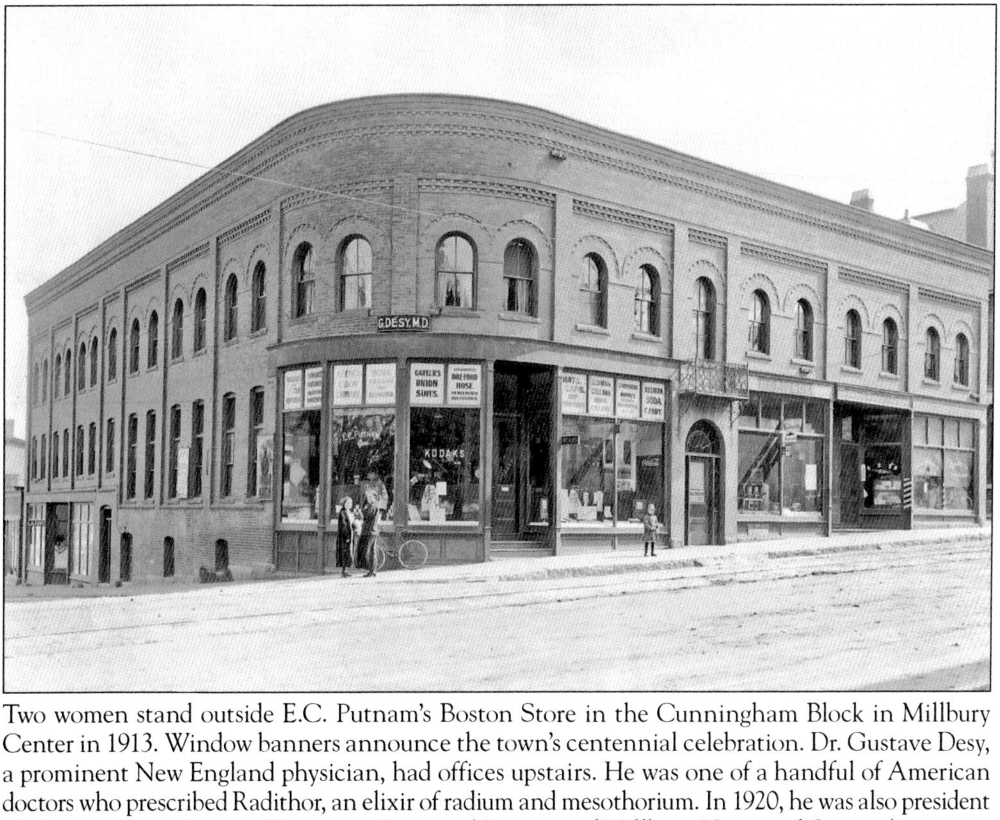

Two women stand outside E.C. Putnam's Boston Store in the Cunningham Block in Millbury Center in 1913. Window banners announce the town's centennial celebration. Dr. Gustave Desy, a prominent New England physician, had offices upstairs. He was one of a handful of American doctors who prescribed Radithor, an elixir of radium and mesothorium. In 1920, he was also president of the Worcester County Esperanto Society. (Courtesy of Millbury Historical Society.)

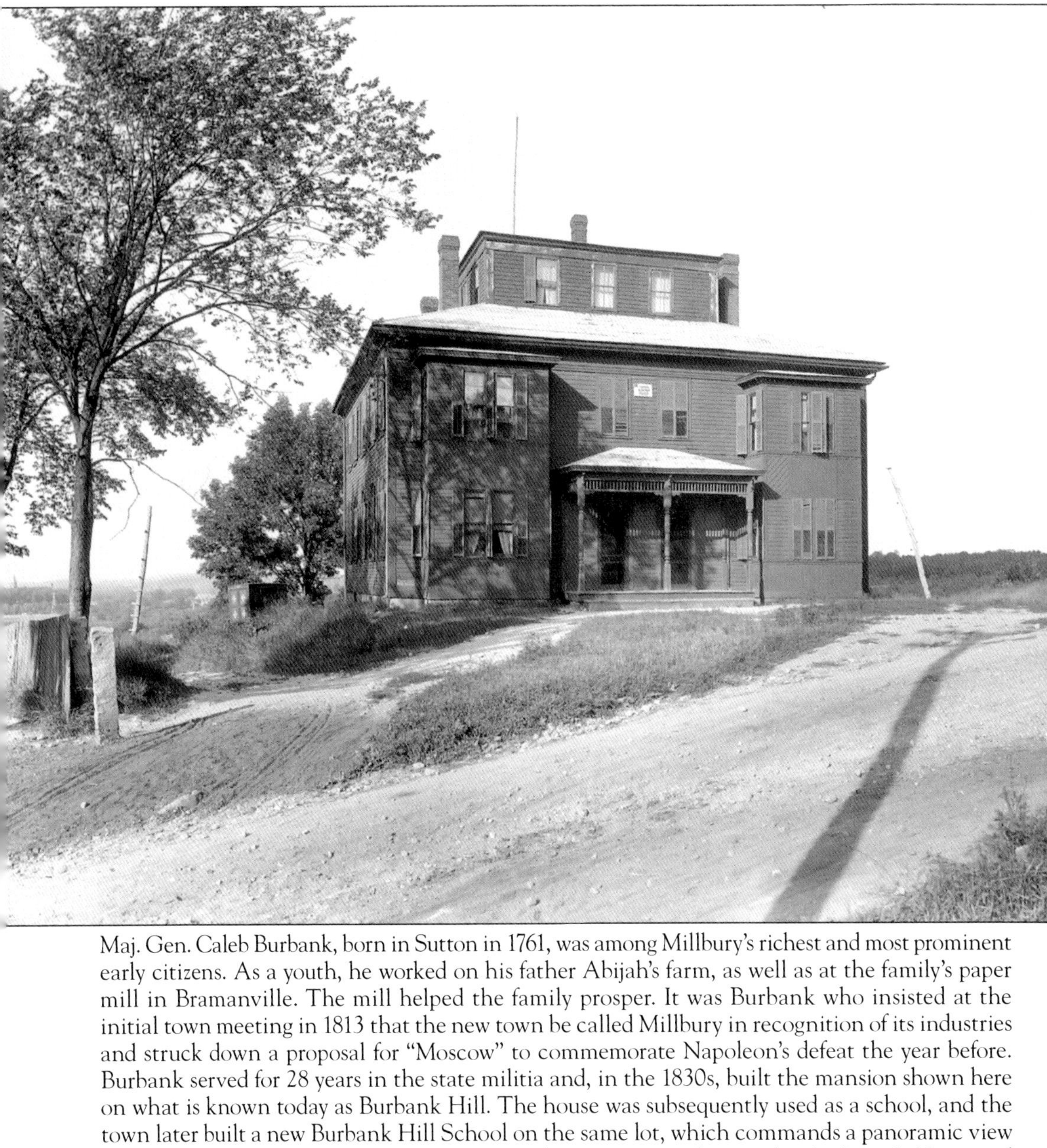

Maj. Gen. Caleb Burbank, born in Sutton in 1761, was among Millbury's richest and most prominent early citizens. As a youth, he worked on his father Abijah's farm, as well as at the family's paper mill in Bramanville. The mill helped the family prosper. It was Burbank who insisted at the initial town meeting in 1813 that the new town be called Millbury in recognition of its industries and struck down a proposal for "Moscow" to commemorate Napoleon's defeat the year before. Burbank served for 28 years in the state militia and, in the 1830s, built the mansion shown here on what is known today as Burbank Hill. The house was subsequently used as a school, and the town later built a new Burbank Hill School on the same lot, which commands a panoramic view of the town that Burbank did so much to build up. He married twice, but had no children, and died in 1849 at the age 88. (Courtesy of Millbury Historical Society.)

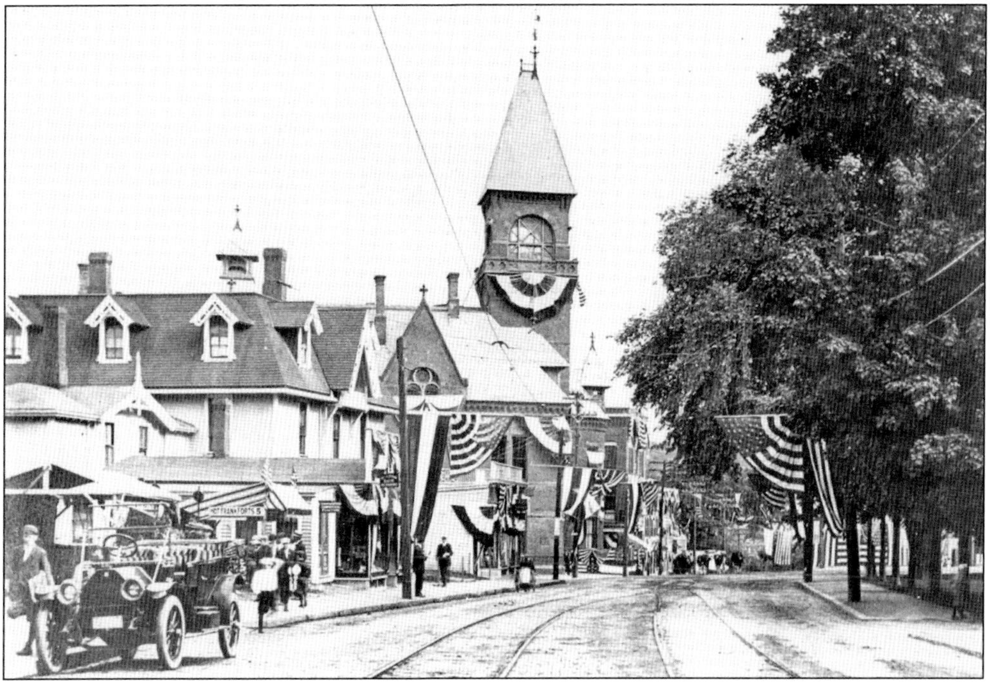

Millbury celebrated its centennial with four days of festivities from June 8 to 11, 1913. The *Centennial History of the Town of Millbury* notes, "The town was prettily decorated on its main streets with bunting by day and with electric lights by night." Residents who could afford cars took riders on routes throughout town, visiting some of the 88 historic spots recorded in the program and marked with placards. (Courtesy of Millbury Historical Society.)

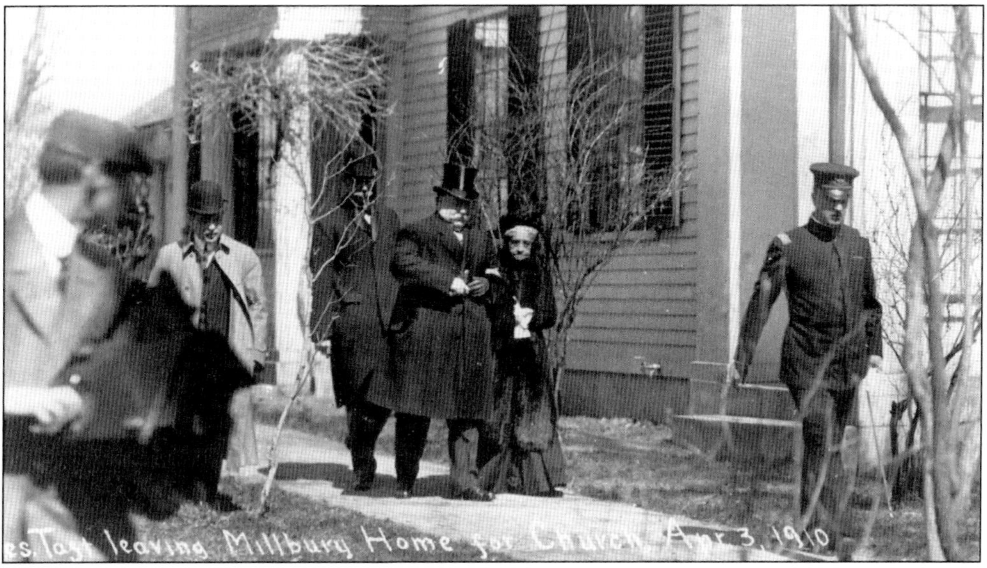

Pres. William Howard Taft's mother, Louisa Maria Torrey, was a descendant of the Waters family. She married Alphonso Taft, attorney general and secretary of war under Pres. Ulysses Grant. The Tafts had five children, of whom the future president was the second. Here, President Taft is pictured accompanying his aunt Delia C. Torrey to church during his visit to Millbury and Worcester on April 3, 1910. (Courtesy of Millbury Historical Society.)

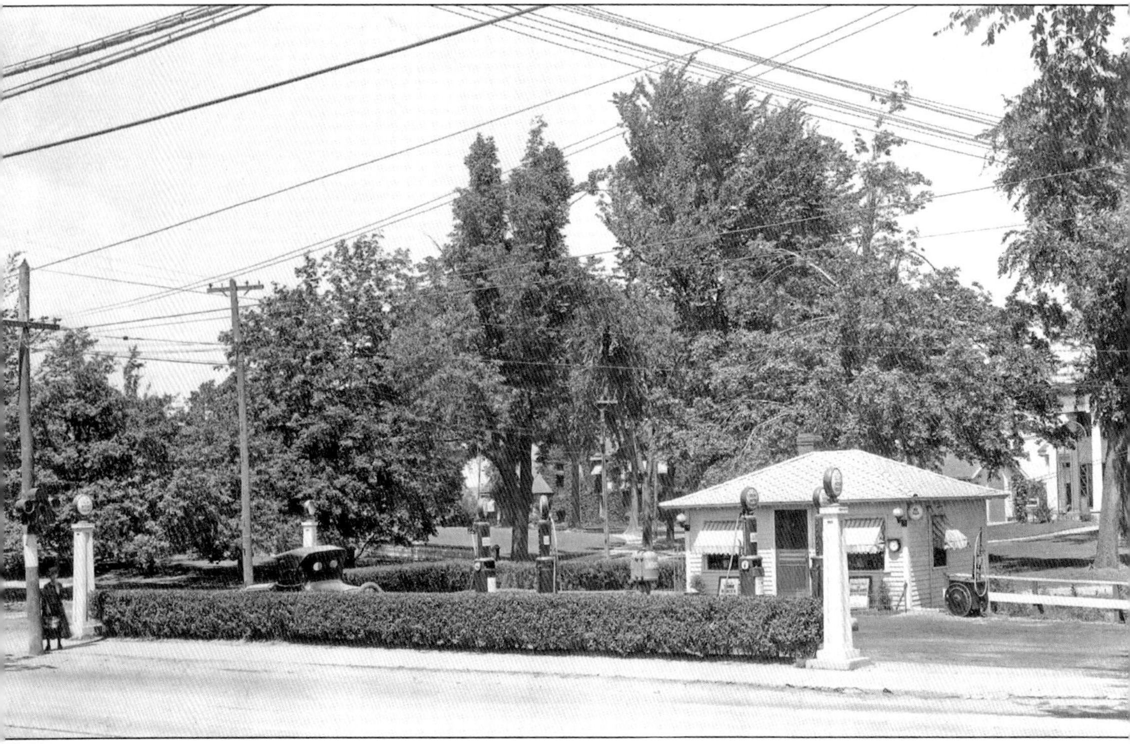

The intersection of Main, Canal, and Miles Streets, seen here (and on the opposite page) in 1913, encapsulates Millbury's history. In the center, behind the gasoline and service station, stands the Walling Mansion, built by Clough R. Miles and owned at this time by Nelson Walling. (Courtesy of Millbury Historical Society.)

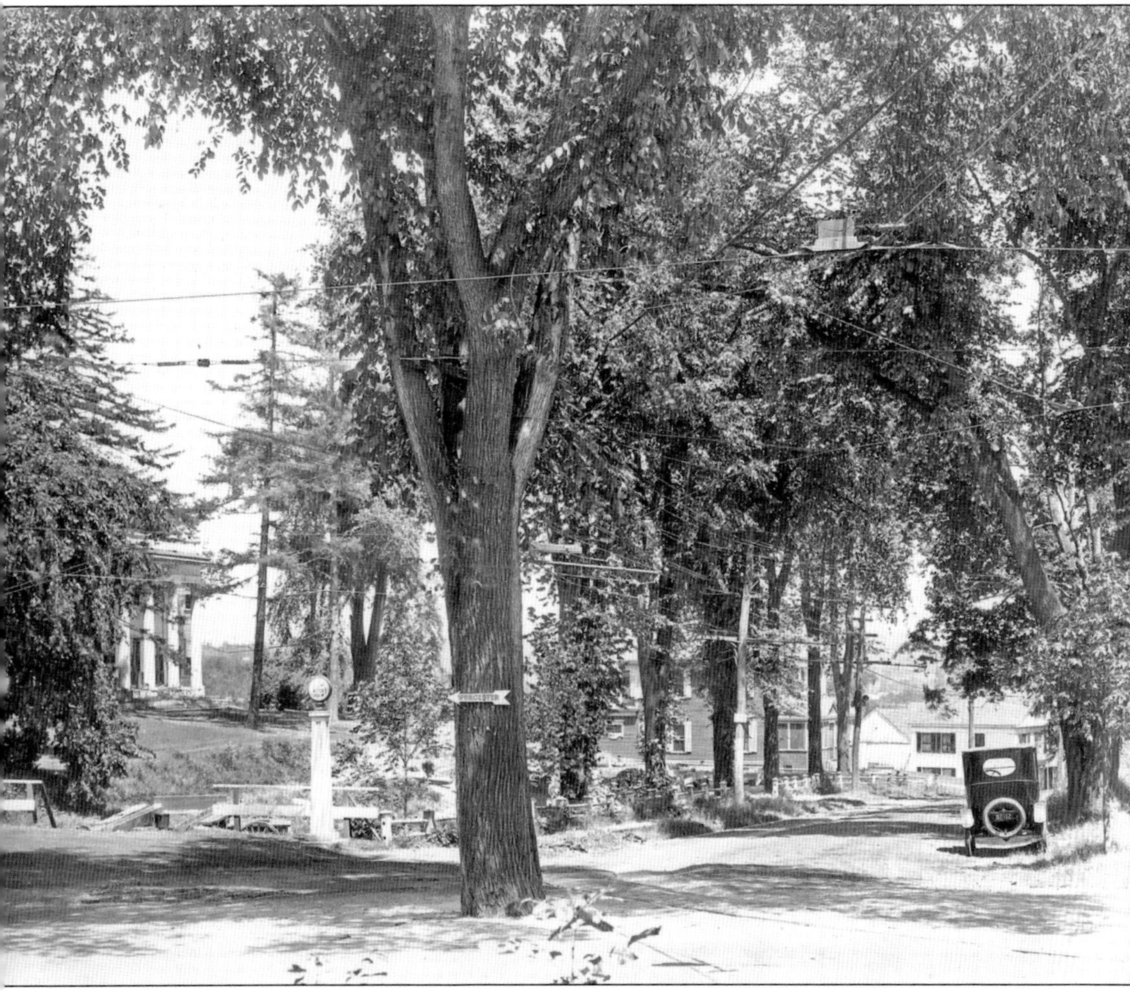

A native of Rhode Island, Walling came to Millbury in 1853, built a mill in Bramanville, and became a leading industrialist. He was a gentleman farmer and cattle breeder and was listed in an 1868 record of pedigreed Ayrshires as the owner of Roxa, Maude, Flora, Jennie Dean, and several other pedigreed cattle. Several locks, gullies, and ditches of the old Blackstone Canal were located on this property, and Walling had the property carefully graded, in keeping with his status as a property owner on Miles Street, home to some of Millbury's leading families. (Courtesy of Millbury Historical Society.)

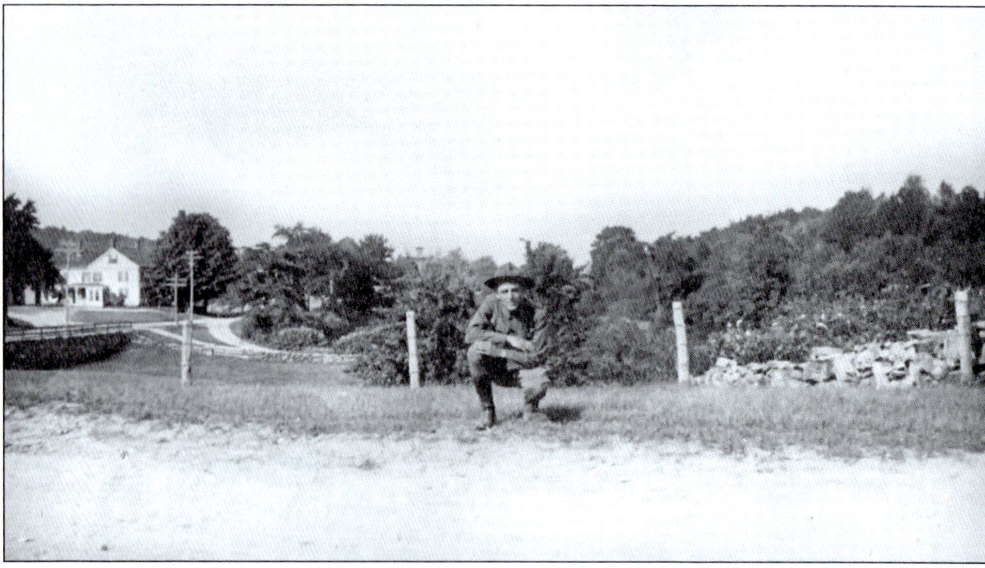

Above, Charles F. Minney is shown near West Main Street and Singletary Lake. The Harris family farm is on the left. Minney, born August 24, 1892, to Arthur and Mary Minney, grew up on Grove Street with his brother and sisters. He fought in France during World War I and escaped serious injury, only to die of pneumonia in France on January 21, 1919, one of seven Millbury residents to die in World War I. Just weeks before his death, he had written his parents, saying he was looking forward to coming home soon. Fellow soldiers, including Frederick H. Vulter (foreground) honored him at his funeral, pictured below. The Charles F. Minney Post, Veterans of Foreign Wars, located on South Main Street, was named for him, along with a square at Elmwood and West Main Streets. (Both, courtesy of Millbury Historical Society.)

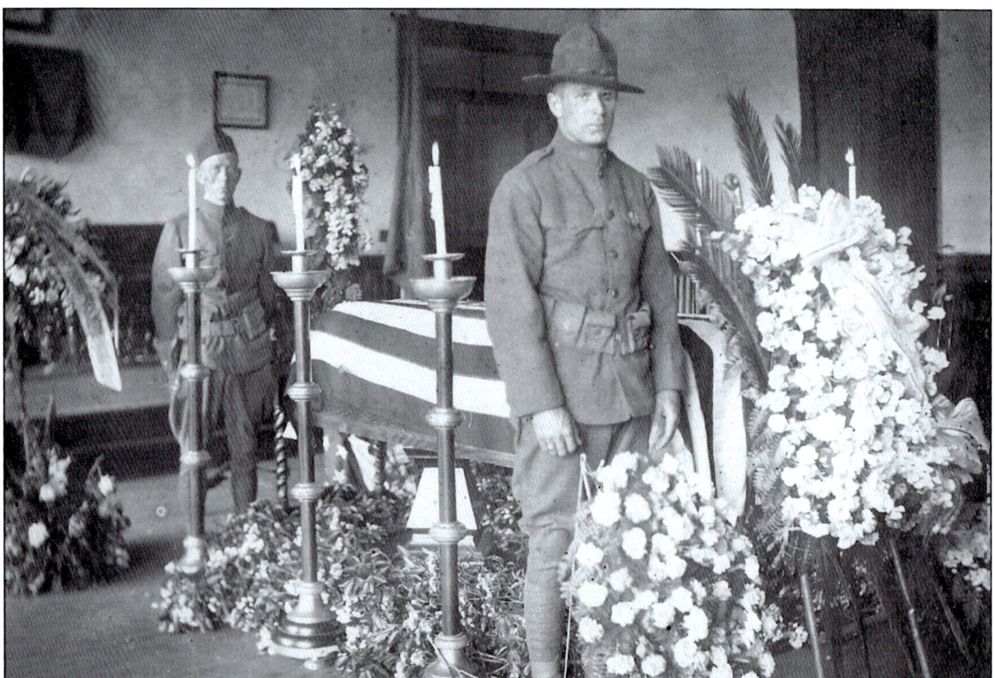

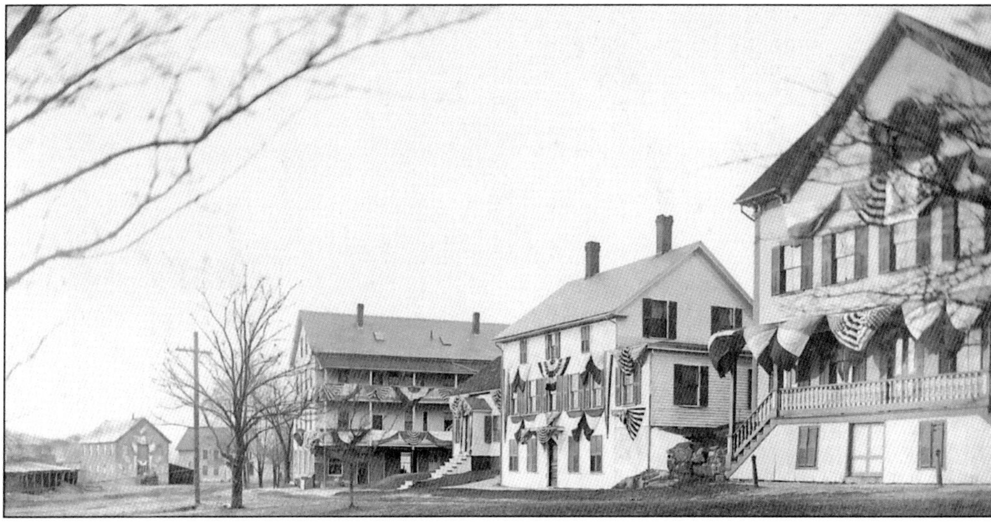

In January 1919, selectmen named a committee of leading citizens to organize a welcome home for Millbury servicemen who had fought with the American Expeditionary Force in France. That celebration was postponed until October 1919, giving all the surviving soldiers ample time to return home. Here, millhouses on River Street are decorated for the occasion. (Courtesy of Millbury Historical Society.)

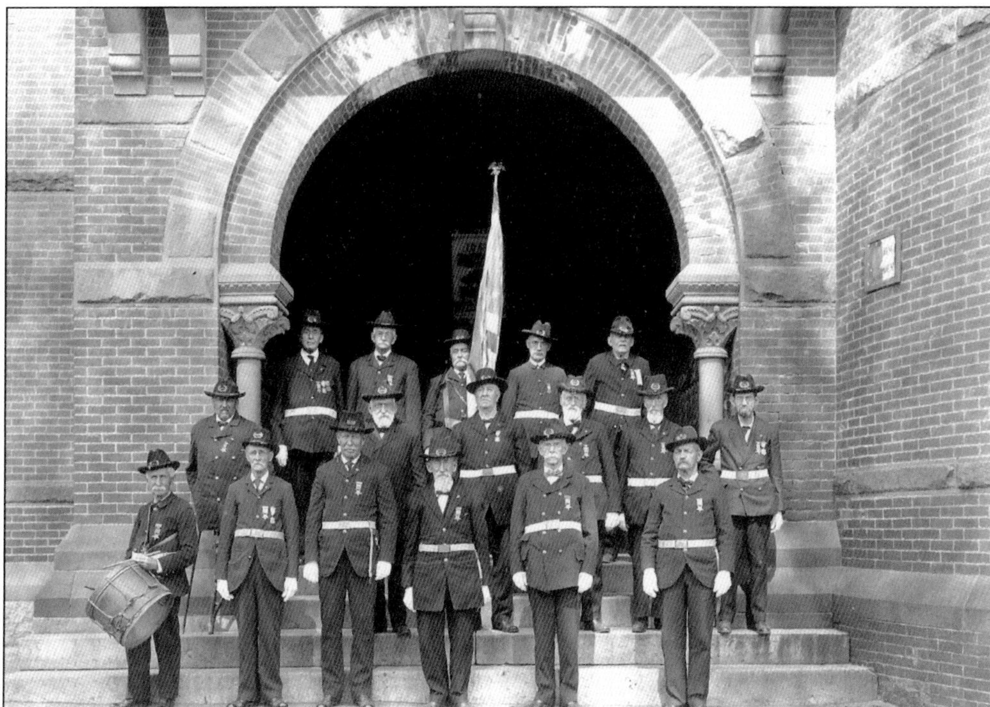

Members of the George A. Custer Post No. 70, Grand Army of the Republic, assemble at town hall for the 1913 centennial. Millbury furnished 346 men for the Union army during the Civil War, including seven officers. The Custer Post was organized August 10, 1876. Charter members included Pvt. Roland E. Bowen of the 15th Massachusetts Infantry, whose letters contain firsthand accounts of battle and camp experiences. (Courtesy of Millbury Historical Society.)

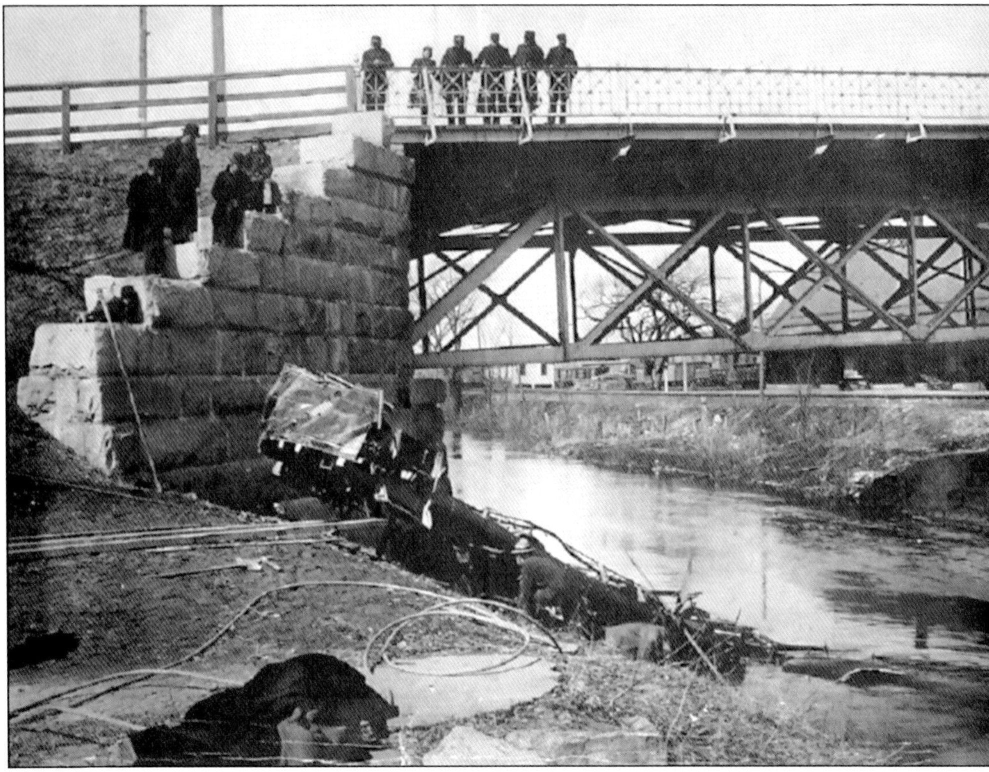

At 9:25 p.m. on March 15, 1899, car No. 63 of the Worcester & Suburban Electric Street Railway jumped the tracks while traversing the McGowan Bridge over the Blackstone River, broke through an iron railing, and plunged 35 feet into the river. Three railway employees died, including motorman Michael Shea, 35, conductor C. Fred White, 26, and spare motorman Maurice E. Walsh, 21, who had left the rooms of the Millbury Young Men's Literary Association to catch the streetcar, ignoring his brother James's request that he wait until he finished his game of whist and could join him. Passenger Louis Plouff of West Bramanville was rescued after firefighters and townspeople braved the darkness and freezing water. Police chief Thomas Dolan attributed the accident to ice that had built up between the rails and planks of the bridge. (Both, courtesy of Millbury Historical Society.)

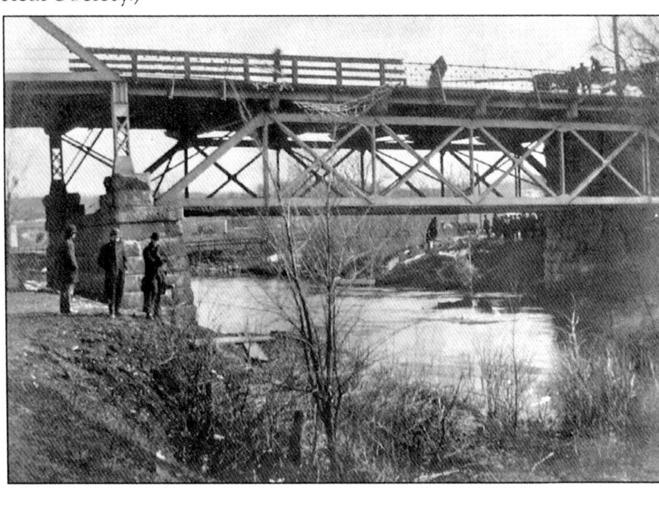

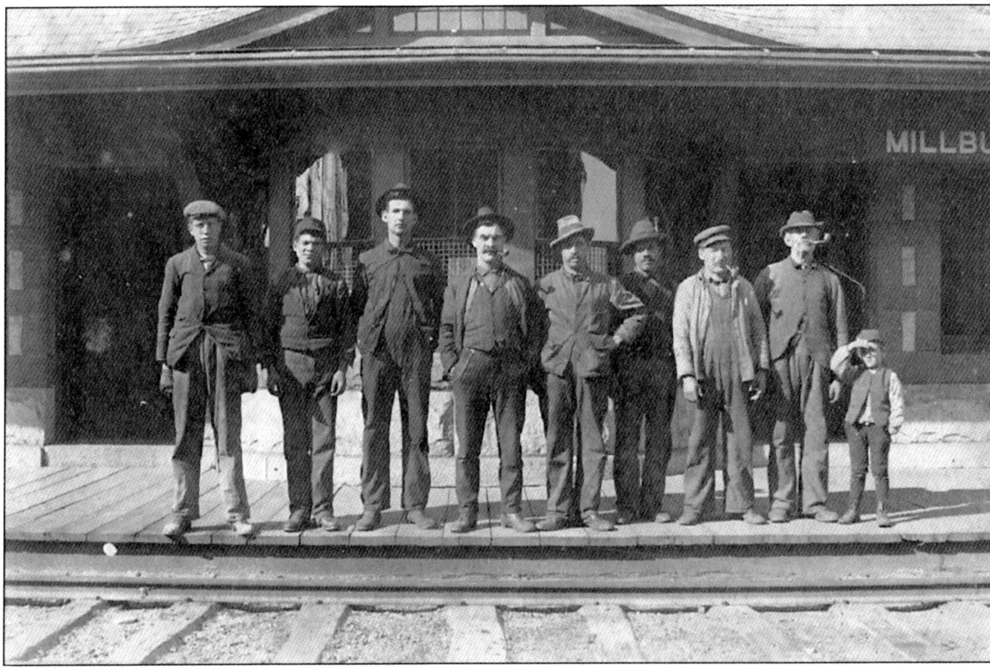

In 1834, work began for a branch line of the Boston and Albany Railroad, which would extend from the Millbury Junction in the northeastern corner of town to Canal Street in the center. A parcel of land belonging to the Cordis Mills was deeded to the railroad for a depot. The branch opened in 1846. Railroad employees are shown here at the depot about 1900. (Courtesy of Millbury Historical Society.)

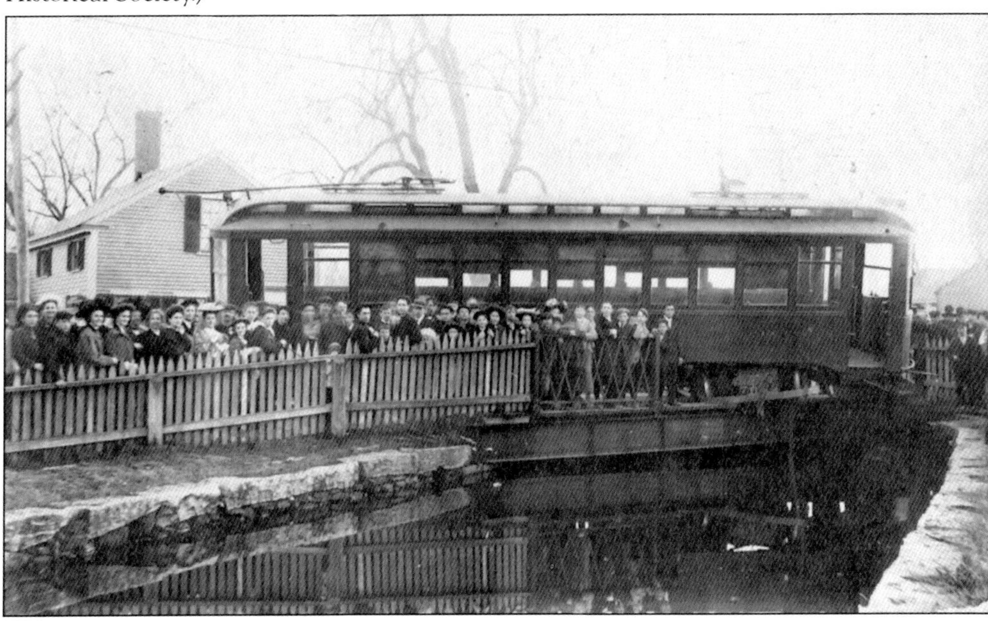

Millbury was well served by railroad and streetcar lines, but accidents, serious and minor, did occur. Here, in c. 1910 photograph, a streetcar has gone off the rails at the diversion channel, which carried water from the Blackstone River under Canal Street to supply the Cordis Mill with power. (Courtesy of Millbury Historical Society.)

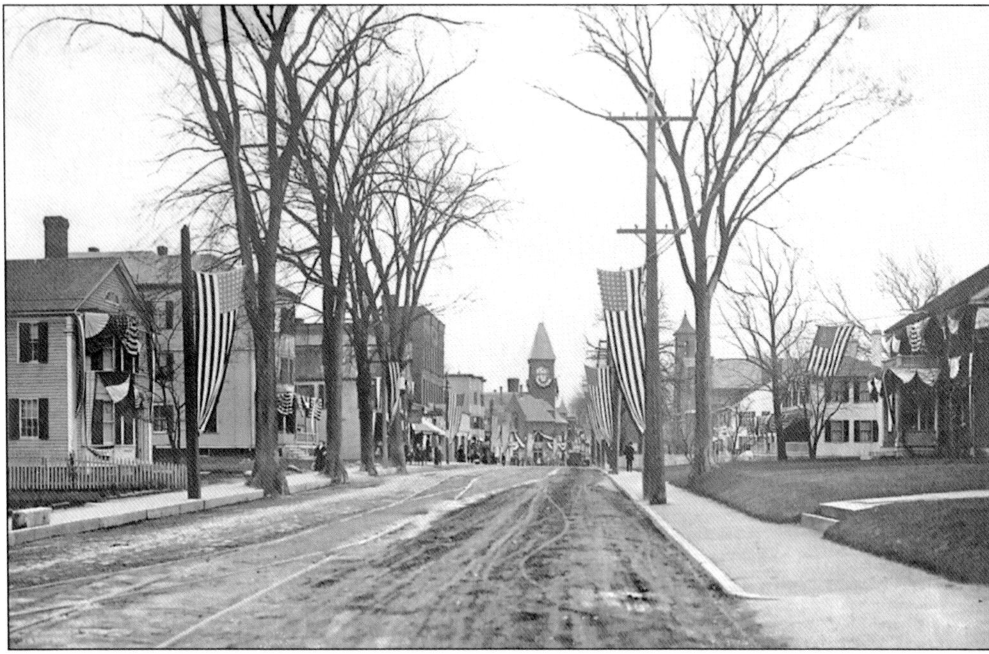

Main Street residents hang flags and bunting for the 1913 centennial. The town history reports, "From the very first the crowds were orderly and appreciative of the superior attractions which the Centennial presented and the serious, wholesome spirit in which all was given. There was an utter absence of roughness and rowdyism." (Courtesy of Paula Beauregard.)

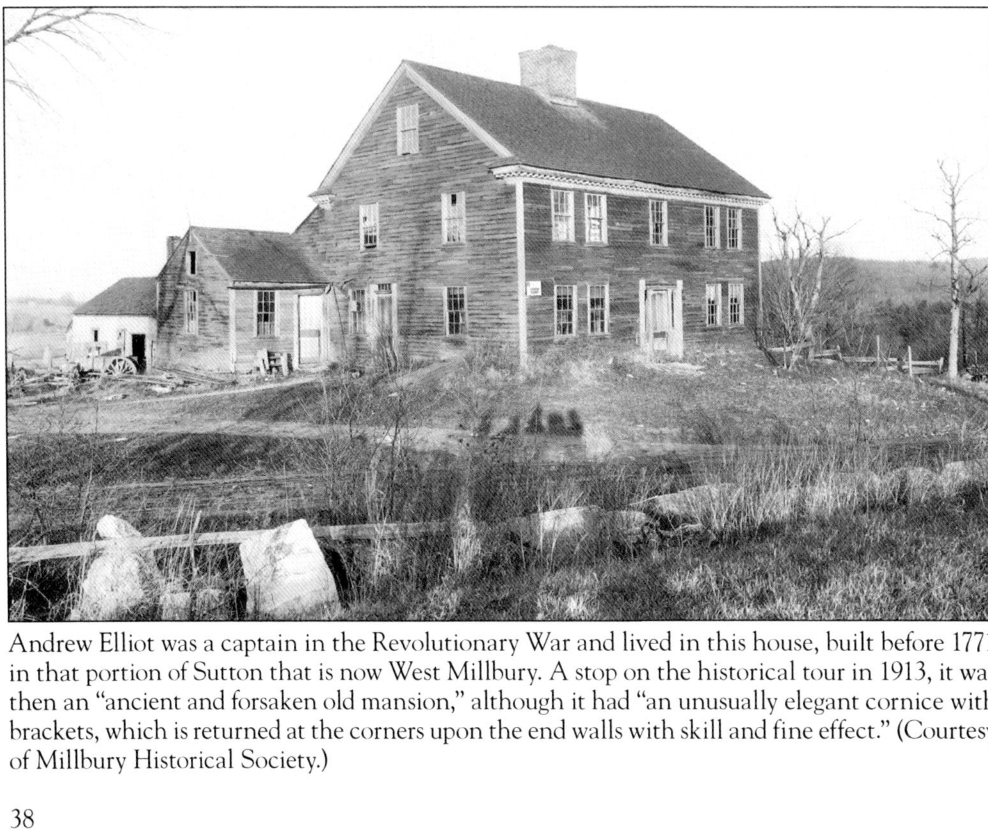

Andrew Elliot was a captain in the Revolutionary War and lived in this house, built before 1771 in that portion of Sutton that is now West Millbury. A stop on the historical tour in 1913, it was then an "ancient and forsaken old mansion," although it had "an unusually elegant cornice with brackets, which is returned at the corners upon the end walls with skill and fine effect." (Courtesy of Millbury Historical Society.)

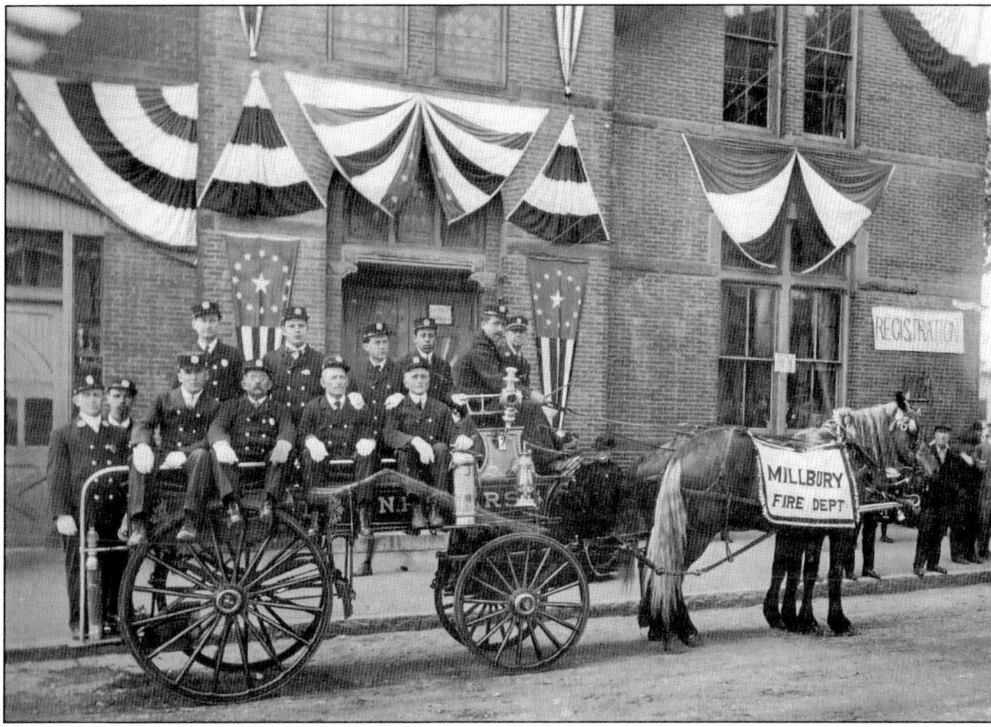

Members of the Millbury Fire Department are shown outside town hall during the 1913 centennial. In addition to lending pomp and dignity to the four-day celebrations, they kept an eye on the public safety, including during a fireworks display and evening bonfire atop Burbank Hill. (Courtesy of Millbury Historical Society.)

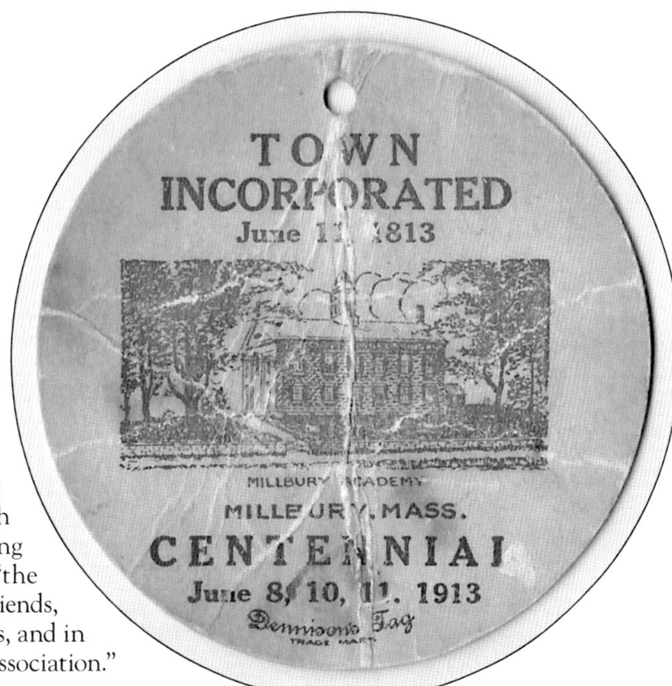

Cardboard tags were issued at the time of the 1913 centennial, bearing the image of the Millbury Academy, which opened in 1832. The tag omits June 9, apparently because there were no official centennial events during the daytime hours, although preparations for the remaining two days went ahead, and "the hours were spent in visiting friends, in renewing old acquaintances, and in visiting the scenes of former association." (Courtesy of Janice Fortin.)

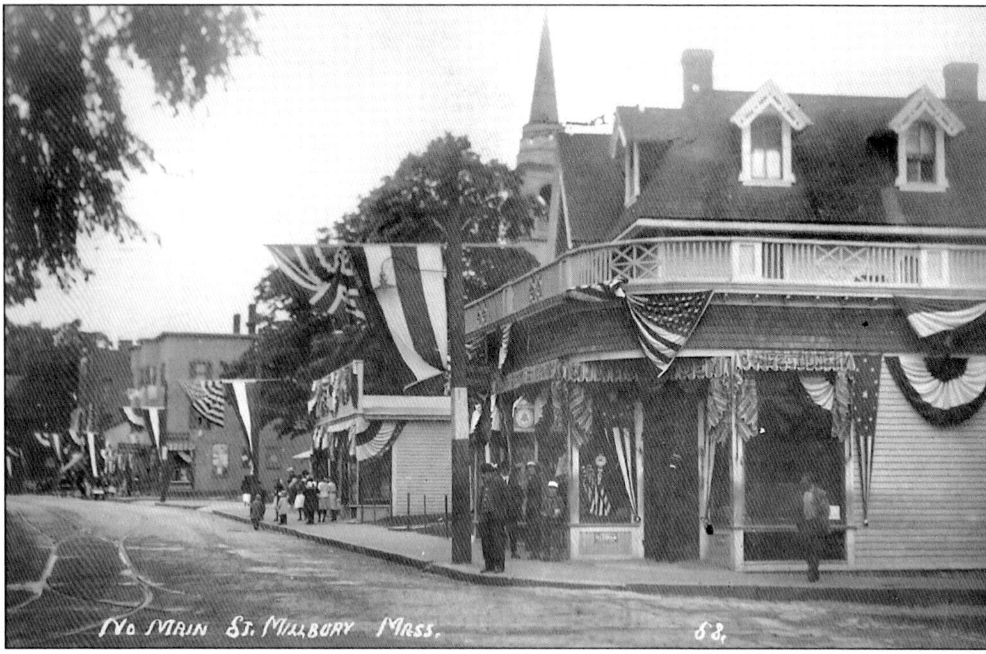

Daniel J. Dempsey ran a news depot, confectionary, and tobacco shop at the northeast corner of Central Square in downtown Millbury. The building remained a newsstand and coffee shop for many years and under various owners. Dempsey served as a selectman from 1902 until 1908. (Courtesy of Rich Hamilton.)

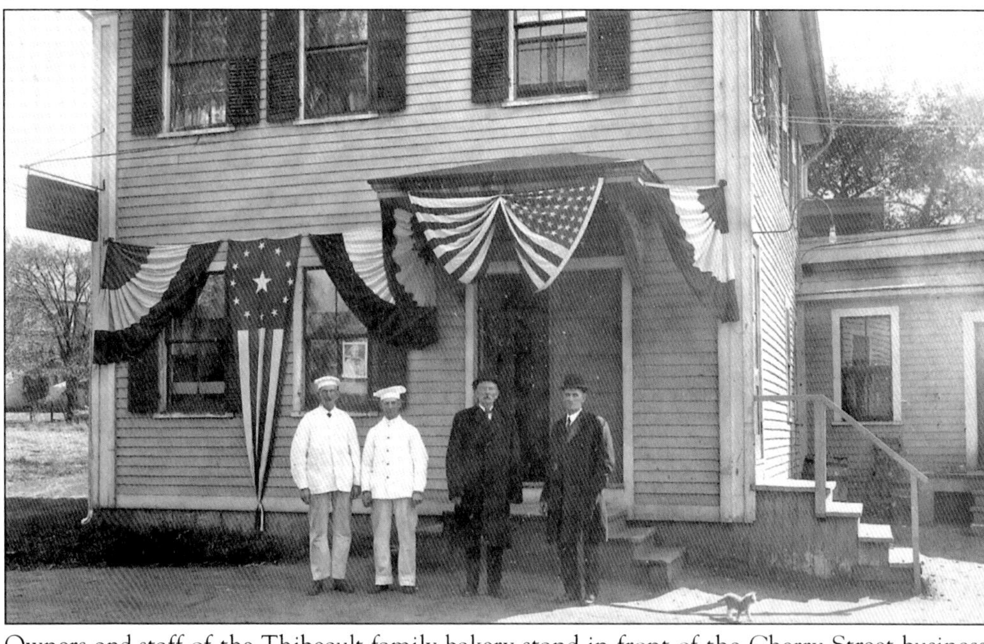

Owners and staff of the Thibeault family bakery stand in front of the Cherry Street business, decorated for the centennial in 1913. On the far left is Arthur Cofske, who came to Millbury from Waterbury, Connecticut, about 1910, worked at the bakery for a time, then owned a shop in Spencer before purchasing this business from Elisabeth Thibeault in 1919. (Courtesy of Millbury Historical Society.)

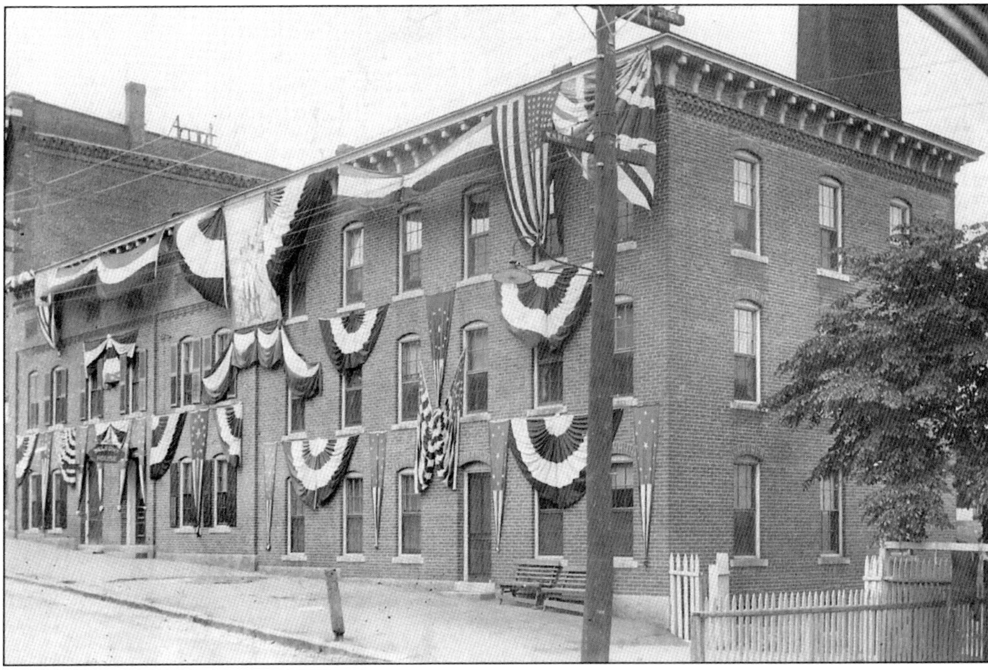

The Belfont House, located on South Main Street, was built in 1883 along with the neighboring Armsby Building, which is visible at top left in this photograph. It was a rooming house and hotel and would have helped meet the needs of workers at the large cotton and linen mill that used to stand immediately to its south on the bank of the Blackstone River. (Courtesy of Millbury Historical Society.)

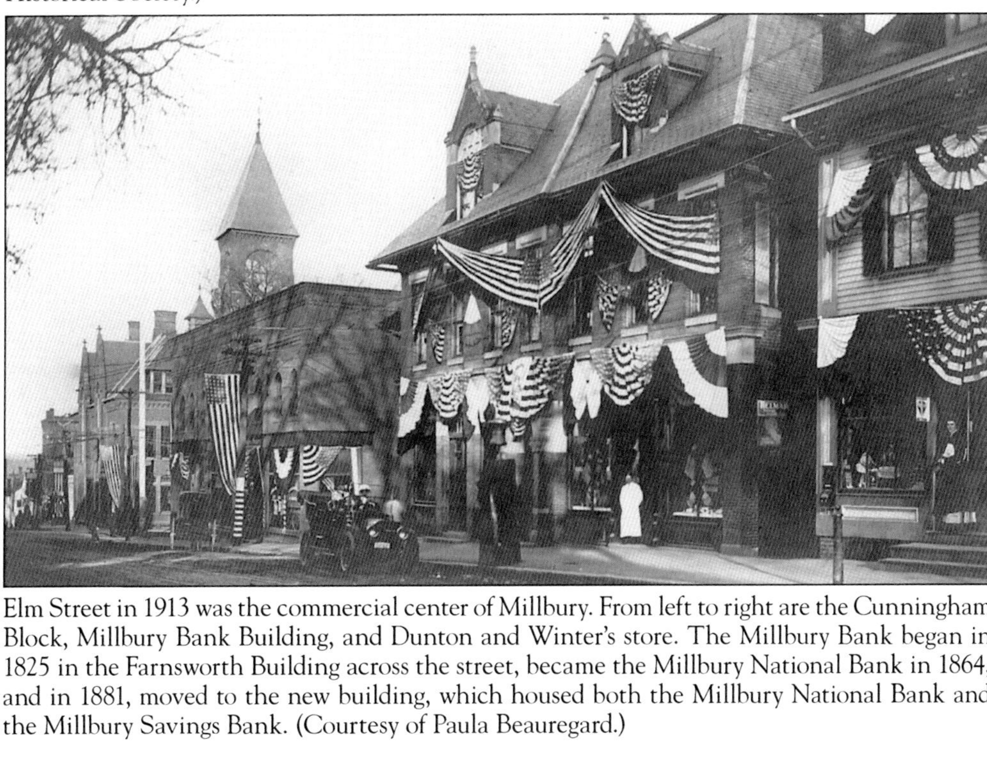

Elm Street in 1913 was the commercial center of Millbury. From left to right are the Cunningham Block, Millbury Bank Building, and Dunton and Winter's store. The Millbury Bank began in 1825 in the Farnsworth Building across the street, became the Millbury National Bank in 1864, and in 1881, moved to the new building, which housed both the Millbury National Bank and the Millbury Savings Bank. (Courtesy of Paula Beauregard.)

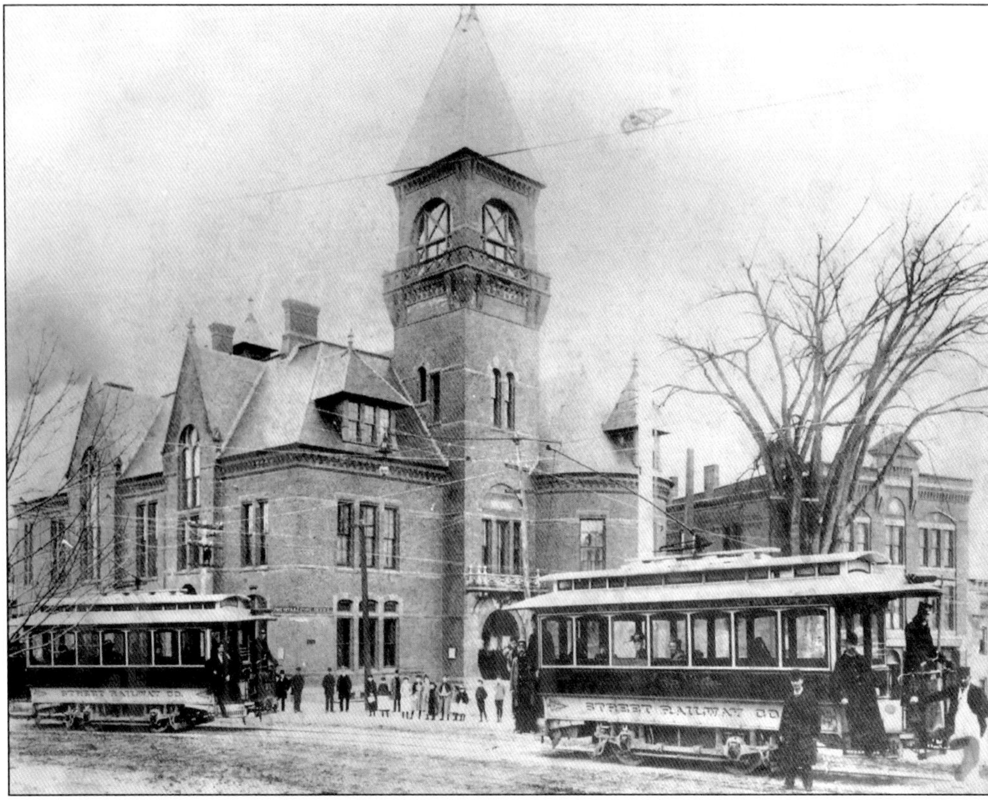

The expansion of street railway and trolley service from Millbury to Worcester took place in the late 19th century, opening new opportunities for residents, workers, and business owners. Several companies extended their lines and service, including the Millbury and Worcester Street Railway Company, whose cars are doing a brisk business in this photograph from about 1900 at Central Square downtown. (Courtesy of Millbury Historical Society.)

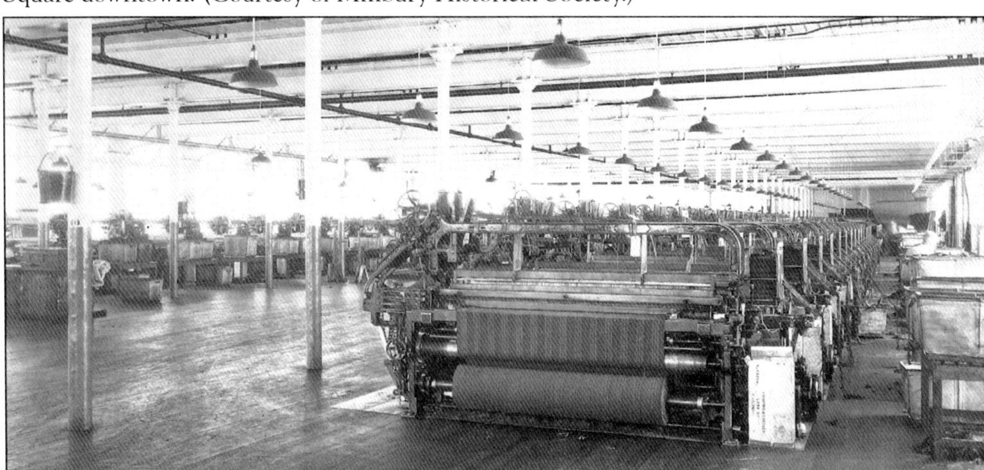

Millbury's economy a century ago was largely dependent upon mills, and the town had long produced a dizzying array of woolen goods. This view from inside the Millbury Woolen Company on South Main Street shows one of the workhorses of the industry—worsted looms from Crompton and Knowles Loom Works in Worcester. (Courtesy of Millbury Historical Society.)

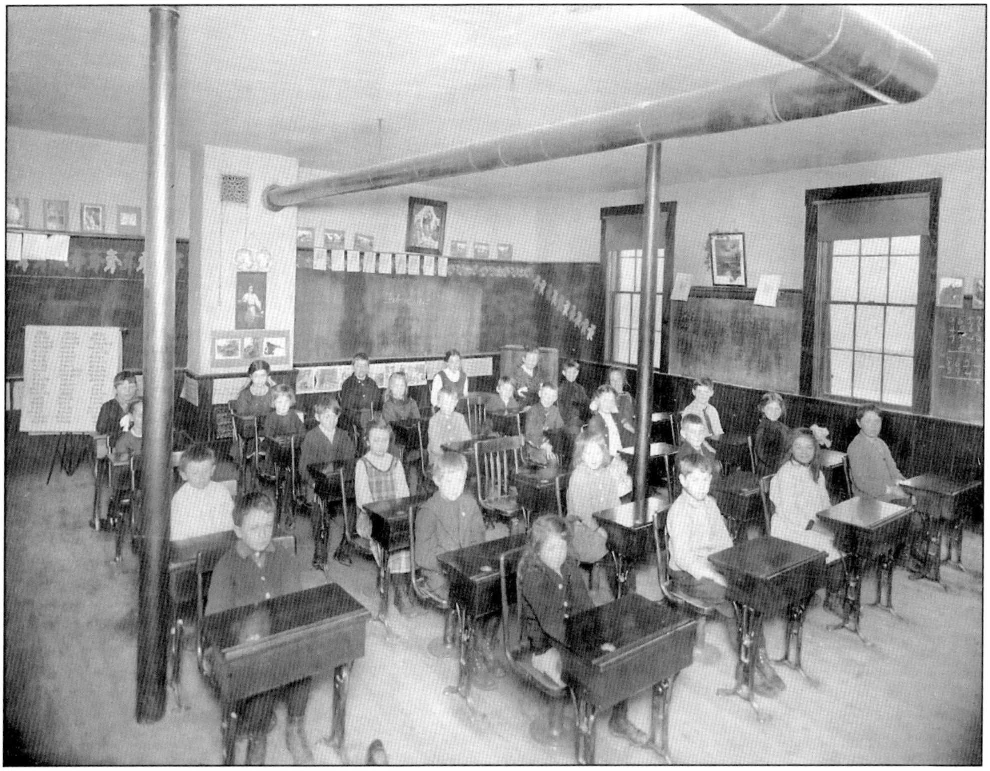

The two-story Grass Hill School was built in West Millbury in 1861 and remained in service until 1968. It was not quite a one-room schoolhouse, but upper and lower grades alike shared the large classrooms, often with just a handful of students in each grade, arranged by rows. The blackboard at the back reveals this photograph was taken on Monday, February 15, 1915. (Courtesy of Millbury Historical Society.)

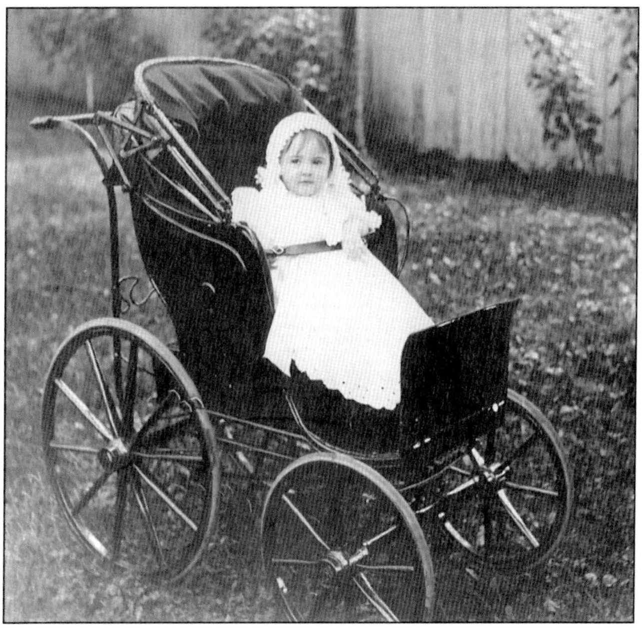

Eva M. Ballard (Malo), born in 1906, enjoys the view from her baby carriage. The daughter of Louis M. Ballard, who founded Ballard Motor Sales, Eva spent her whole life in Millbury, was president of the Millbury District Nursing Society, a charter member of the Millbury Historical Society, and clerk for the Board of Health. She died at age 100, leaving three children, nine grandchildren, and 10 great-grandchildren. (Courtesy of Mary Lou Mulhane.)

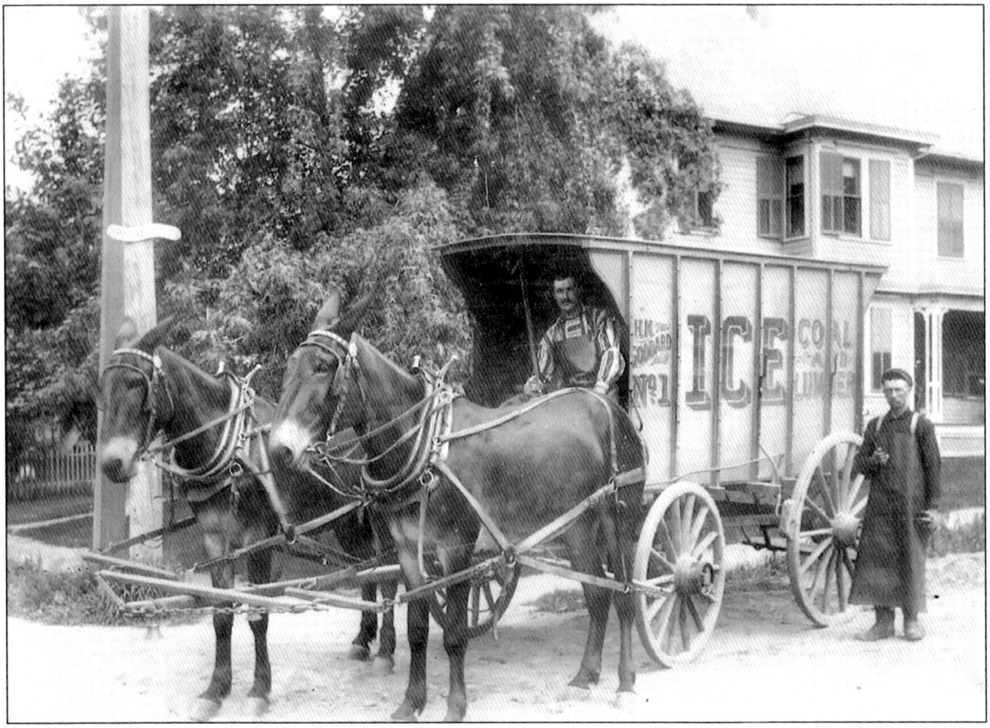

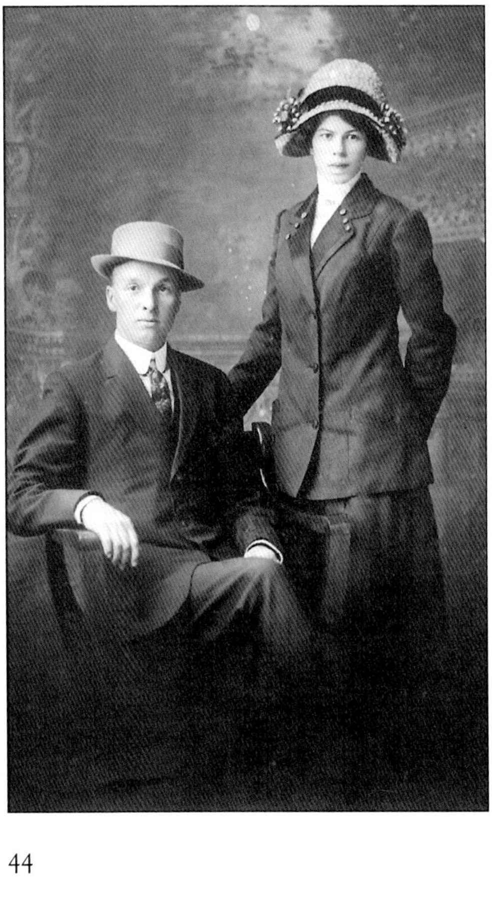

Born in 1859, Harry Merritt Goddard was the son of longtime town clerk Ira Nathaniel Goddard. The son ran an ice, coal, and lumber business and in 1890, bought out Frank E. Powers's business near the Providence and Worcester rail depot. Goddard harvested ice from Singletary Lake. Here, his team makes a delivery at North Main and Orchard Streets about 1900. (Courtesy of Millbury Historical Society.)

Charles M. Kilmer, born in upstate New York, served with the US Marine Corps aboard the USS *Delaware* from 1908 to 1912. While on leave at Provincetown, Massachusetts, he met Achsah Paine, who was living at that time with the Winter family on Elmwood Street in Millbury. The couple is shown here following their marriage in the fall of 1912. (Courtesy of Judy O'Connor, from the Harold C. Kilmer collection.)

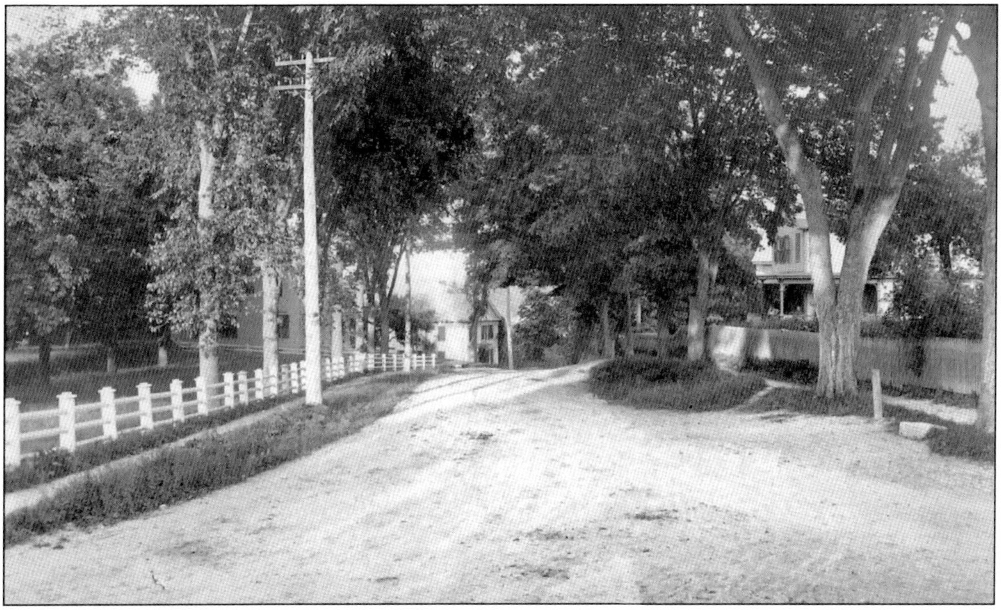

A 1910 view of Canal Street shows the Barton family house in the center and, obscured by trees at left, the home of Charles B. Perry, court official in Worcester and Millbury's town moderator for 25 years. On the right, the home of Samuel Neal was later taken down, and the site is now a parking lot for the Millbury Credit Union. (Courtesy of Millbury Historical Society.)

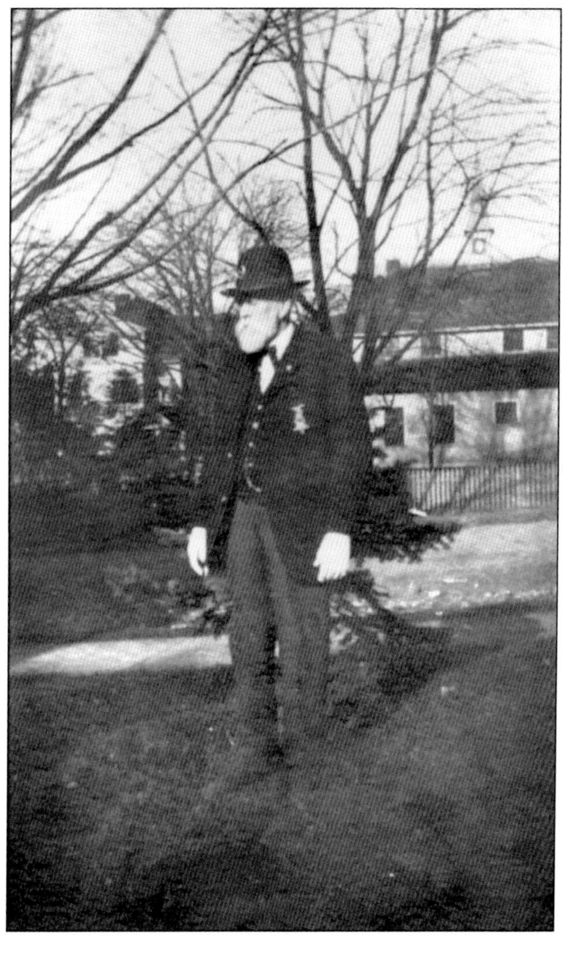

Simeon E. King, born in Sutton in 1844, served in the 57th Regiment Massachusetts Voluntary Infantry during the Civil War. The regiment took part in many battles, including the Wilderness, Spotsylvania, Cold Harbor, and the Battle of the Crater at Petersburg, Virginia, in 1864. King, shown here in 1917, lived at West Main Street and Carleton Road in West Millbury. (Courtesy of Judy O'Connor, from the Harold C. Kilmer collection.)

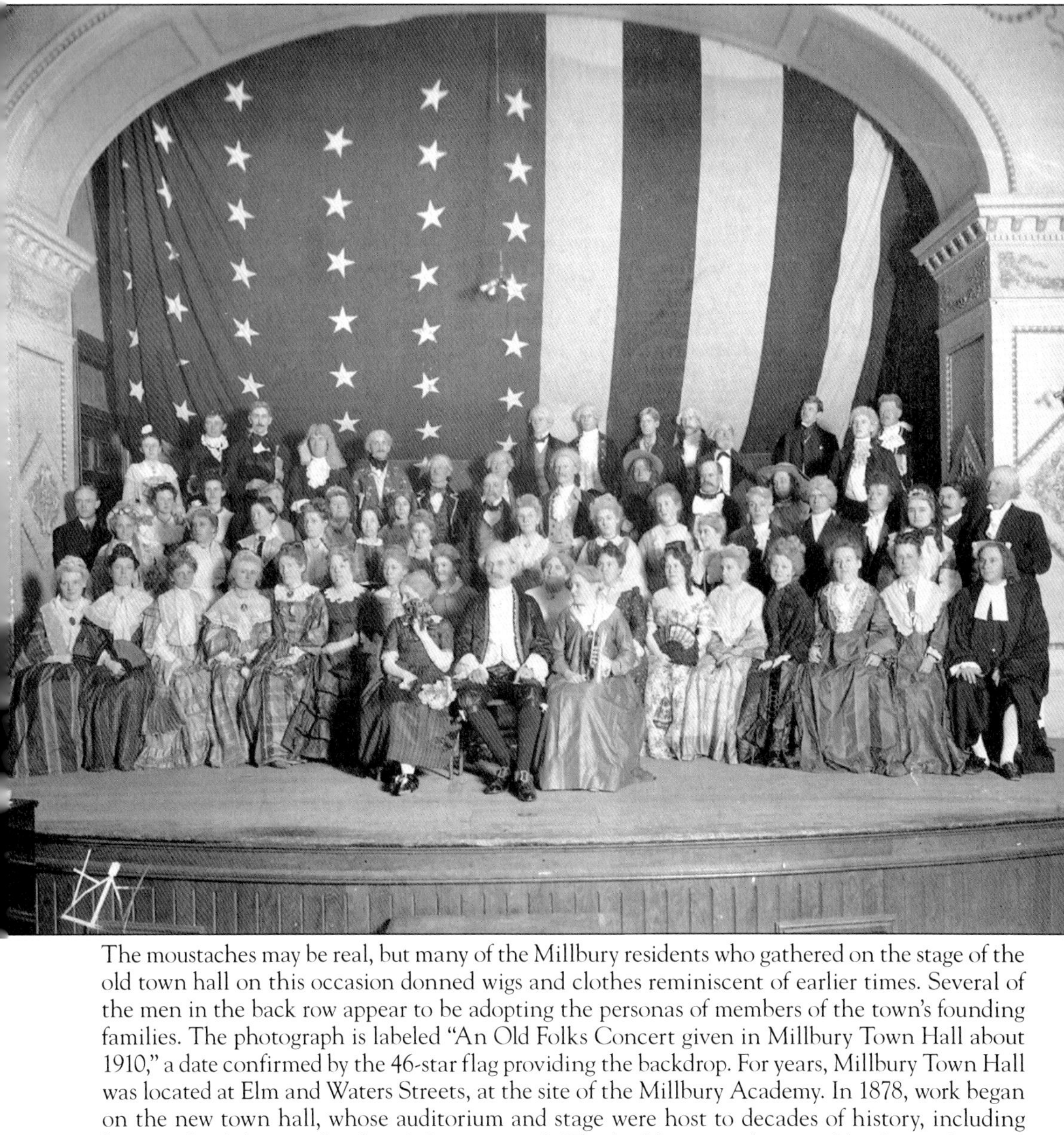

The moustaches may be real, but many of the Millbury residents who gathered on the stage of the old town hall on this occasion donned wigs and clothes reminiscent of earlier times. Several of the men in the back row appear to be adopting the personas of members of the town's founding families. The photograph is labeled "An Old Folks Concert given in Millbury Town Hall about 1910," a date confirmed by the 46-star flag providing the backdrop. For years, Millbury Town Hall was located at Elm and Waters Streets, at the site of the Millbury Academy. In 1878, work began on the new town hall, whose auditorium and stage were host to decades of history, including historical exhibitions for the 1913 centennial. The building was destroyed by fire on January 28, 1971, and a new municipal office building was constructed on Elm Street. A portion of the mahogany stairway railing from the old town hall was salvaged and made into a gavel for town meetings, and the 1878 cornerstone sits outside the new town offices. (Courtesy of Millbury Historical Society.)

Three

Mill Legacy

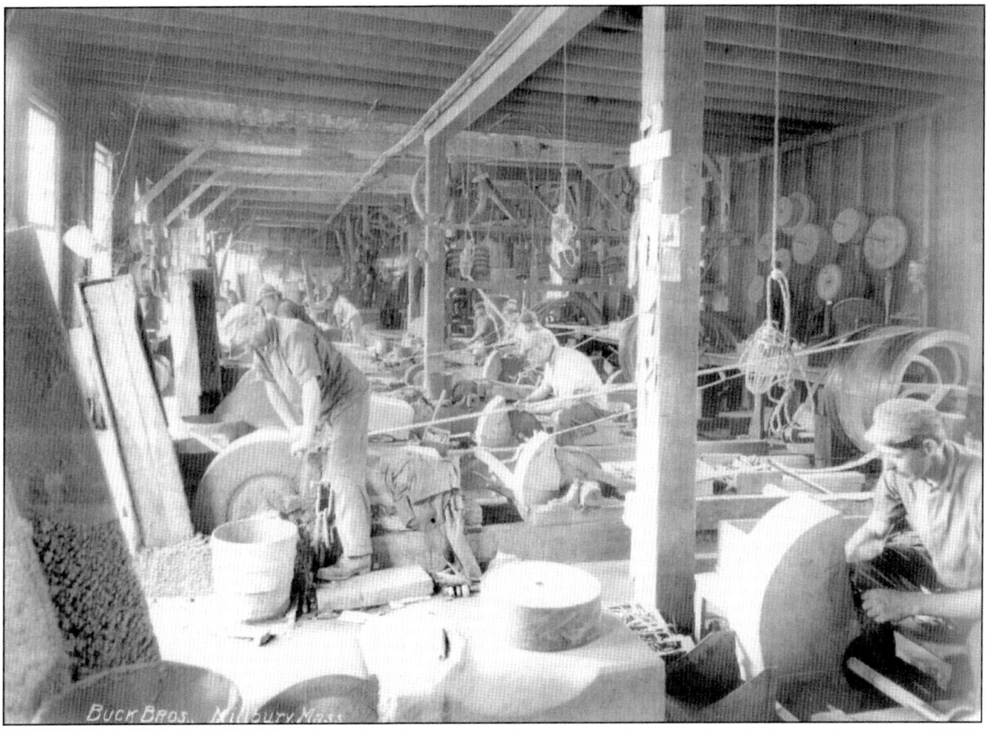

Workers at Buck Brothers on Riverlin Street are shown grinding and polishing chisels in 1912. Brothers John and Charles Buck began working in Rochester, New York, and in 1853, began an edge tool business in Worcester, Massachusetts. In 1857, a third brother, Richard, joined them. The company's expansion led to a move to Millbury in 1864, where it occupied the first water privilege on Dorothy Stream. (Courtesy of Buck Brothers.)

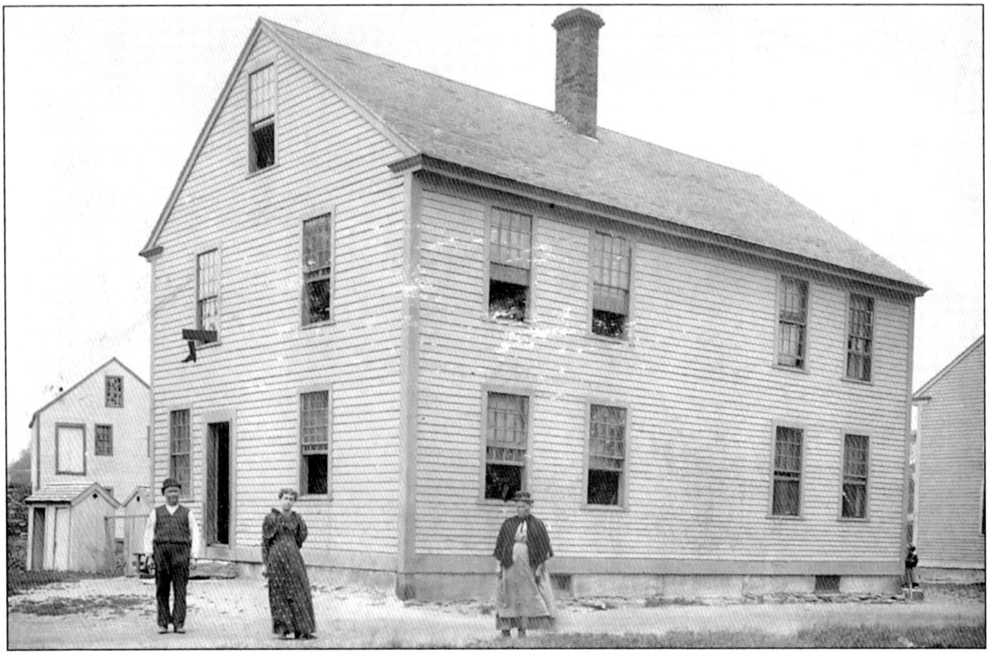

Millbury's rise to industrial prominence in the late 19th and early 20th centuries provided jobs for laborers of all skill levels and backgrounds, whether in the spinning and weaving mills or as shopkeepers and craftsmen serving the needs of a growing town. This 1890 photograph shows the St. George family, who ran their cobbler's shop on Riverlin Street near the Cordis Mill. (Courtesy of Millbury Historical Society.)

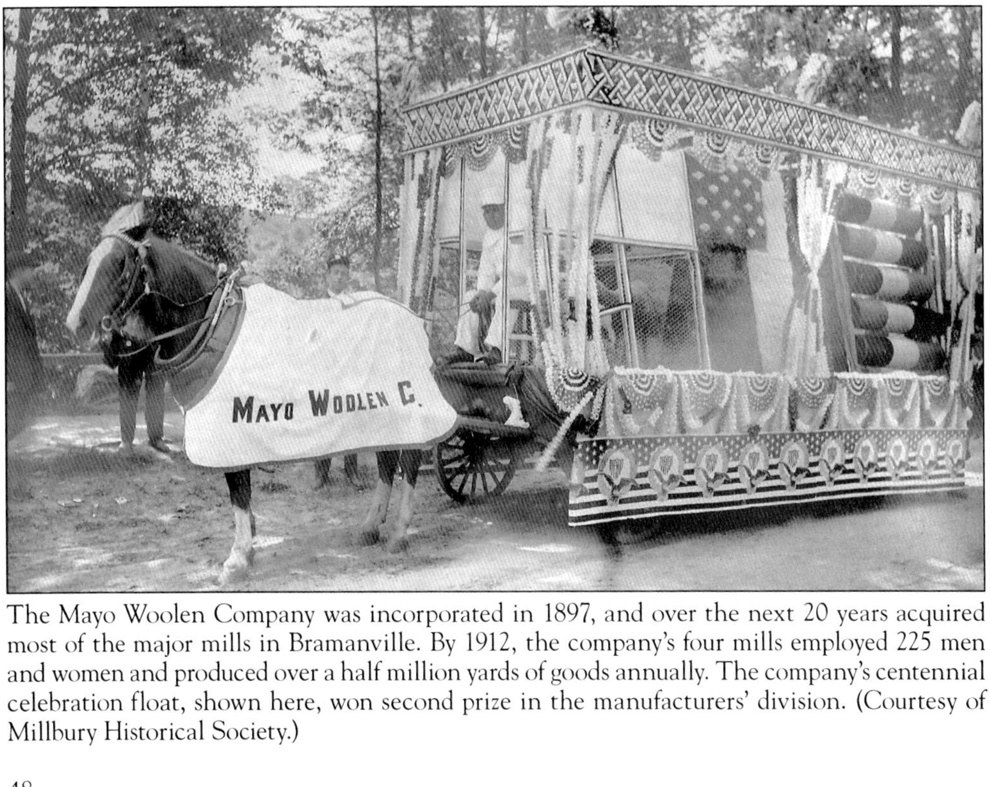

The Mayo Woolen Company was incorporated in 1897, and over the next 20 years acquired most of the major mills in Bramanville. By 1912, the company's four mills employed 225 men and women and produced over a half million yards of goods annually. The company's centennial celebration float, shown here, won second prize in the manufacturers' division. (Courtesy of Millbury Historical Society.)

George C. Dewey, a 54-year employee of Buck Brothers, is shown in 1912 using a helve hammer to draw out the tang of a chisel so that it can be inserted into a handle. By then, this hammer was considered antiquated and was removed that same year. (Courtesy of Buck Brothers.)

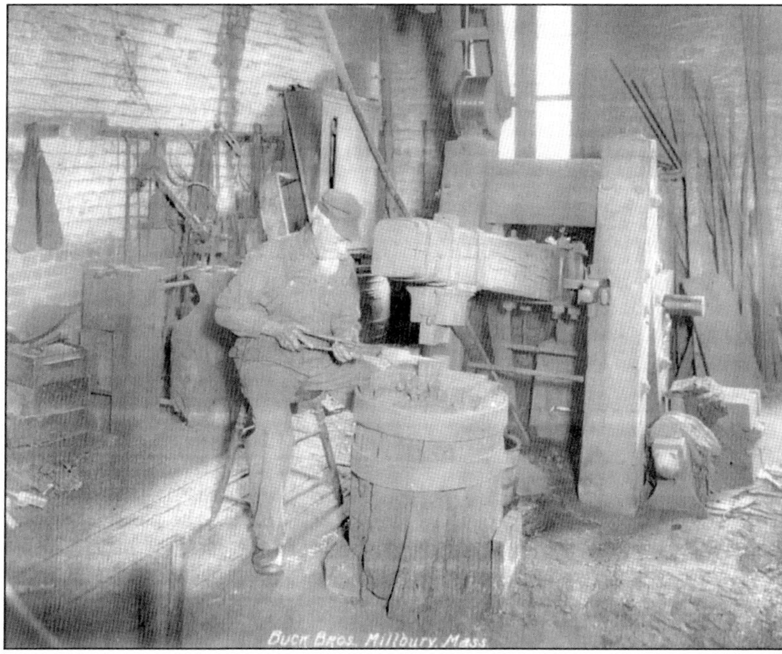

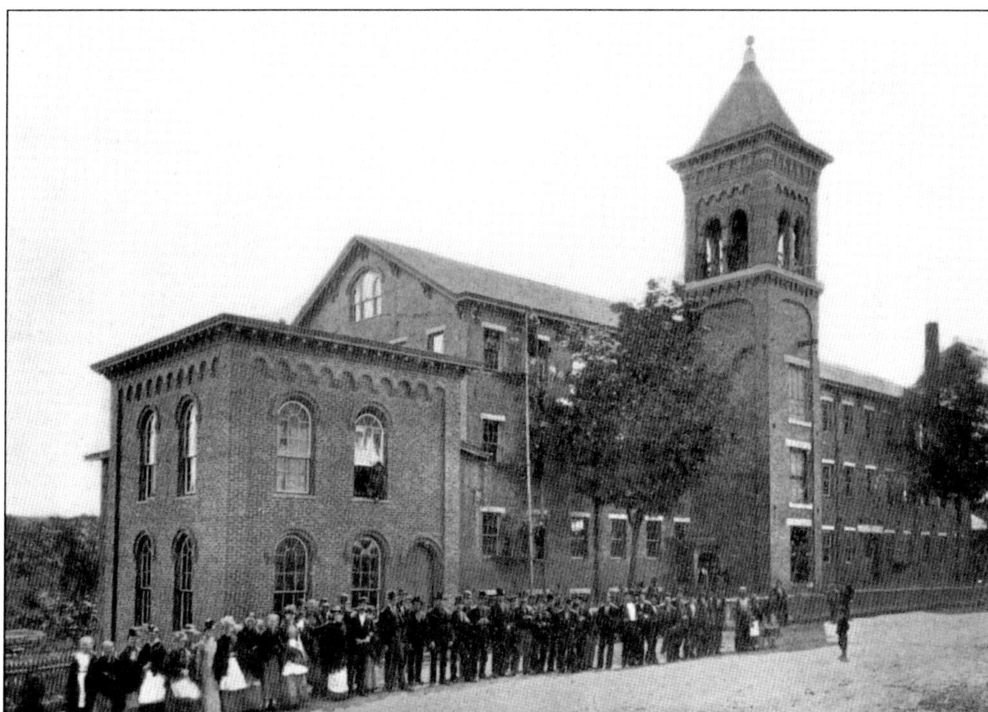

Nelson Walling, born in 1813 in Burrillville, Rhode Island, moved to Millbury in 1853 and built a mill on the Singletary Stream that became a leading manufacturer of woolen cloth. Workers are shown outside the mill in 1886. (Courtesy of Chris Sinacola, from *Centennial History of the Town of Millbury.*)

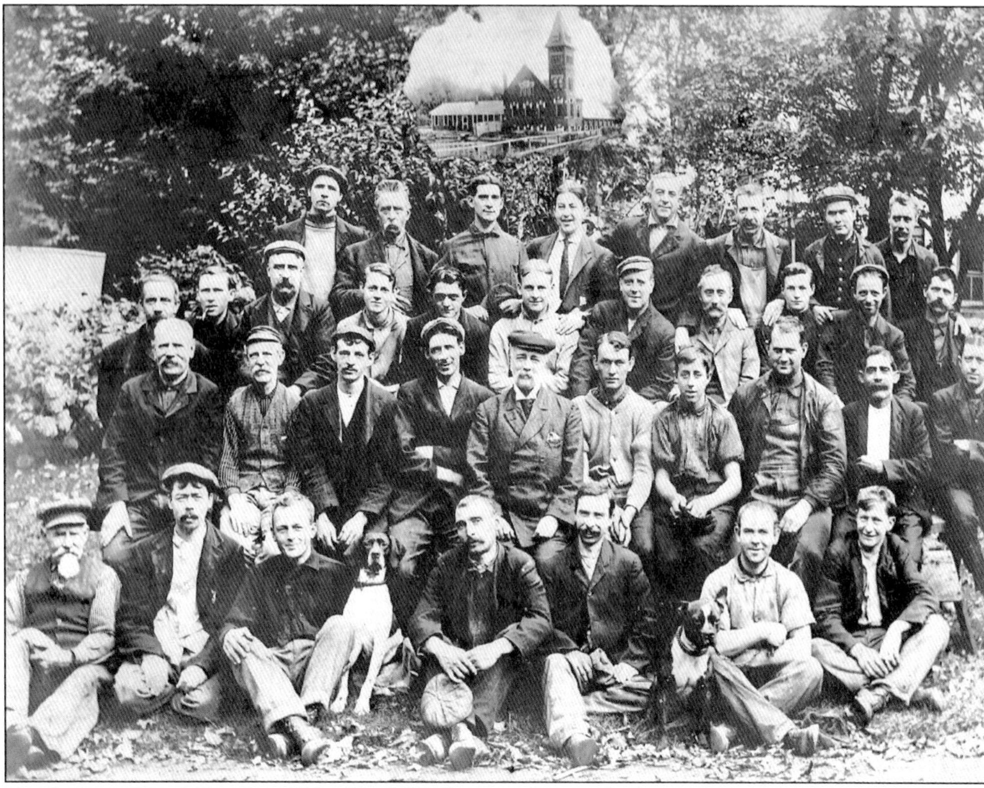

Employees of Buck Brothers Edge Tool Works, together with their canine companions, gather for a 1912 company photograph. Buck Brothers had, by this time, built its reputation as one of the finest makers of chisels and edge tools in the world and provided housing for many of its workers in Buck's Village, constructed near the tool works. (Courtesy of Buck Brothers.)

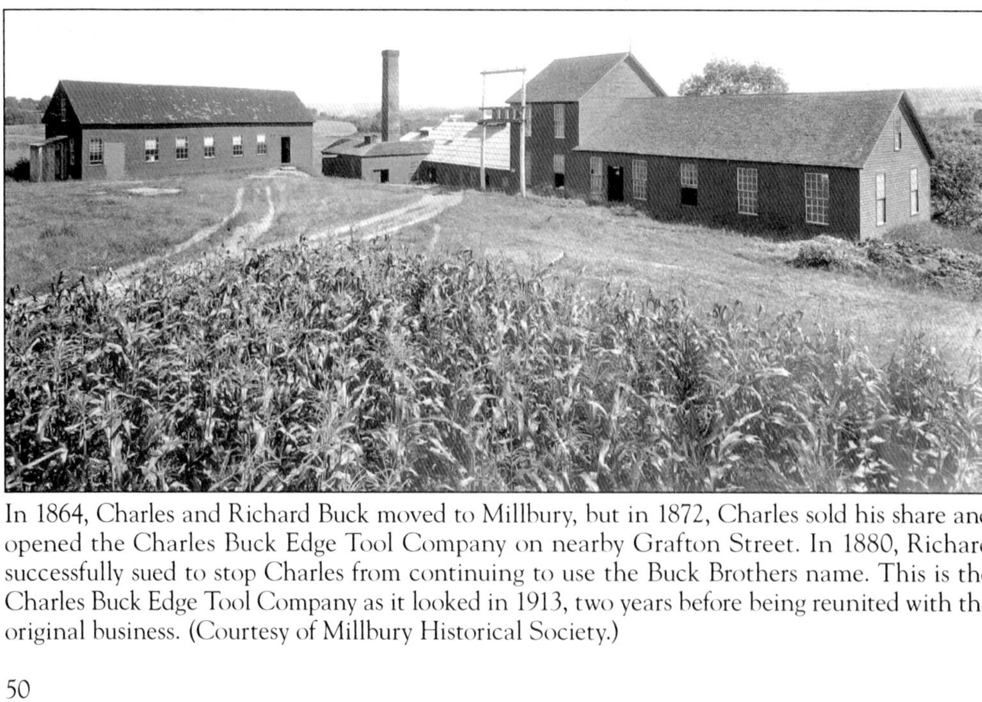

In 1864, Charles and Richard Buck moved to Millbury, but in 1872, Charles sold his share and opened the Charles Buck Edge Tool Company on nearby Grafton Street. In 1880, Richard successfully sued to stop Charles from continuing to use the Buck Brothers name. This is the Charles Buck Edge Tool Company as it looked in 1913, two years before being reunited with the original business. (Courtesy of Millbury Historical Society.)

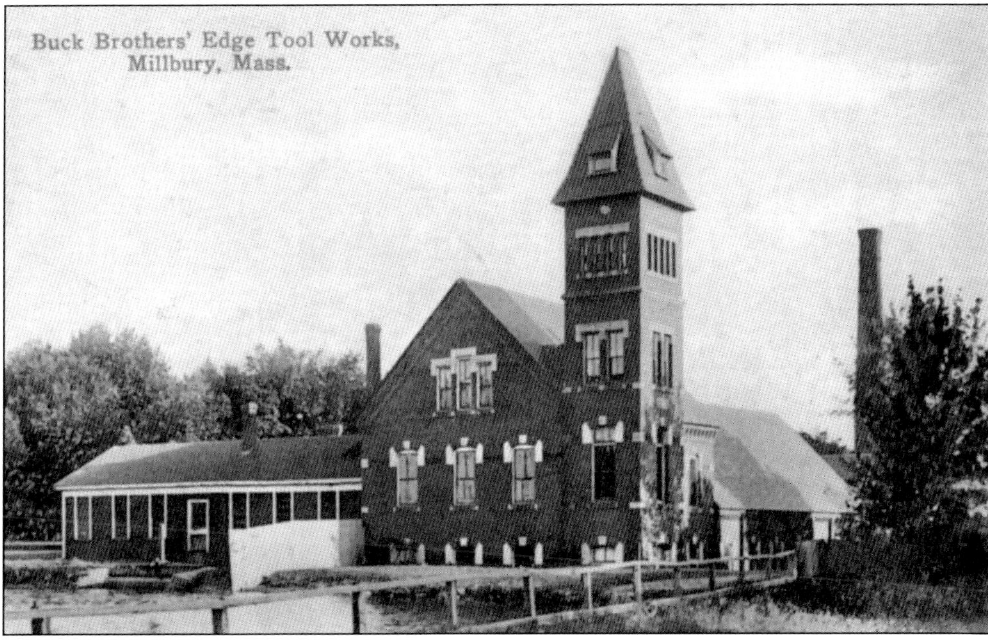

In 1878, Richard Buck built the Riverlin Works, described in Ellery B. Crane's 1907 history of Worcester County as "a handsome brick structure . . . two stories high, thirty-five feet wide and one hundred and twenty feet long." The tower portion was impractical, modeled on a church in the Bucks' native Sheffield, England, and the Riverlin name was derived from the Rivelin River near that city. (Courtesy of Rich Hamilton.)

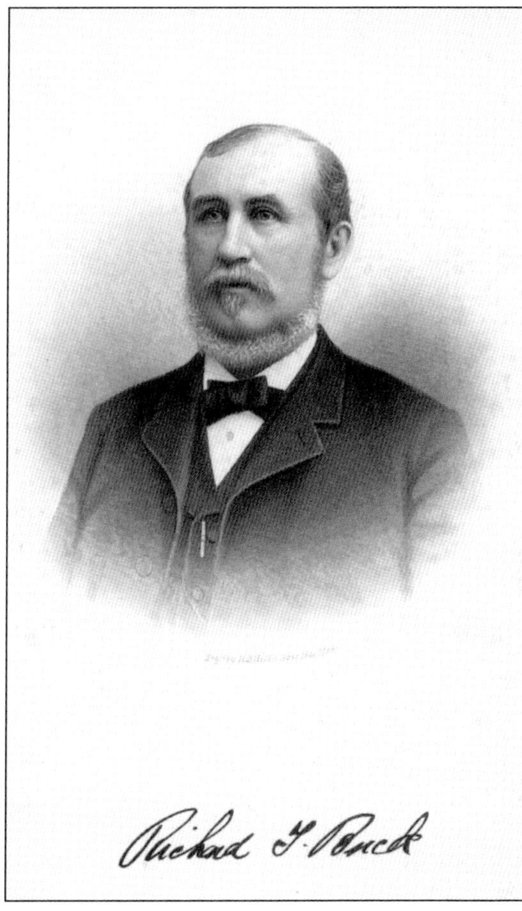

Richard Buck was both a prosperous and a generous business owner, was active in the community, and traveled and read widely. He married Elizabeth Edge and had four children. Their daughter Sarah married William L. Proctor, who later became owner of Buck Brothers. Richard died in 1893, the same year his company won a gold medal for its products at the World's Columbian Exposition in Chicago. (Courtesy of Buck Brothers.)

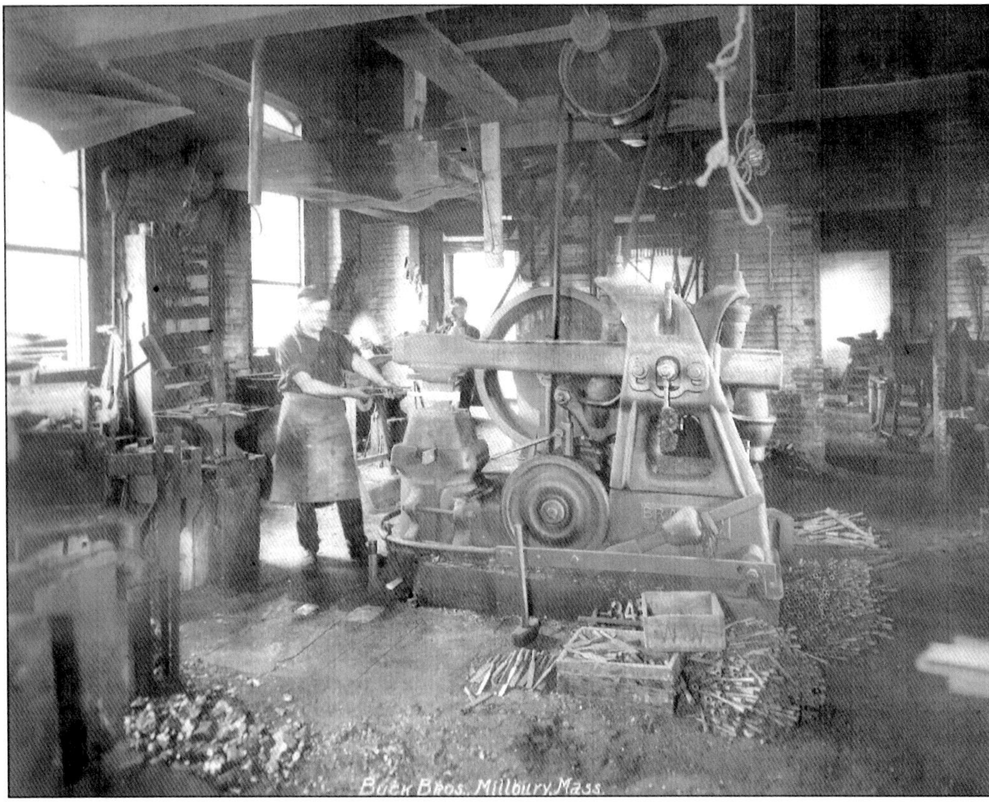

William White, standing to the left in the center, is operating a Bradley Power Hammer in the forge shop at Buck Brothers tool works on Riverlin Street in 1912. In the background, Marshall Russell is welding barrels for sockets. Manufacturers throughout the Northeast competed to supply equipment to tool-making factories. C.C. Bradley & Son was located in Syracuse, New York. (Courtesy of Buck Brothers.)

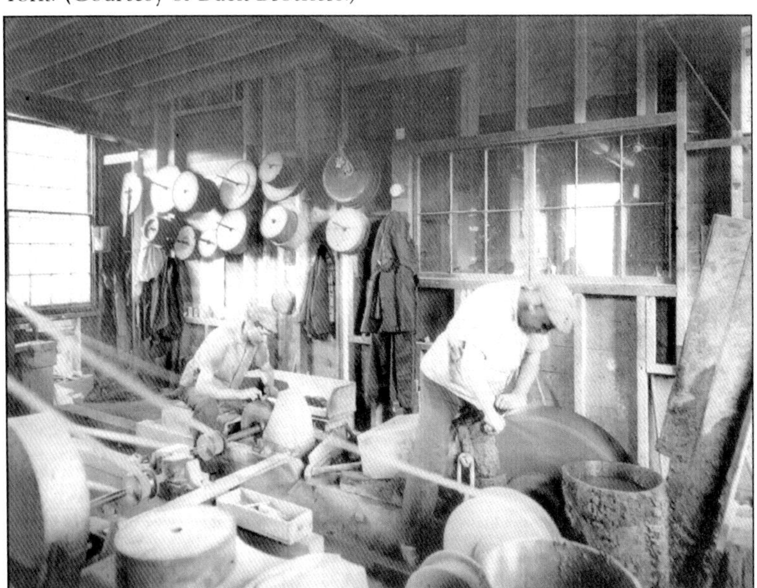

William Barratt, on the left, and Walter Clayton are show grinding tang chisels on imported English grindstones at Buck Brothers in 1912. Workers would sit at "arse boards" as the wheels spun furiously, just inches away. It was precise and dangerous work, for stones could fracture and explode, causing serious injury or death. (Courtesy of Buck Brothers.)

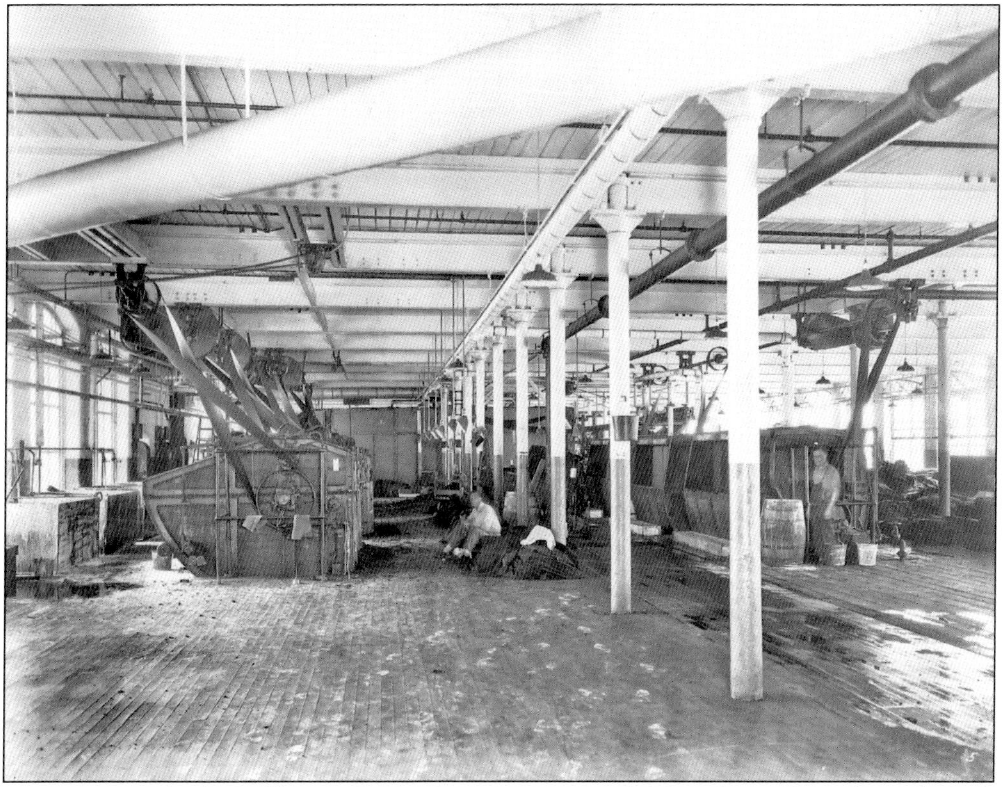

Two views inside the Millbury Woolen Company on South Main Street from the early 20th century capture some of the atmosphere of life in the mills during that era. In the photograph above, workers pause amid some of the wool processing machinery. The men appear somewhat indistinct or ghostlike, because they did not remain still long enough for the long exposure required for the equipment of that era. In the photograph below, a factory floor is covered with scraps, indicating the vast production of goods at this time. A careful look reveals one worker crouching behind the pile of rags at center, playfully eyeing the camera. (Both, courtesy of Millbury Historical Society.)

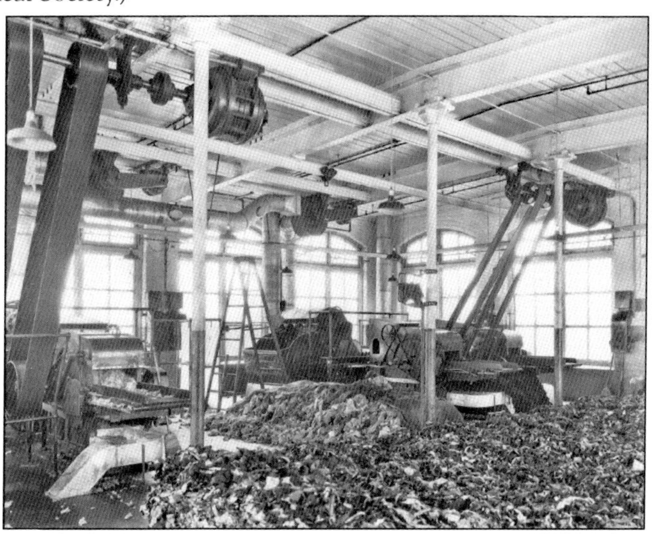

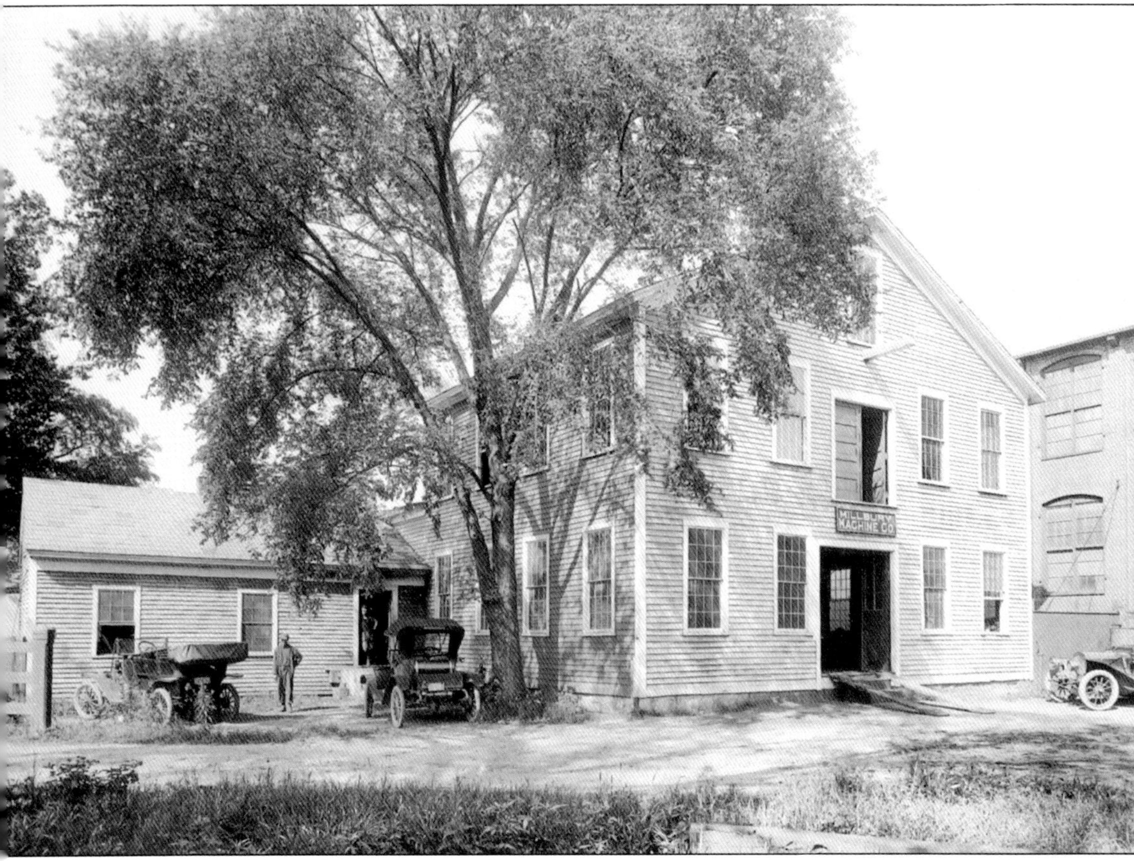

The Millbury Machine Company, shown here about 1913, was located between the Felters Mill and the Blackstone River, on property that was formerly occupied by the Stillwater Mill, constructed by Col. Asa H. Waters following the loss of government arms contracts in 1845. Millbury Machine Company was operated for 30 years by C.D. Morse and E.J. Humphries and in 1907 was sold to Warren B. Harris. It conducted general machine work, welding, cutting, and pattern-making. In 1914, it acquired the dobby chain business belonging to Henry F. Rice of Sutton. Dobby chain looms had begun to appear in the 1840s and vastly increased the number of patterns that weaving companies could create. This building was destroyed by fire in the 1970s. (Courtesy of Millbury Historical Society.)

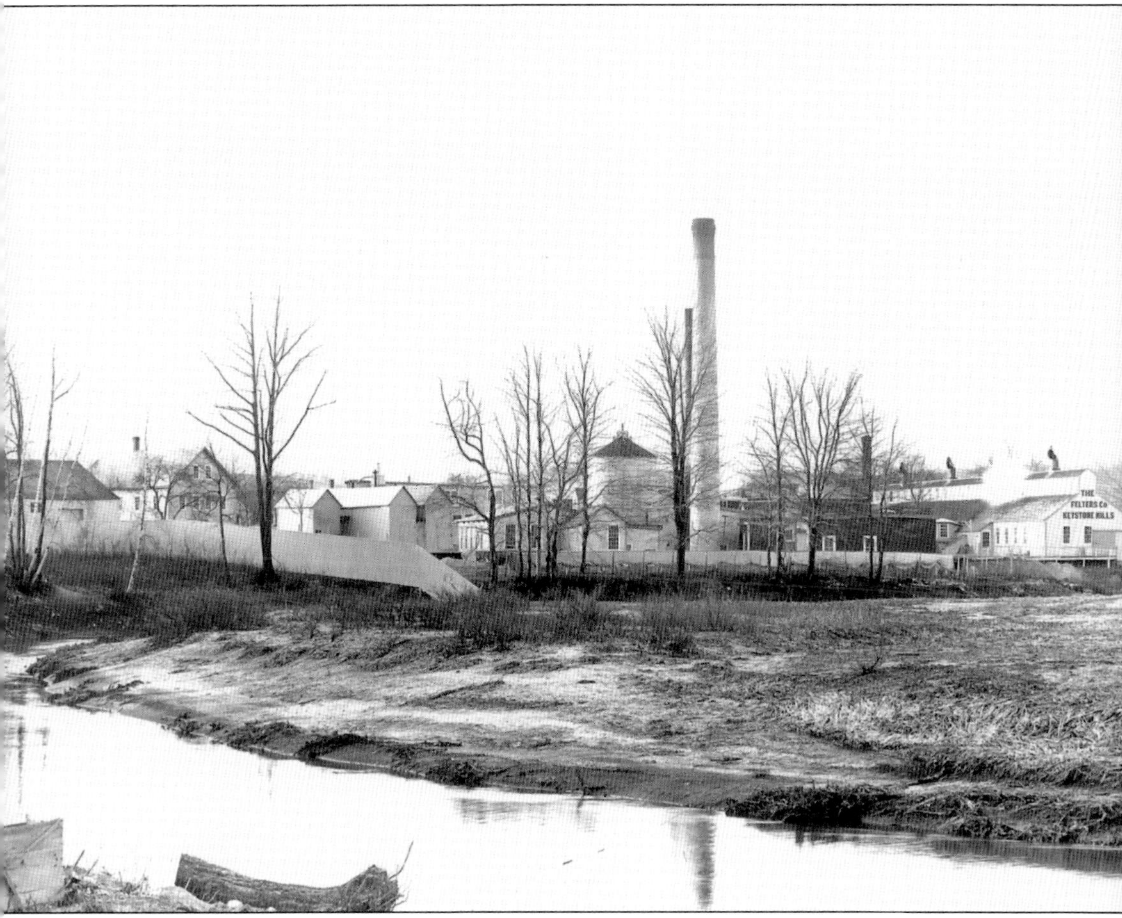

In 1898, H.L. Bowden, a Boston industrialist, purchased property and water privilege along the Blackstone River that had once belonged to the C.D. Morse Company & Shop, which had been destroyed by fire in February of that year, and began the Bowden Felt Mills Company. In 1910, it merged with other companies to become the Felters Company. It operated mills in Middleville and Leicester in New York State—in addition to Millbury. This 1913 view was taken from the west side of the Blackstone River. (Courtesy of Millbury Historical Society.)

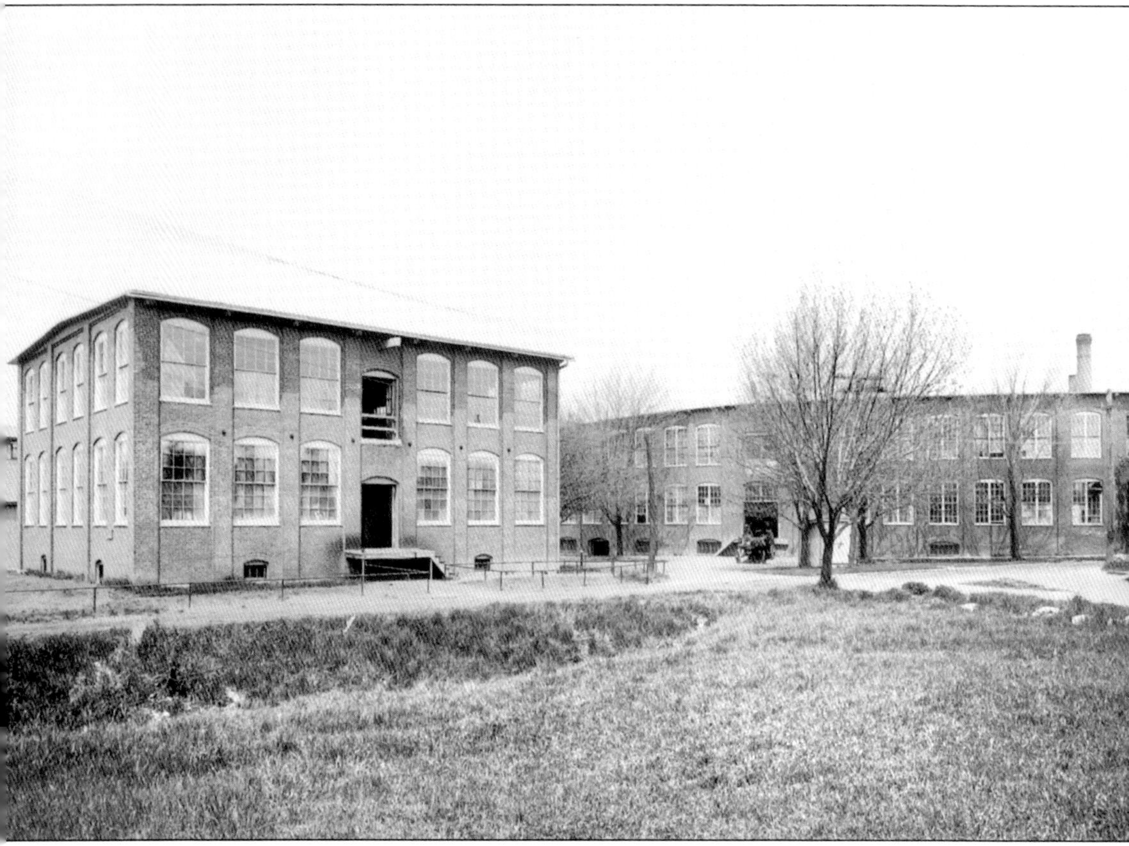

This is another view of the Felters Company plant in 1913. Sometimes, as in the spring of 1919, the future was uncertain. The Worcester Telegram reported that with the end of World War I, the company "is running on a short-time basis of seven hours a day," but added that "officials of the company expect a big boom in the felt business, and the big plant is being reequipped with new electrical machinery." (Courtesy of Millbury Historical Society.)

The Felters Company provided solid, steady employment to generations of Millbury families during the 85 years it operated in town. Often, a young man's first job would turn into his career. Here, five Gagliardi brothers, with 244 years of Felters experience among them, attend the 1971 retirement dinner for George Gagliardi. From left to right are Joseph, George, John, Frank, and Albert Gagliardi. (Courtesy of Millbury Historical Society.)

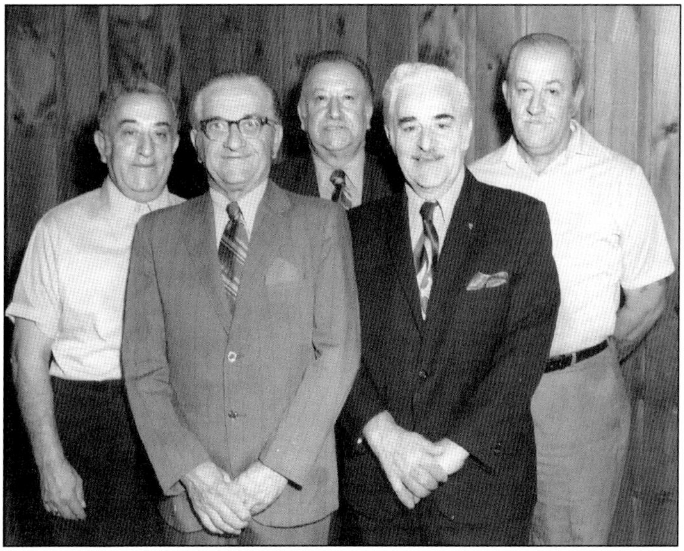

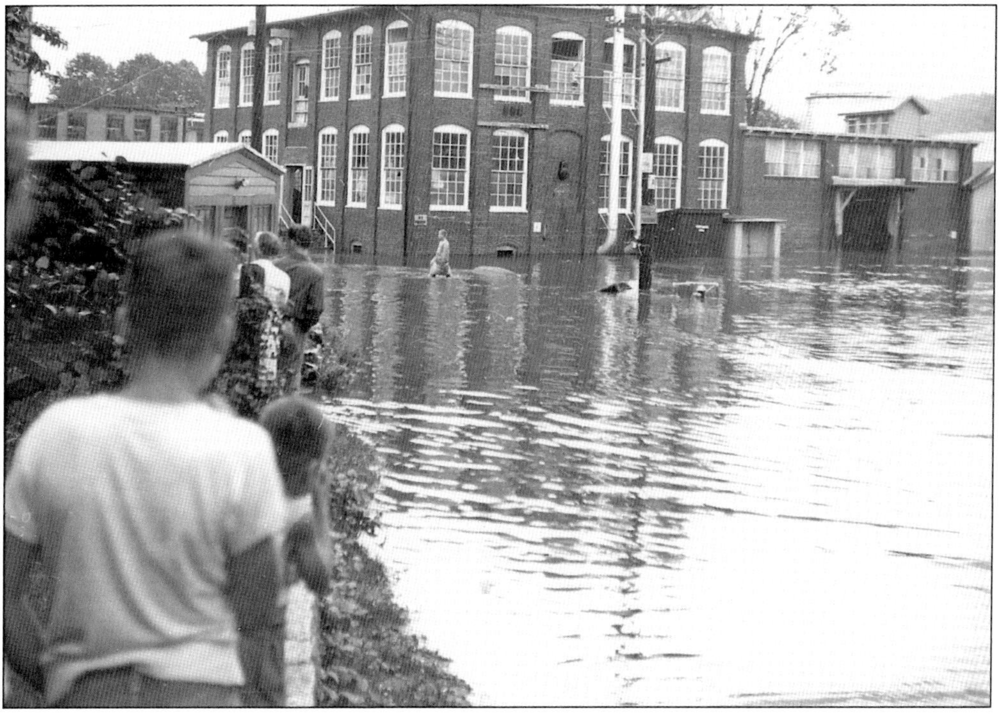

Very little slowed production at the Felters Company, which survived recessions, war, fires, and floods, including this one brought on by the heavy rains from Hurricane Diane in 1955. In the end, it was economic considerations that forced the closure of the company's Millbury production plant in 1996, sending 67 jobs to South Carolina, where the Felters Group carries on the company's legacy. (Courtesy of Millbury Historical Society.)

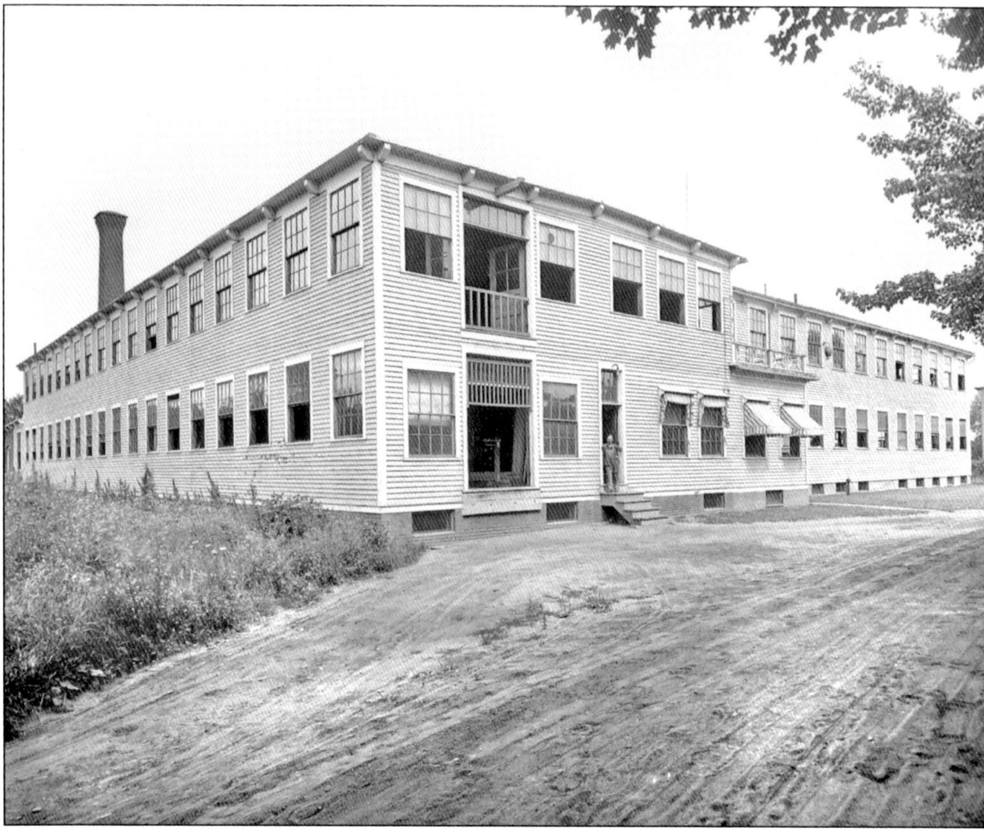

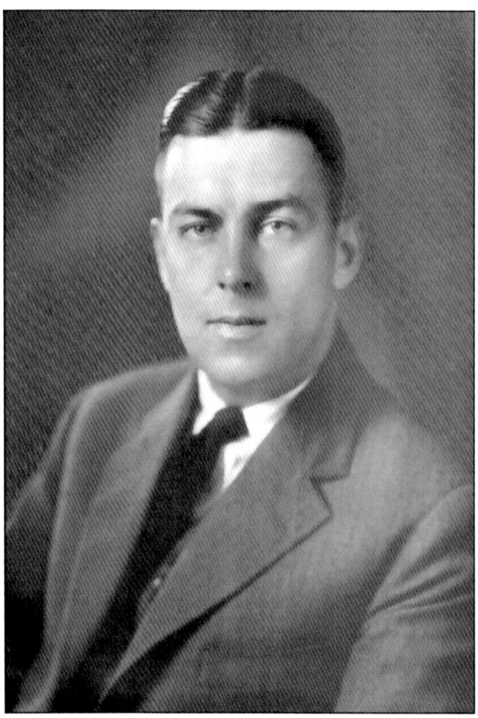

Behind every successful Millbury business stood an entrepreneur with vision and determination. Hudson Warren Hakes, son of a Civil War veteran, was born in Millbury and watered tobacco on the very same land where, in 1881, he constructed the building shown here, the H.W. Hakes Manufacturing Company Shop, producing heddle frames and other materials for many of the town's mills. (Courtesy of Millbury Historical Society.)

The Hakes Manufacturing Company was purchased by L.S. Watson Manufacturing Company of Leicester in 1890, and in 1909, acquired the J.H. Williams Company of Utica, New York. The combined companies were known as Watson-Williams. Clifton E. Watson, a graduate of Dartmouth College and a gunnery sergeant in the US Marine Flying Corps during World War I, served as vice president and general manager. (Courtesy of *Worcester Telegram & Gazette*, from Ellery B. Crane's 1907 history of Worcester County.)

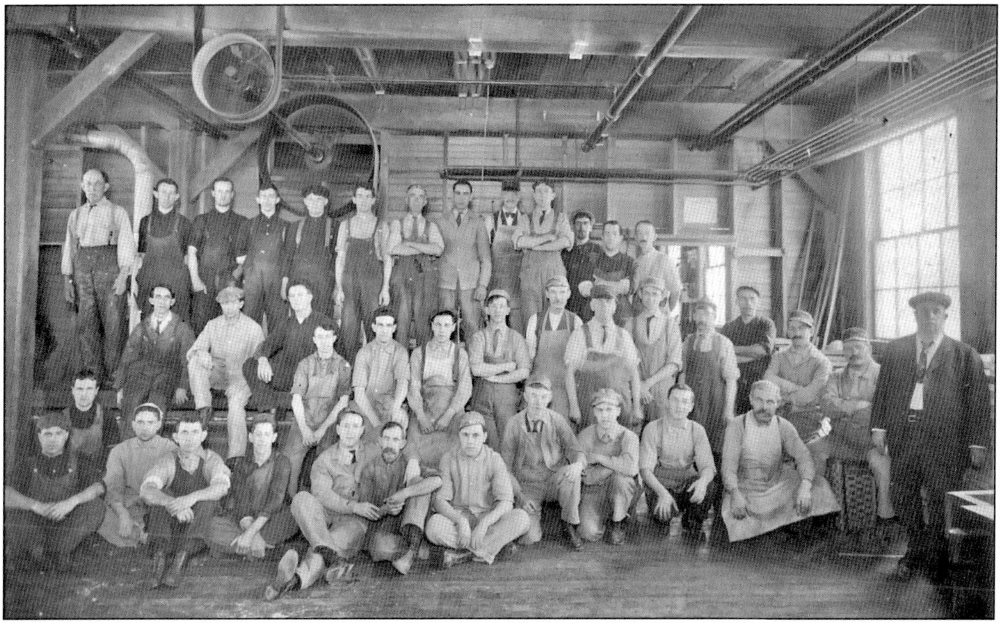

Above, employees of the Watson-Williams Company gather for a c. 1913 company photograph inside the manufacturing facility on River Street. Seated in the front row, second from left, is August Malhoit of Elm Court, and also seated in the front row, seventh from left, with a mustache, is Pierre Commayer, also a resident of Elm Court. The photograph below captures some of the workers at their stations. The company made shuttles and heddle frames for looms and a variety of other products for mills. (Both, courtesy of Millbury Historical Society.)

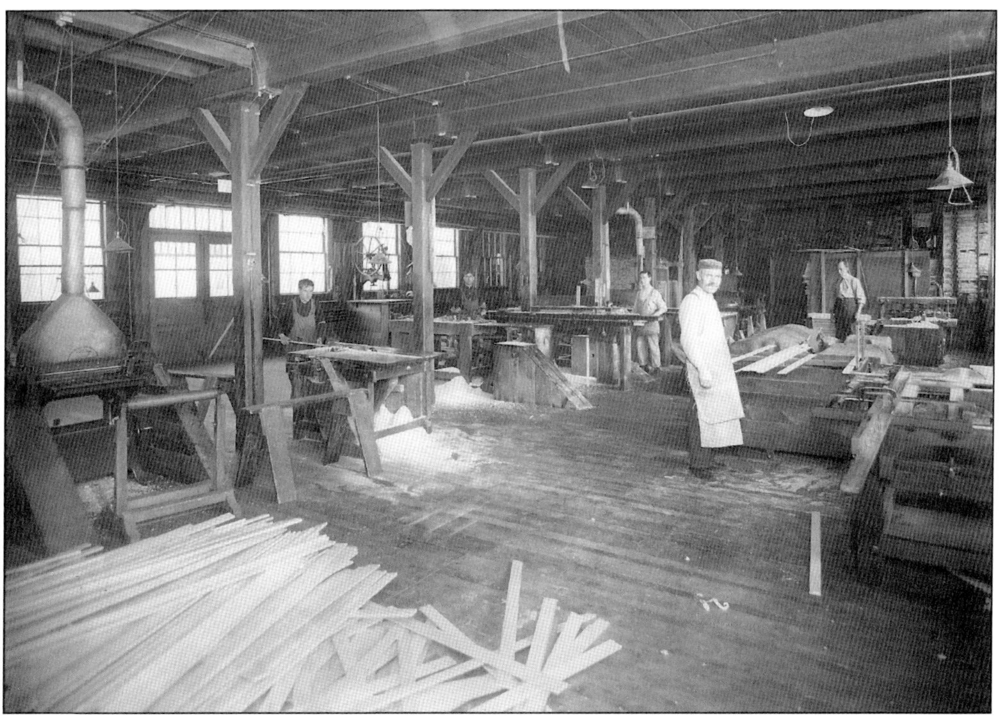

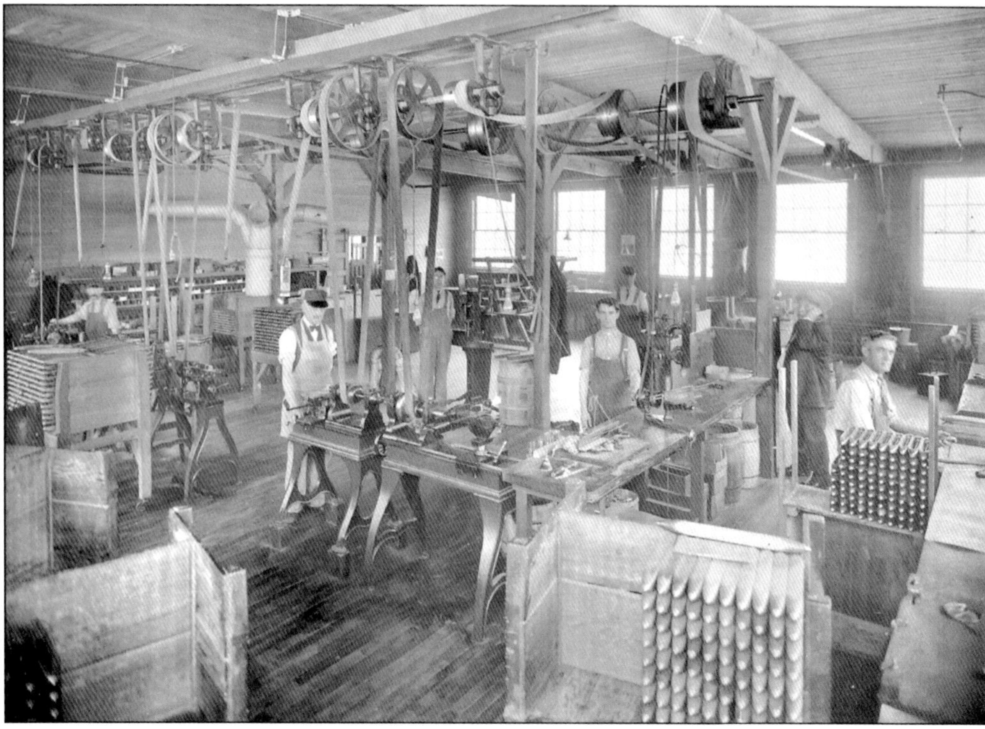

Workers of the Watson-Williams Company are shown about 1913, manufacturing shuttles for looms. Millbury was for many years a leading supplier of shuttles. During the Civil War, when it was prohibitively expensive to import porcelain shuttle eyes, Moses D. Garfield developed a process of making the eyes from clay, producing a superior shuttle in his shop on Millbury's Tainter Hill that enabled cloth manufacturers to keep producing the goods needed by the Union army. In the photograph below, Fred Caplette is standing second from left. The Watson-Williams Company filed for bankruptcy in 1962, and the company's assets, including a plant in North Carolina, were sold to Fletcher Industries. (Both, courtesy of Millbury Historical Society.)

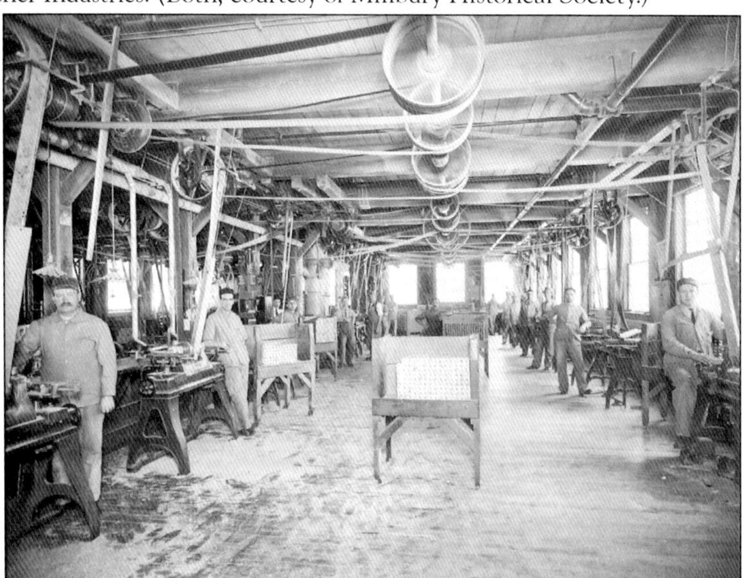

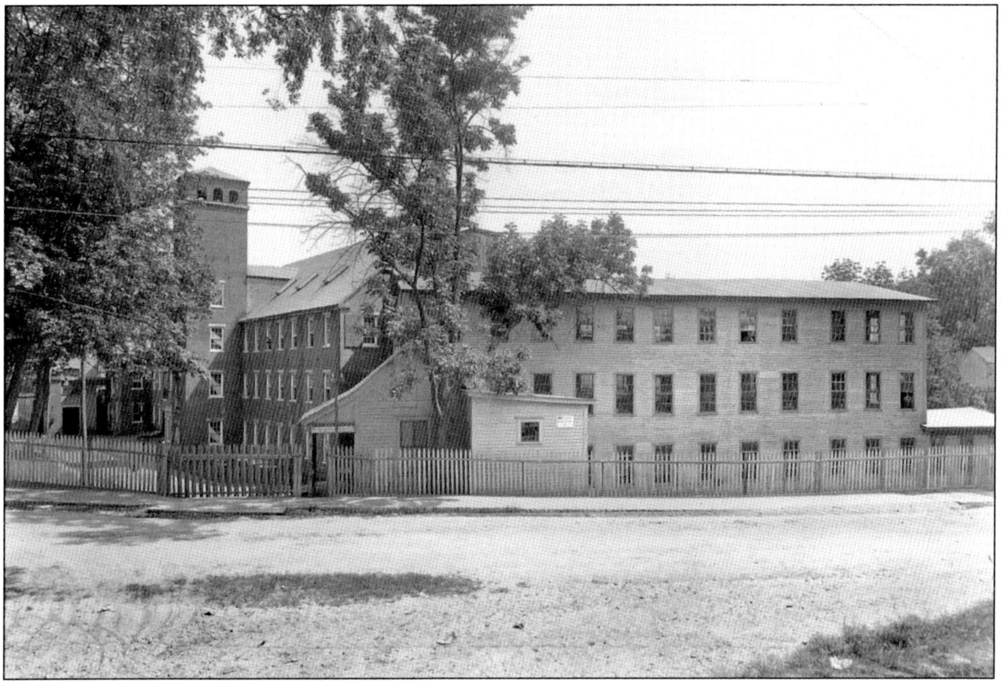

The National Crash Manufacturing Company, shown in 1913, was located on South Main Street, just beyond Belfont House. At this site, before 1740, Benjamin Gowing had an iron foundry, the first industry on the Blackstone in Millbury. Later mills changed hands and specialties several times. Crash is coarse cotton or linen used for towels and curtains and comes from the Russian *krashenina*, meaning "colored linen." (Courtesy of Millbury Historical Society.)

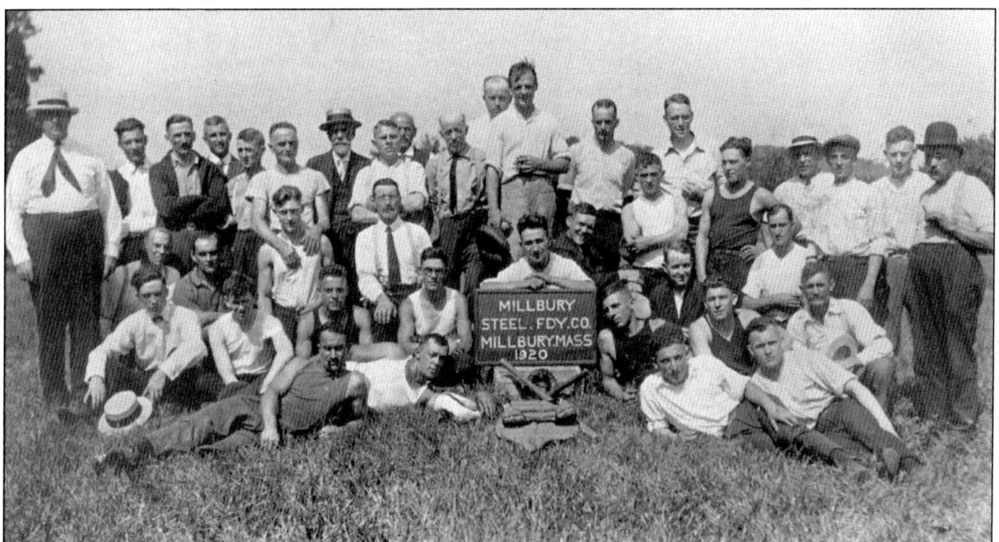

Millbury Steel Foundry Company employees are shown here on a company picnic in 1920. The business was incorporated in 1908 as the Oakley Steel Foundry Company, occupying the former Millbury Foundry Company near the Boston and Albany Railroad line, along what is now Howe Avenue. It specialized in Monel metal, an alloy of nickel, copper, and iron that resists corrosion by seawater, acids, and oxygen. (Courtesy of Millbury Historical Society.)

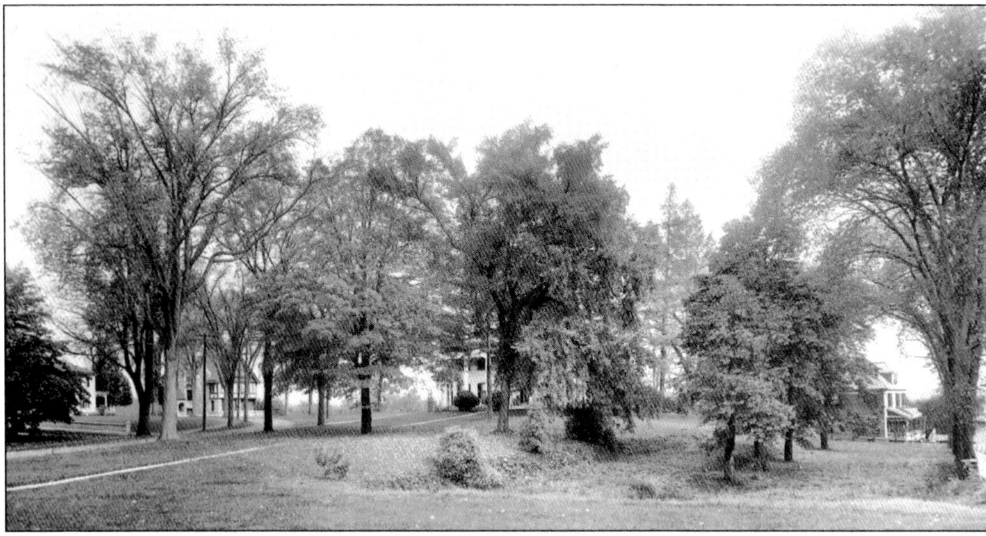

The legacy of Millbury's mills can be seen to this day, both in ongoing industrial operations and in the architecture of the comfortable homes and mansions that belonged to mill owners and other influential families. This 1913 view of Miles Street shows homes belonging to the Atwood, Windle, Walling, and Perry families, who were leaders in industry, law, local government, and their churches. (Courtesy of Millbury Historical Society.)

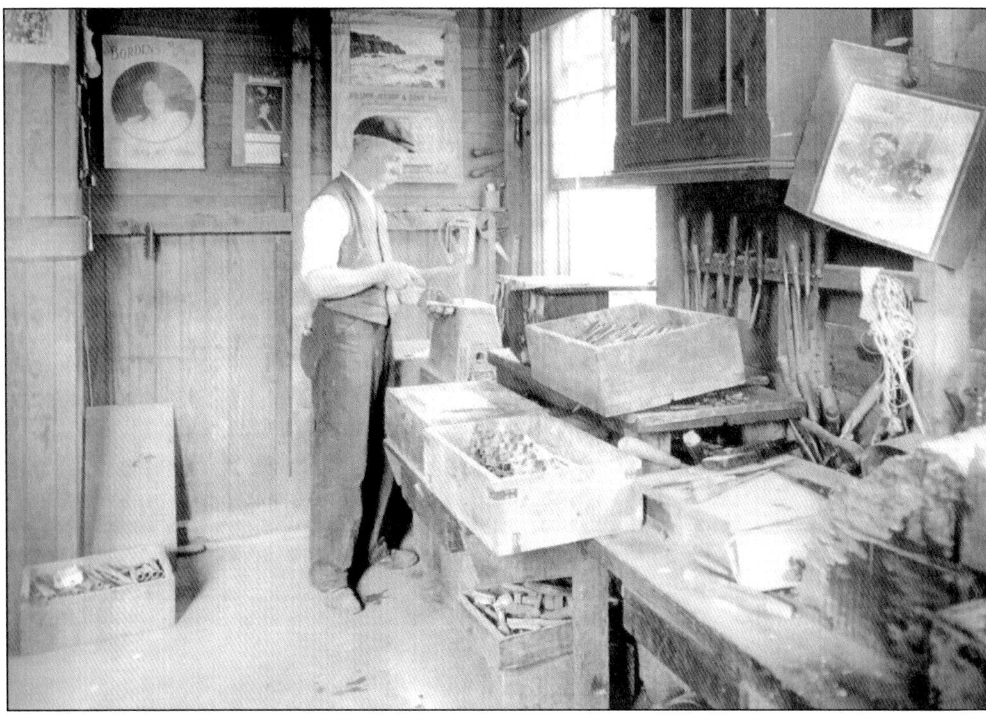

Joseph Ashton of Buck Brothers is shown in 1912 using a ball-peen hammer to set tools that he has heated. According to Gerald Sortor, just the fifth general manager in the company's history, the calendar on the wall behind Ashton was still hanging in this room when the old factory was torn down in the late 1970s, more than 65 years after this photograph was taken. (Courtesy of Buck Brothers.)

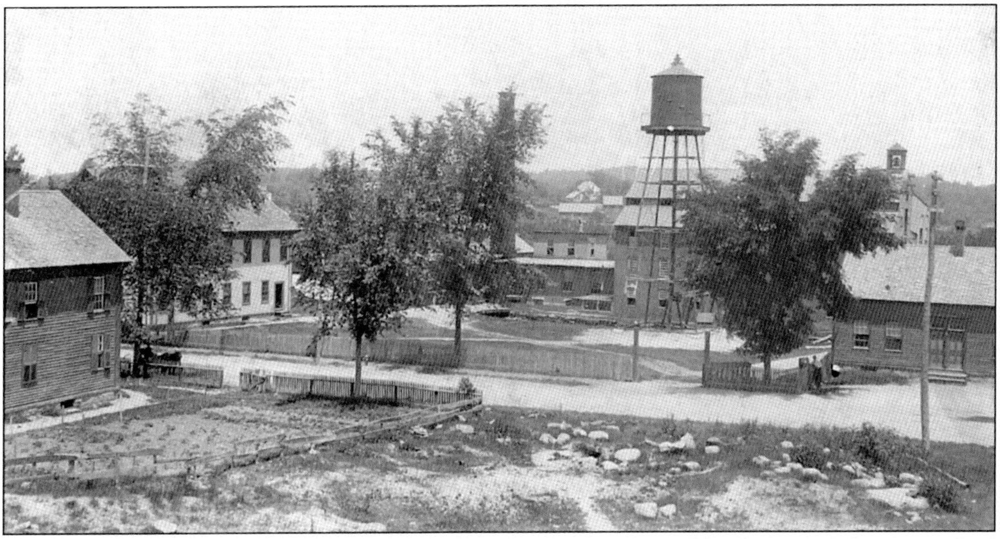

Millbury's industries grew up on waterpower, but the growing town, like the rest of the nation, had growing energy needs. In the photograph above, the Consolidated Power Company's power station is shown in 1895. It occupied the site of the former Peter Simpson mill on what was Simpson Street in the late 19th century and later Providence Street. Below, an early-20th-century view shows workers at the Millbury Substation No. 1. As the region's electrical transmission grid grew, the area lying between Providence and Grafton Streets and straddling the Blackstone River became a preferred location for bringing together numerous power lines, such that Millbury is sometimes referred to as "the fuse box of New England." (Both, courtesy of Millbury Historical Society.)

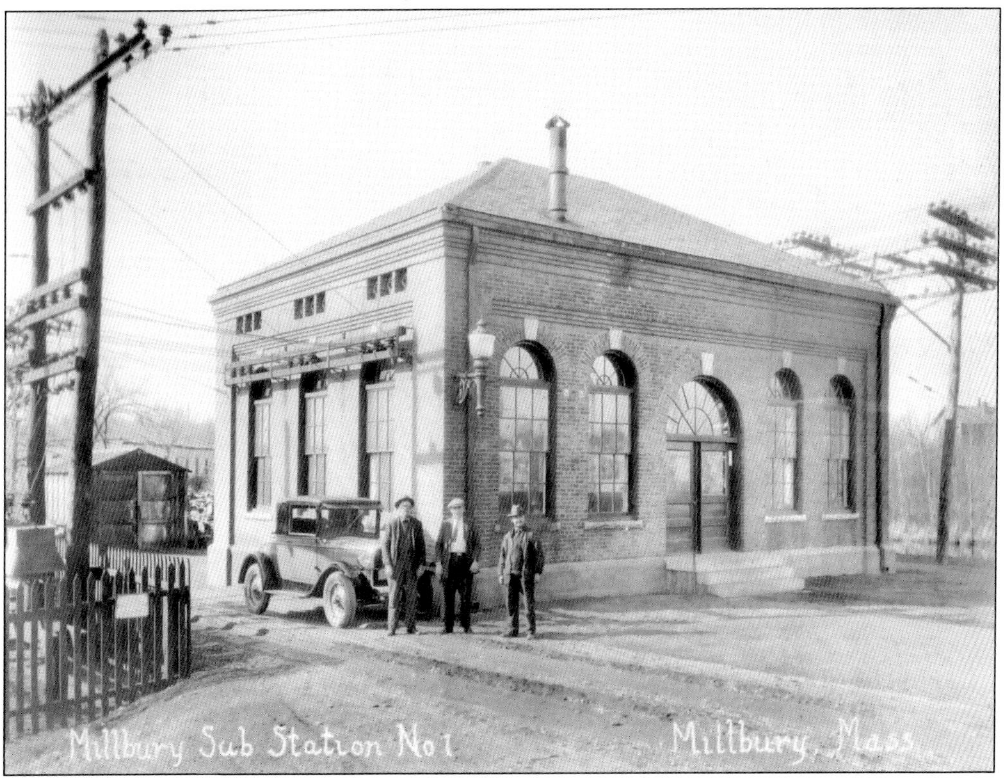

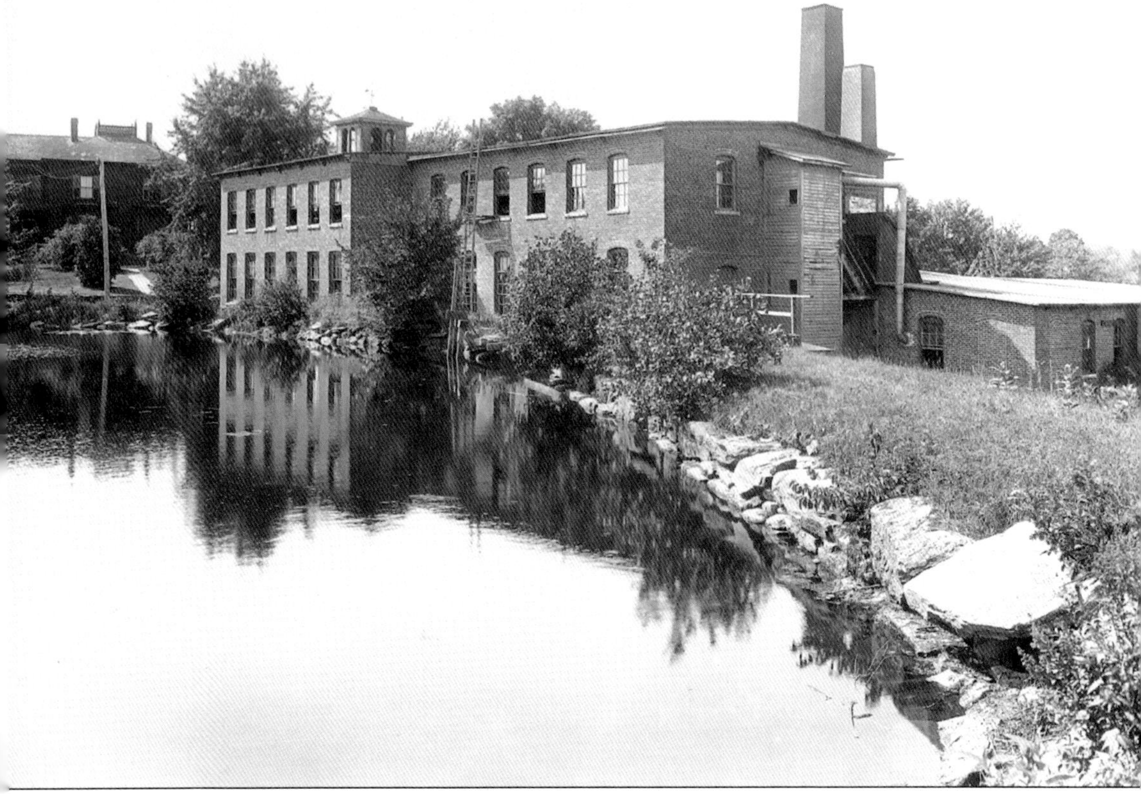

The Hoyle Mill, on the Ramshorn Stream in West Millbury, was heavily damaged by the Ramshorn Dam collapse in 1873. It was rebuilt in 1877 by the partnership of Edwin Hoyle and Thomas Windle. Hoyle, born in England in 1844, came to Millbury at age eight, learned his trade in the cotton mills, and went into business for himself as a pioneer in waste scouring, the process of separating lanolin and impurities from newly shorn "greasy wool" and treating the wastes. In January 1904, the mill was damaged but not destroyed by fire. Villagers and members of the Lion hand tub firefighting company kept the blaze at bay until steamers could arrive from Millbury Center. The *Worcester Telegram* reported the fire "will be a hard blow to many families who worked in the mill, and had children dependent upon their earnings . . . many of the operatives looking at the blazing structure with tears streaming down their faces, as they realized it meant privation for them, unless they can find work in some other mill at once." (Courtesy of Millbury Historical Society.)

Four

MILLBURY CENTER

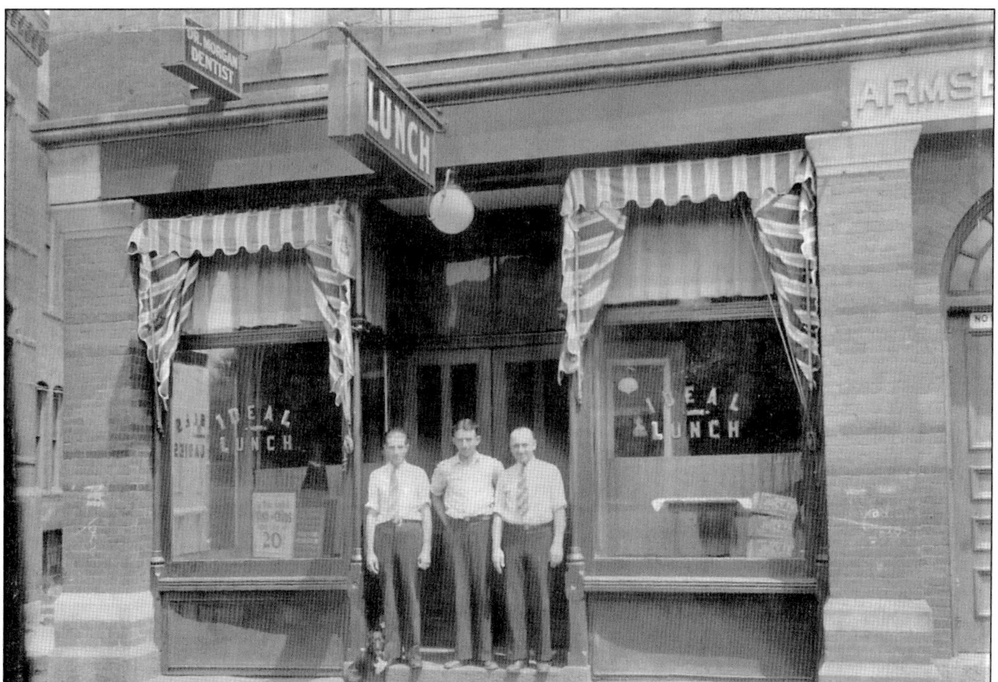

A trio of friends stands outside Ideal Lunch in Millbury Center in 1931. The restaurant was located in the 1883 Armsby Building, next to the old town hall. The eatery occupied space that began as Lyman S. Waters's grocery shop. From left to right are Ed Cofsky (with his dog, Jiggs), Lester Minor, and Del Lavallee. (Courtesy of Millbury Historical Society.)

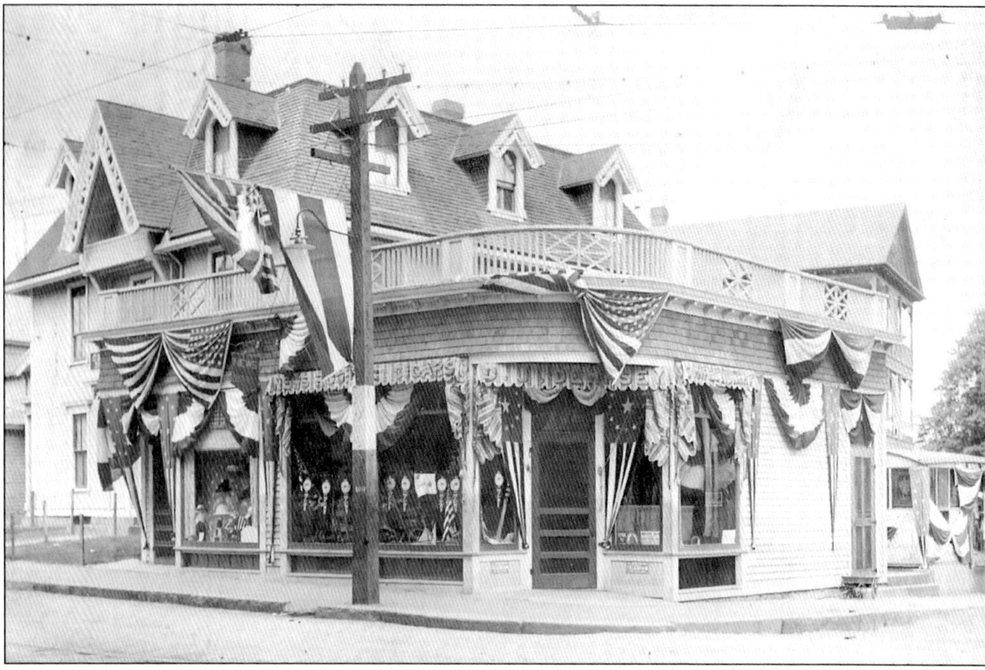

Daniel J. Dempsey's news depot and confectionary occupied prime real estate in Central Square downtown and sold newspapers, cigars, Coca-Cola, confections, and sundries. The photograph above shows two neighboring businesses. On the left is the Jacques Millinery Shop on Main Street, and just visible on the right is the Central Diner, around the corner on Elm Street. In the photograph below, Dempsey's son Paul is shown behind the counter in May 1932. The current issue of *Popular Science* on the far wall features a cover story on the dynasphere, while the latest issue of *Screenplay* features Greta Garbo. (Both, courtesy of Paula Beauregard.)

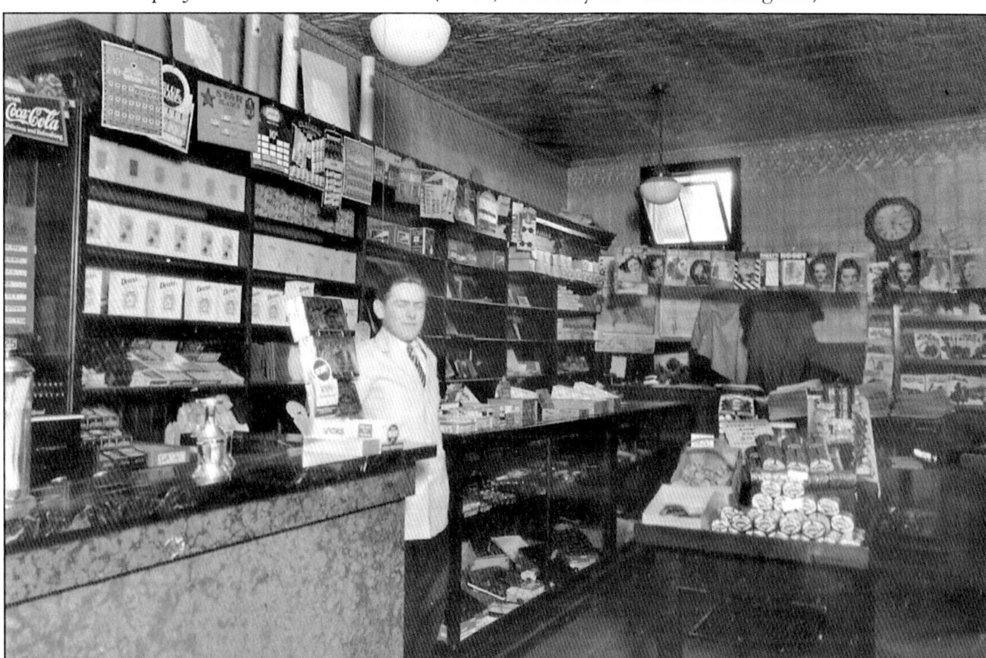

Martin J. Roach was one of the town's original teamsters, running the Millbury and Worcester Express service from Millbury Center—even after streetcar service began. In this 1898 photograph, driver John May holds the reins as the team pauses next to the common. Roach's concern for the roads extended to the entire town, as he served many years as Millbury's highway surveyor. (Courtesy of Millbury Historical Society.)

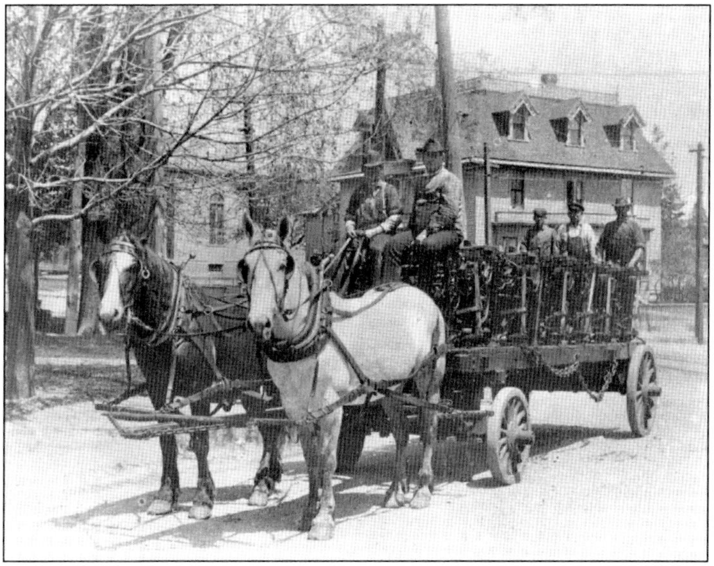

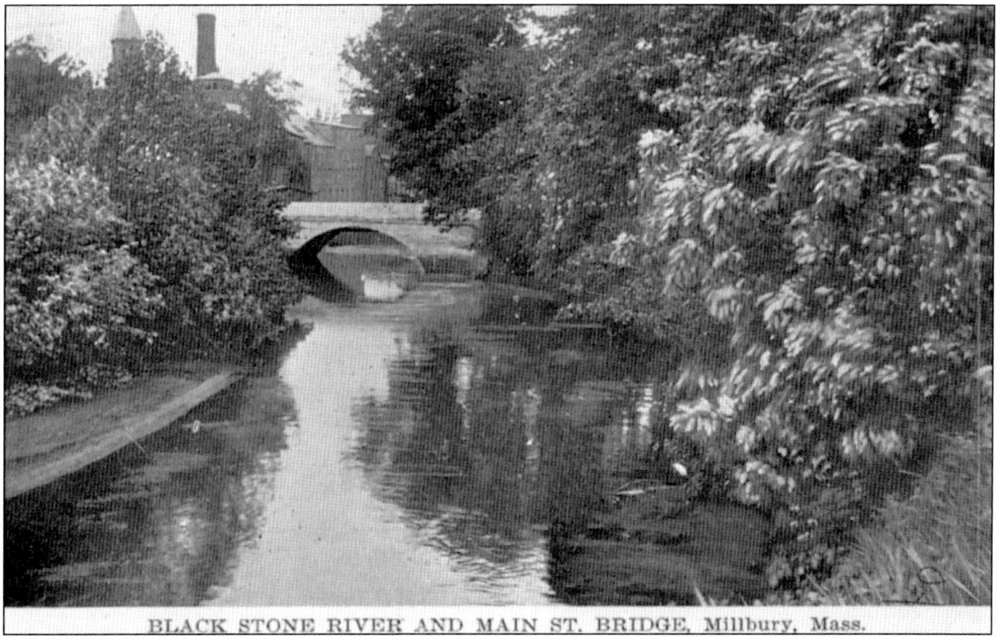

One of the earliest names for the Blackstone River was the "Halfway River," a name that was applied only to its stretch through Millbury, and which leads some historians to surmise that Indian tribes frequently traversed the river here. This c. 1930 view, looking downriver as it bends south of Millbury Center, shows the National Crash Manufacturing Company on South Main Street. (Courtesy of Rich Hamilton.)

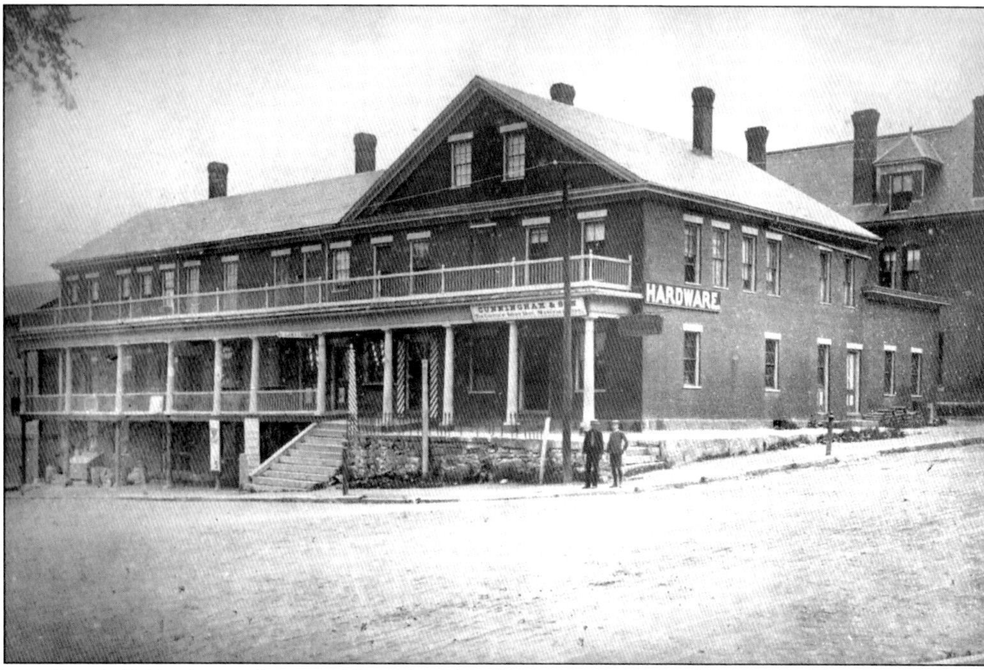

The Randall Block was destroyed by a fire that broke out early in the morning of Monday, May 7, 1894, in the adjacent Forester House boardinghouse. Fifteen people escaped the blaze, which was spread quickly by high winds. Worcester firefighters helped their Millbury counterparts save the nearby Millbury Savings Bank, town hall, and Armsby Building. The Cunningham Block was built on the spot the next year. (Courtesy of Millbury Historical Society.)

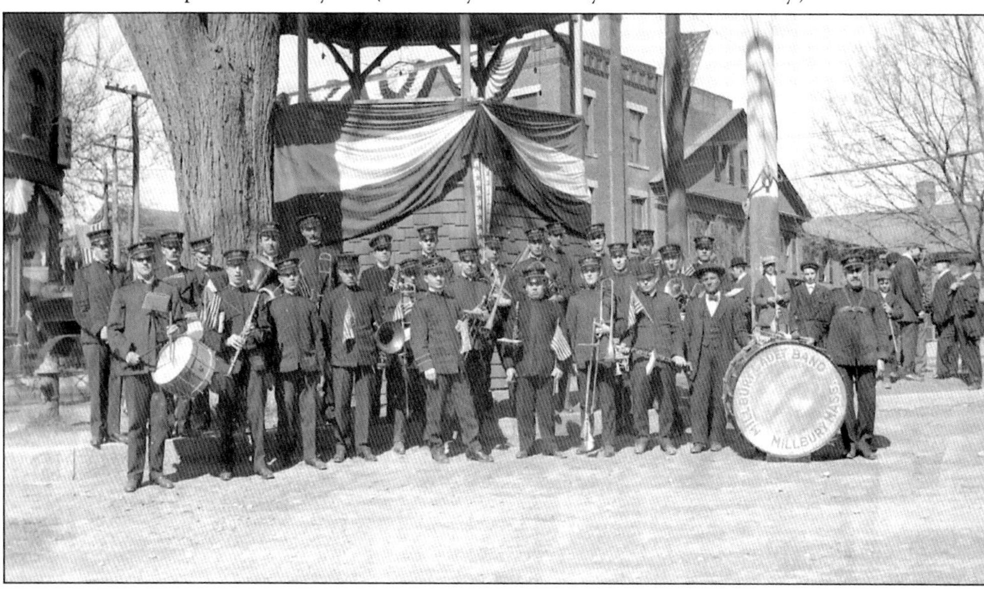

Wednesday, June 11, 1913, the "great day of the celebration, dawned fair and mild," according to the *Centennial History of the Town of Millbury*, and a "Trades and Historic" parade stepped off from Burbank Square in Bramanville at 9:00 a.m., proceeding to Central Square. The parade included the Salem Cadet Band, the Worcester Brass Band, and the Millbury Cadet Band, shown here midway through its route. (Courtesy of Millbury Historical Society.)

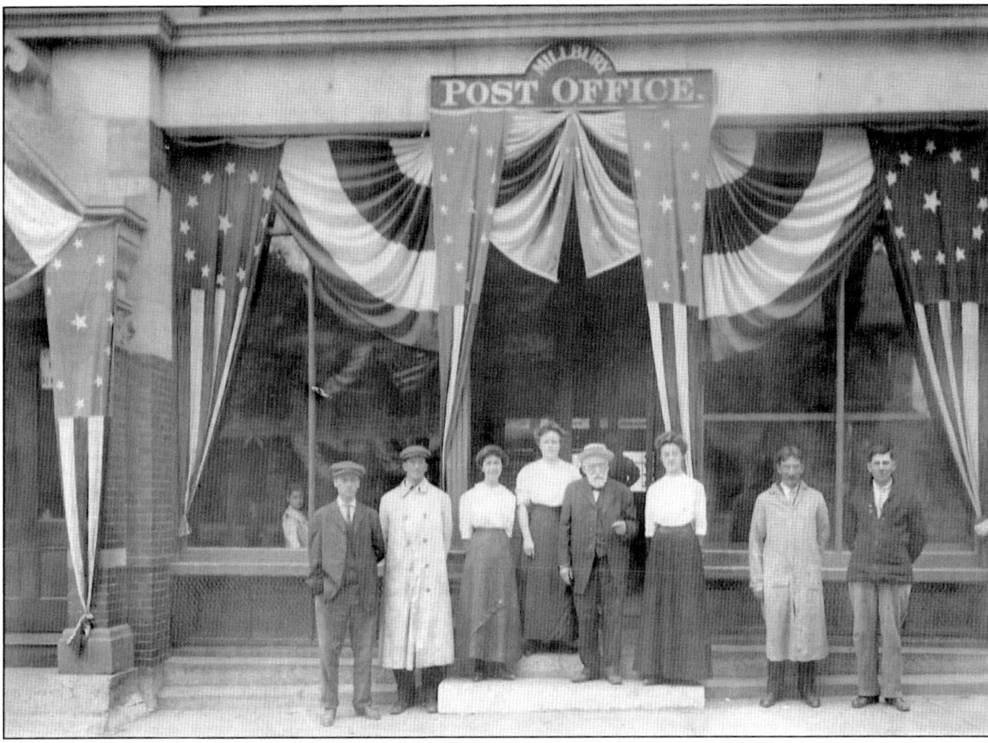

A post office was established in Millbury Center in 1816 and in 1870 was located in the Randall Block at Central Square. By the time of the centennial in 1913, it had moved a few doors west to the Millbury Bank Building, shown here. In 1940, the current post office in Millbury Center was built, and operations again moved a bit further west on Elm Street. (Courtesy of Millbury Historical Society.)

Millbury's development meant it would lack the large central common with residences typical of many towns of Worcester County, including its parent, Sutton. The town center shifted early on from Old Common to Millbury Center, seen here about 1920. The commercial Farnsworth Building on the left and Baptist church, built in 1864, ensured that the town center would have a largely commercial and institutional flavor. (Courtesy of Millbury Historical Society.)

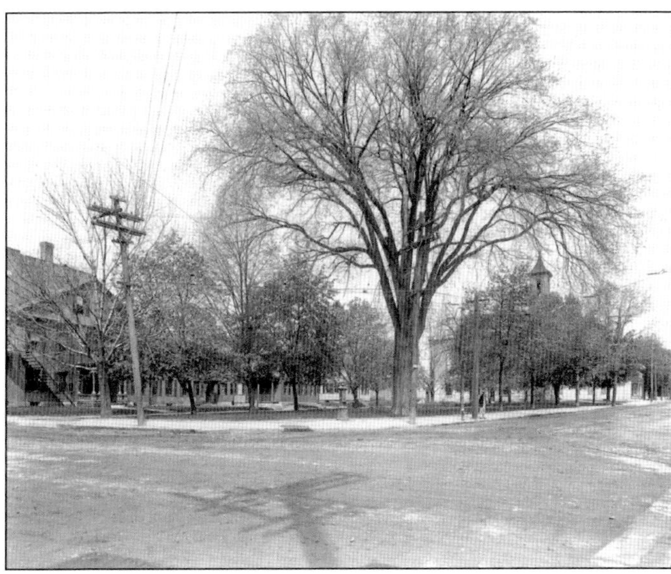

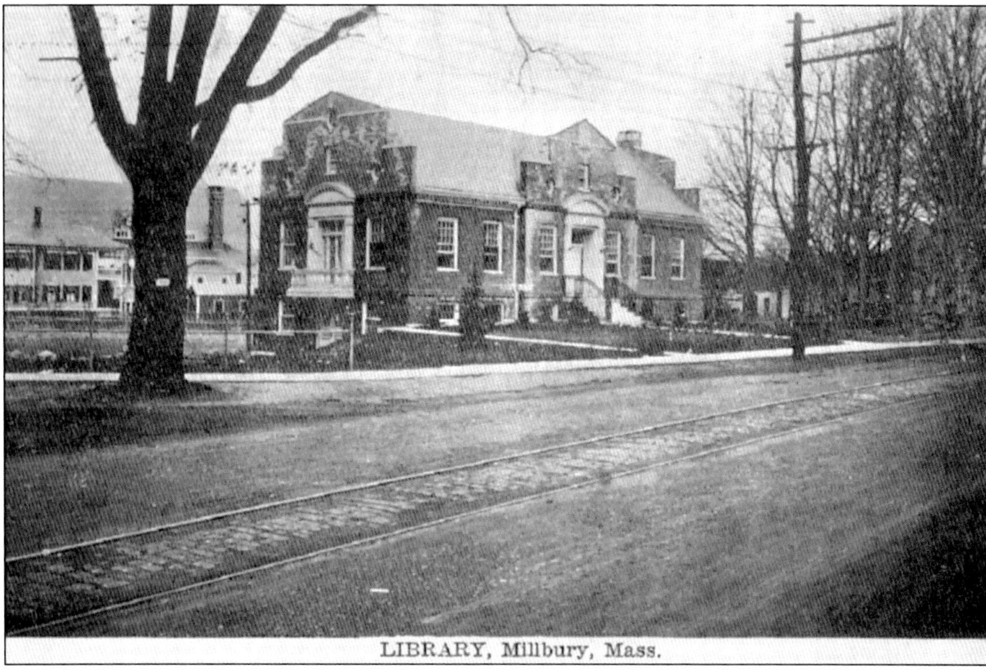

The Society of Social Friends met on April 7, 1864, and members voted to donate their books to the town "for the purpose of founding a free public library." Selectmen accepted the gift that same month. In 1915, Andrew Carnegie gave Millbury $12,500 for a new public library, shown here, which was built on an Elm Street parcel donated by President Taft's aunt, Delia Torrey. (Courtesy of Rich Hamilton.)

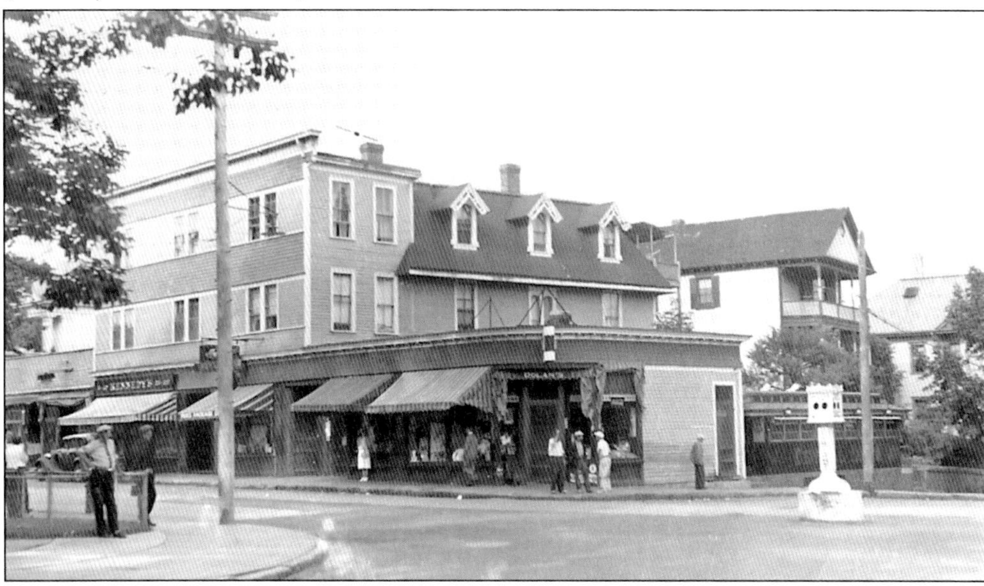

The post–World War II era brought new growth and prosperity to Millbury Center. In this 1948 photograph, a new commercial block has been added to Dolan's corner store (formerly Dempsey's). Such growth was good for business but would cause headaches and heartache for architectural purists for decades to come. The elegant former Rhodes residence has been literally tied into the much later commercial spaces. (Courtesy of Millbury Historical Society.)

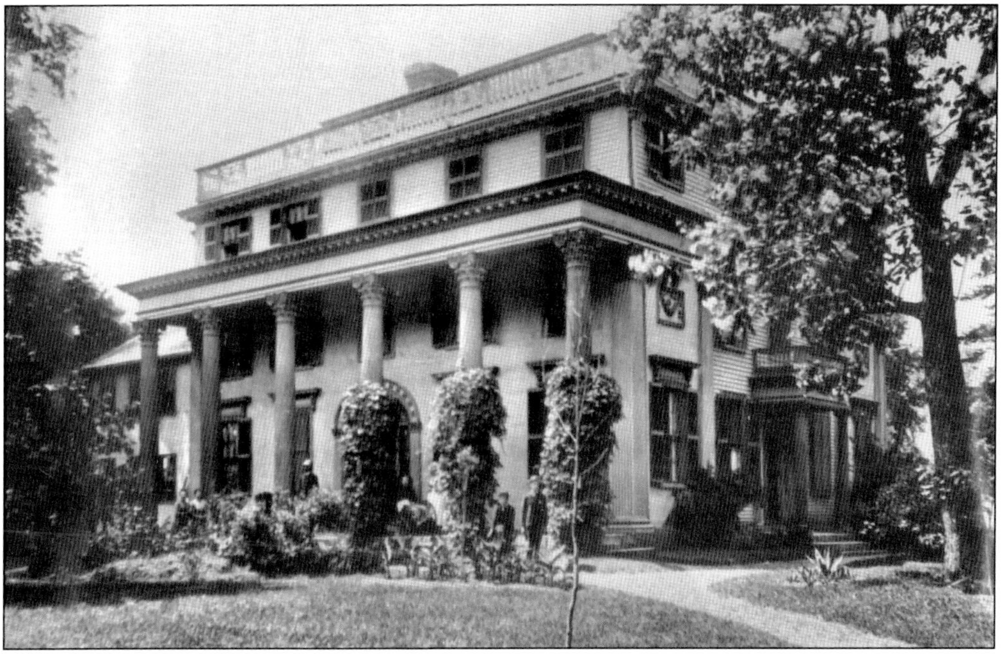

Asa Waters II constructed Millbury's signature mansion for his wife, Susan Holman Waters, between 1824 and 1826. Visitors included Daniel Webster, Henry Clay, Henry David Thoreau, Pres. William Howard Taft, and Alexander Graham Bell. This is how the mansion appeared about 1890. Once in danger of demolition, it is now town-owned, hosts public and private meetings and weddings, and houses the Millbury Historical Society's museum. (Courtesy of Kay and Roland Lachance.)

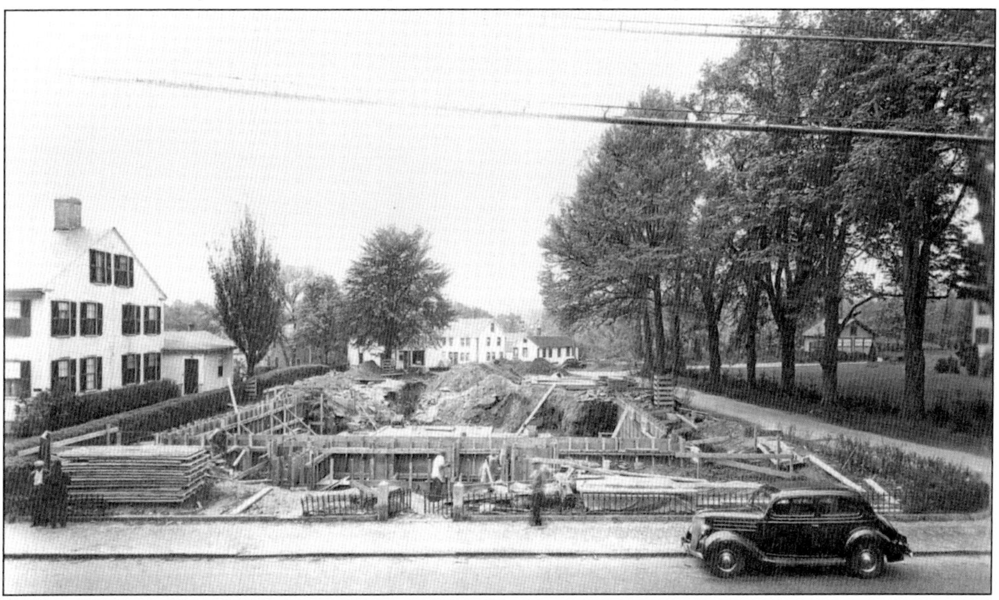

In 1940, the Waters Mansion, at right in this photograph, got a new neighbor with the construction of a new US post office in the Moderne style. The surrounding buildings date to the early 19th century, when the Waters family won the first of many federal contracts for gun manufacturing, leading to the rapid expansion of Armory Village, as Millbury Center was then known. (Courtesy of Millbury Historical Society.)

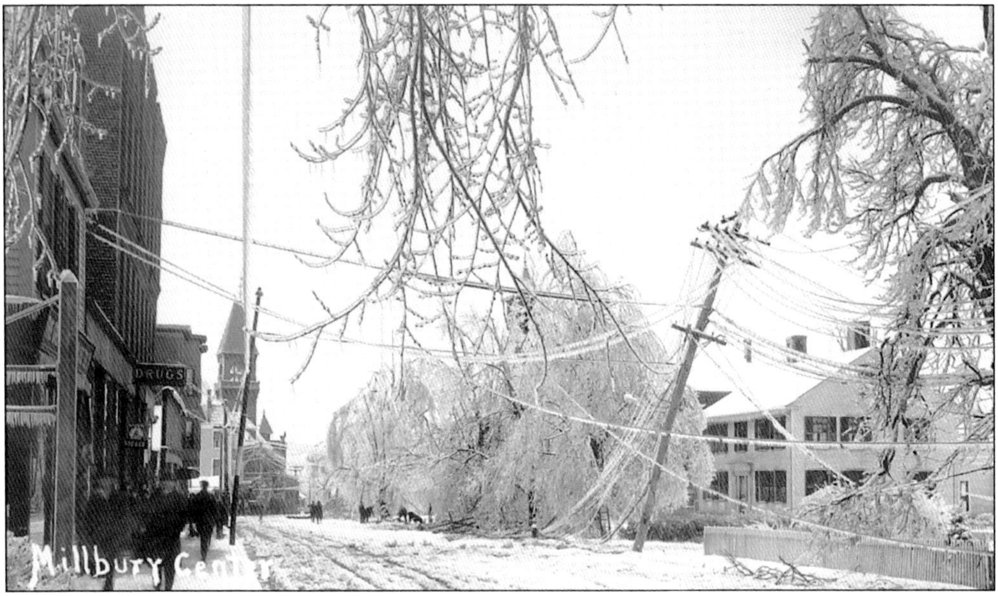

Between November 25 and 29, 1921, a devastating ice storm gripped portions of southern New England. Guy H. Burnham of Clark University in Worcester writes in a spring 1922 article in the *Journal of Geography*: "The rain intermingled with sleet and accompanied at times by a fairly high wind continued unabated for over seventy-two hours. . . . Under this ever-increasing burden the trees and wires groaned and creaked in the wind. Unable to withstand the severe strain, great limbs were torn from thousands of trees and crashed to the ground." Rails, telegraphs, telephones and electricity were knocked out, in some places for over a month, and "the countryside came to look and sound like the shell-torn regions of France!" These photographs show damage along Main Street, looking south (above) and north (below). (Both, courtesy of Paula Beauregard.)

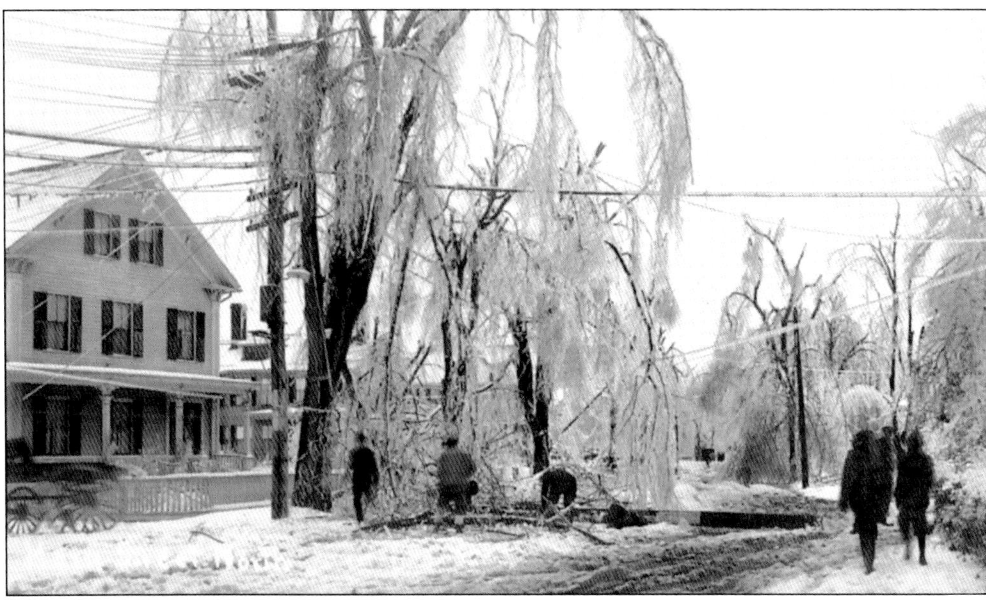

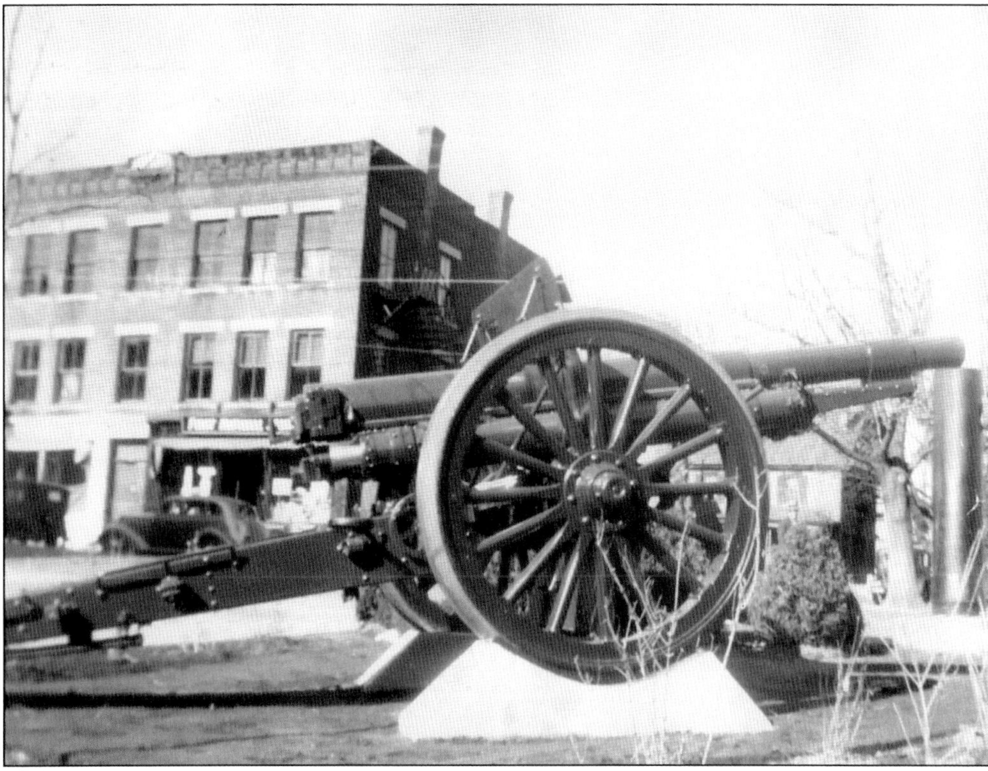

On November 15, 1936, the World War Monument was moved from the common to Central Square, and this recently donated 4.7-inch howitzer was added. This weapon probably never saw action on the Western Front, where American troops were equipped with French 75-mm artillery guns. Following World War II and later conflicts, the memorial was moved to the entrance to the new town hall on Elm Street. (Courtesy of Millbury Historical Society.)

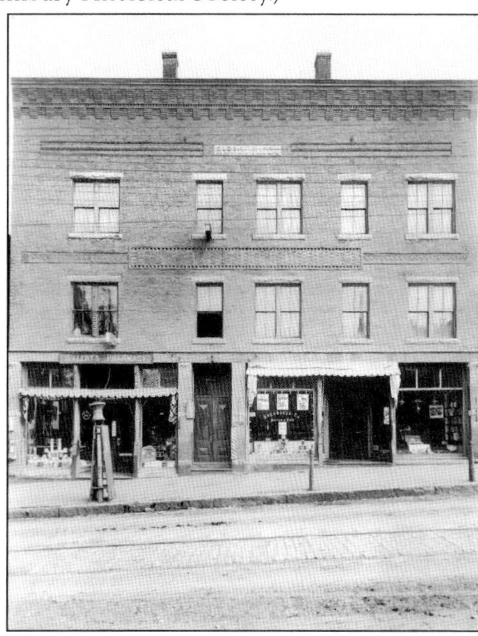

The Barrow Block, located on Elm Street, is typical of the two- and three-story commercial buildings constructed between 1880 and 1900. Although the textile industry slumped in the 1890s, by the end of the decade it had returned, as manufacturers began making linen and woolens. By 1914, storefronts were filled, as here, with businesses such as Arthur J. Gillert's pharmacy and Bresnahan Company grocers. (Courtesy of Millbury Historical Society.)

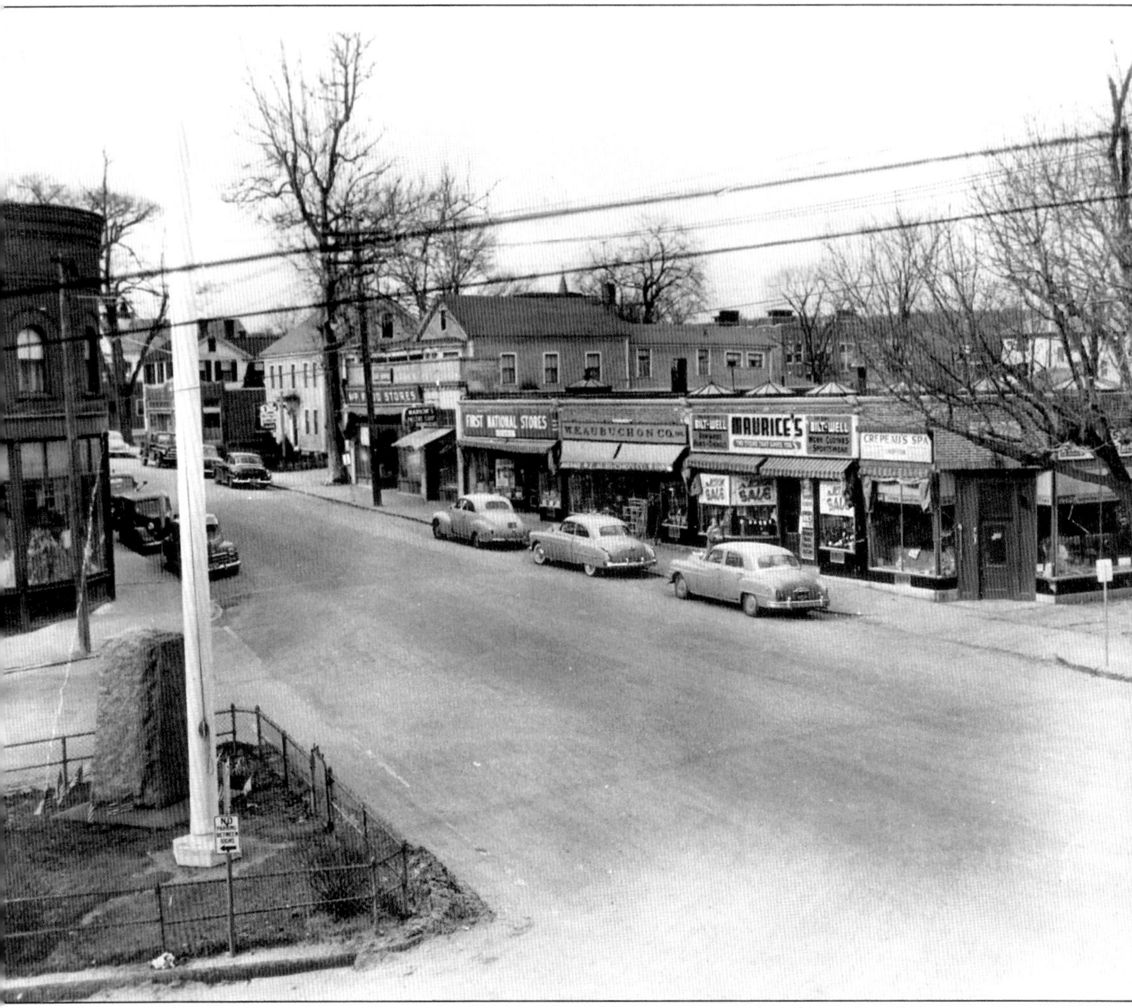

By the early 1950s, Millbury enjoyed strong employment within its borders, abundant manufacturing and service opportunities in the neighboring city of Worcester, steady population growth, and a thriving downtown. This 1952 view of downtown shows Elm Street. The Farnsworth Building that stood for decades adjacent to the common has been taken down, replaced by a variety of stores, including small local spots like Crepeau's Spa and Marion's Pastry Shop, and chains, like W.E. Aubuchon Co. Inc. and A&P Food Stores. In the next half-century, the downtown would continue to change with the nation's economy, but the town has largely maintained its core commercial strength, even with the coming of regional shopping malls. (Courtesy of Millbury Historical Society.)

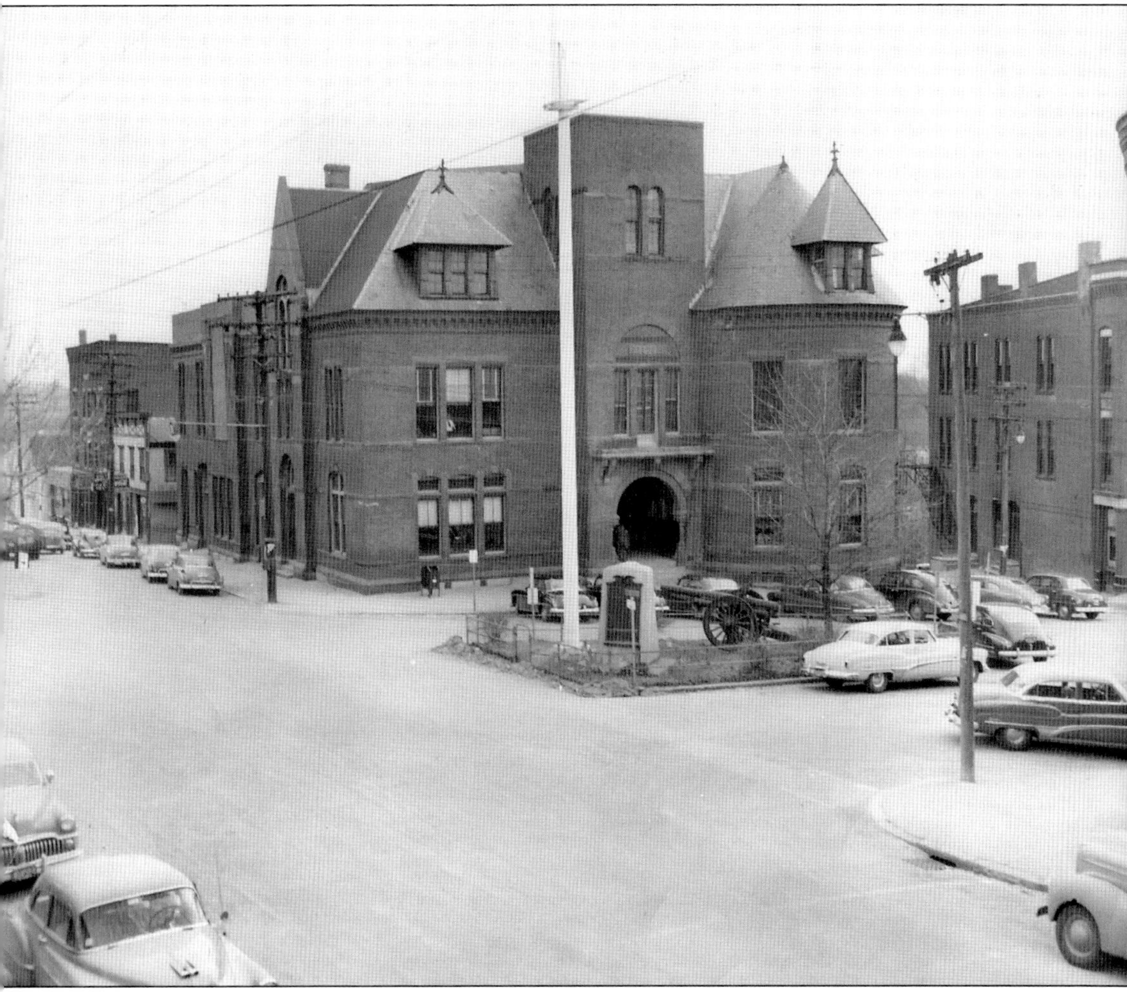

Millbury's town hall, once located in the former Millbury Academy at Elm and Waters Streets, was moved in 1878 to a new brick structure constructed in the Victorian Gothic style. Pictured here on January 24, 1952, the central tower has been taken down from the hall. (Courtesy of Millbury Historical Society.)

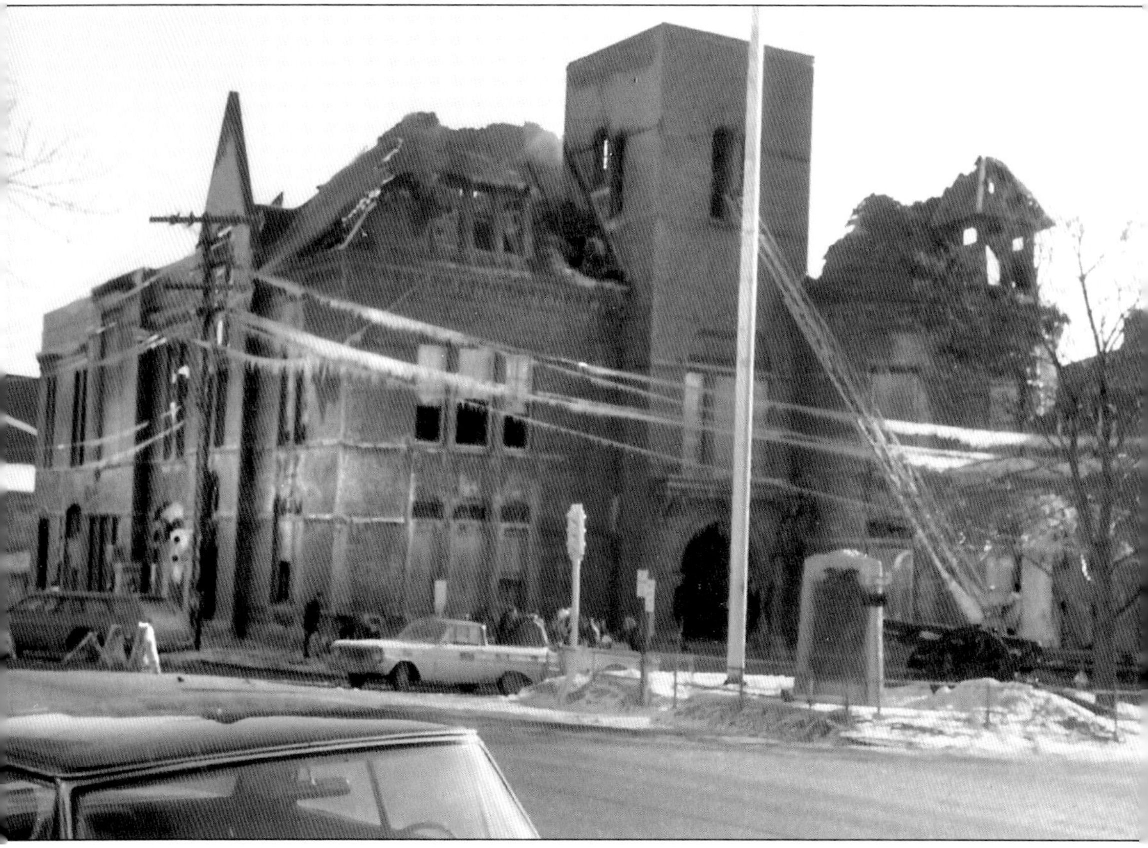

Just before 2:00 p.m. on January 28, 1971, workers in the town hall heard noises in the walls and ceilings of the upper levels of the building. Employees hurriedly put town records into fireproof vaults and evacuated, just before the fire erupted. The cause was faulty wiring over the main west entrance. (Courtesy of Chris Sinacola.)

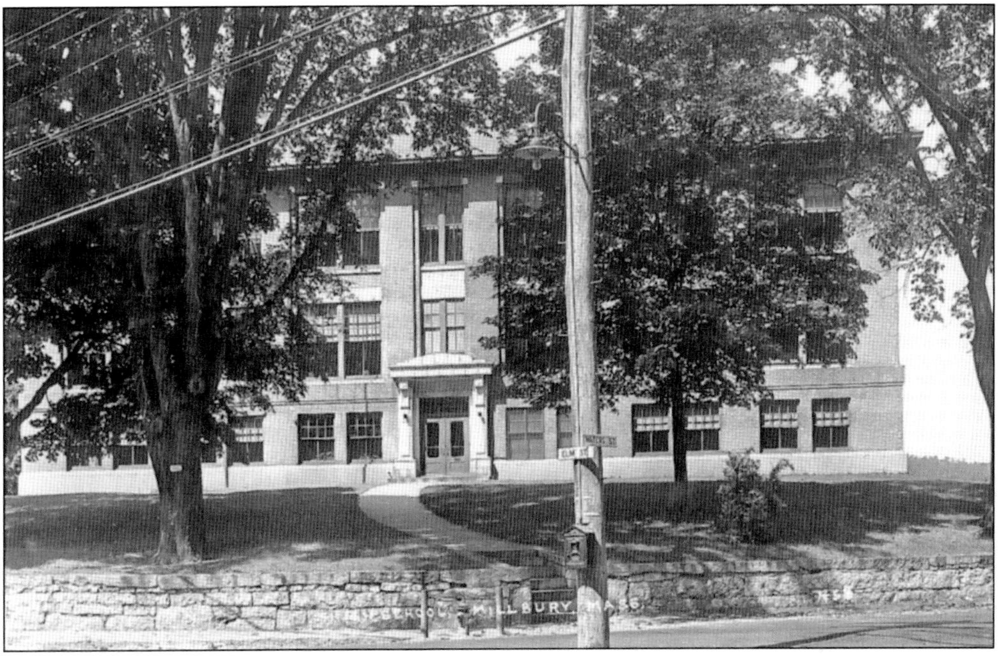

At a special town meeting on September 30, 1912, voters approved a new high school and appropriated $50,000 for its construction. The building was constructed on the knoll between Elm, River, and Waters Streets in downtown Millbury, the same site long occupied by the Millbury Academy. The new school opened in 1914. (Courtesy of Rich Hamilton.)

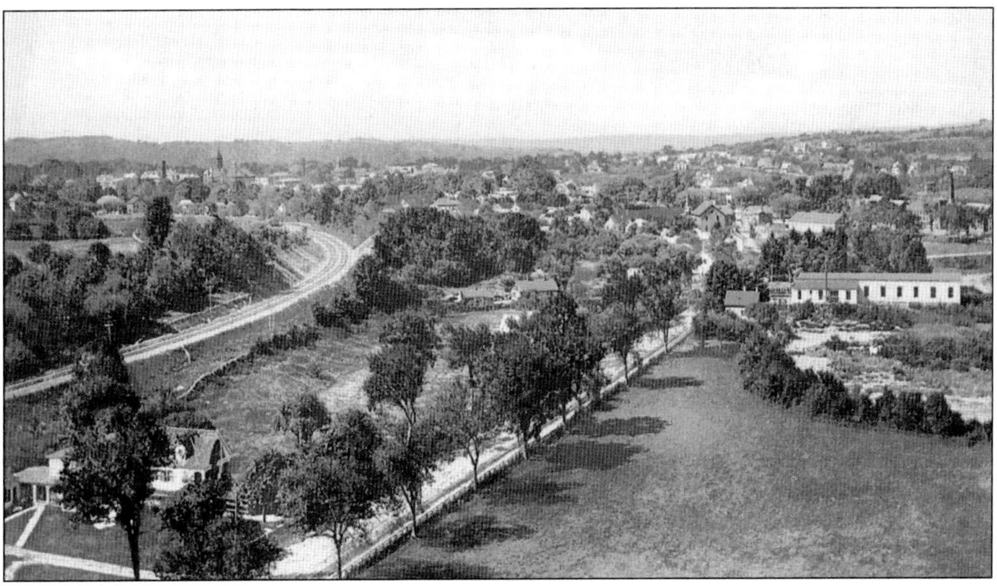

This popular postcard offers a bird's-eye view of Millbury from the southeast, showing Providence Road in the center and what is now the Providence & Worcester Railroad line on the left. This image can be found on cards from 1901 through 1915. In 1907, the US government allowed writing on the back of postcards, which opened the so-called golden age of postcard collecting and mailing. (Courtesy of Chris Sinacola.)

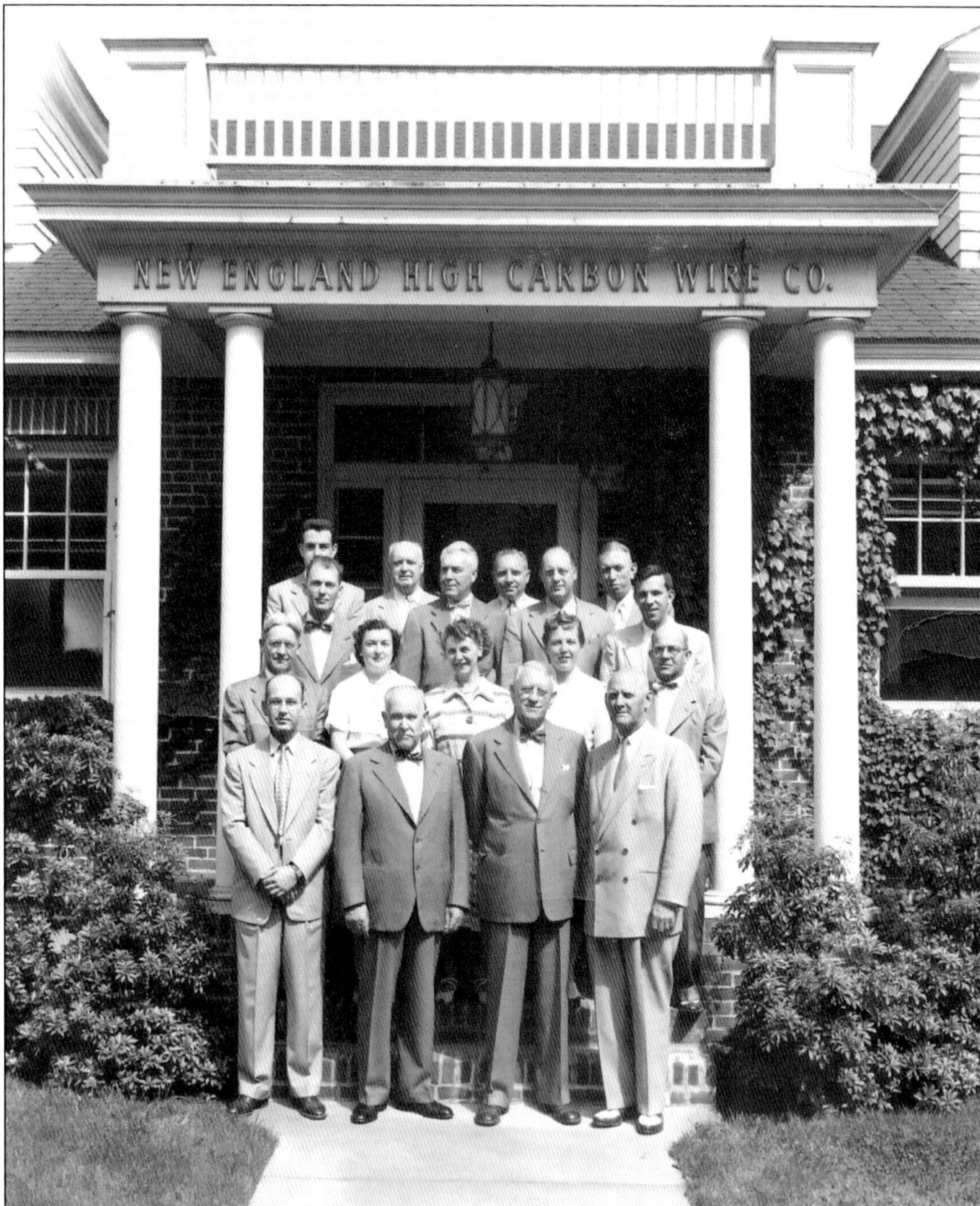

New England High Carbon Wire Company was founded in 1923 by Carl T. Lund of Worcester and operated on Howe Avenue in Millbury for more than 50 years. During World War II, the company produced recoil springs for antiaircraft guns, and following the war, shifted to production of valve spring wires for the automotive industry. As more and more of the nation's industrial production shifted overseas, industrial giants such as New England High Carbon Wire lost sales and trimmed workforces. In 1981, the company filed for bankruptcy. This photograph shows company managers and employees at the height of the company's prosperity. From left to right are (first row) Willard Blanchard, Steen Johnson, John Berg, and Robert Johnson; (second row) Eddie Johnson, Mary Daley, Thekla Bugge, ? Stupera, and Sig Ekstrom; (third row) Andrew Hubbard, John Murray, Jim Ormrod, and James Taparowsky; (fourth row) John Newton, Peter Flemming, Al Beaton, and Stanley Van de Mark. (Courtesy of Millbury Historical Society.)

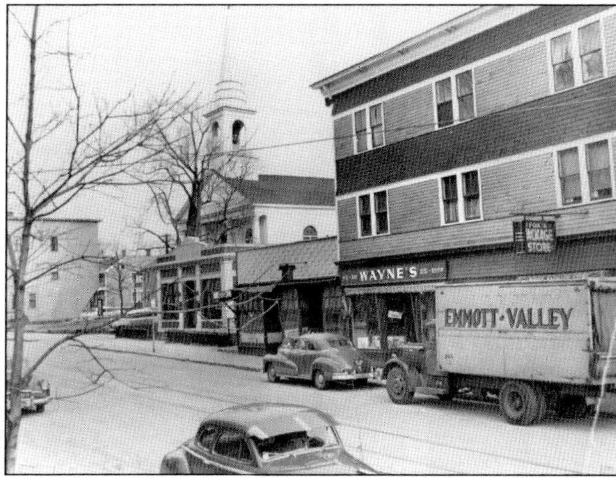

By 1950, Millbury's Main Street was a hodgepodge of architectural styles and storefronts, offering something for most everyone, particularly at Wayne's five-and-dime, operated by Peter Nalbandian from 1951 to 1974. Two doors to the left is the Millbury National Bank, which had separated years earlier from the Millbury Savings Bank on Elm Street. The Second Congregational Church, later the Federated Church, is visible in the background. (Courtesy of Millbury Historical Society.)

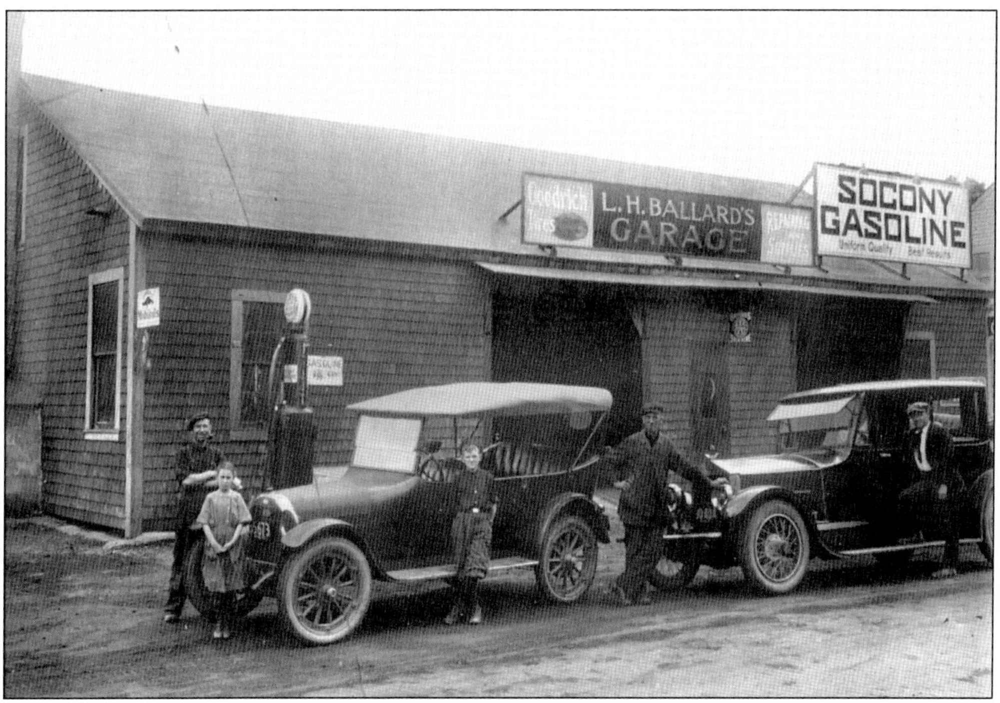

Louis Ballard opened a horse carriage repair shop in 1906 but soon changed along with the times to selling and repairing automobiles. The business prospered on Howe Avenue for many years, was taken over by his son Harold, and in 1957 was incorporated as Ballard Motors. In 1988, Harold purchased the Mack franchise in Worcester, where the business continues as Ballard Mack Sales & Service. (Courtesy of Mary Lou Mulhane.)

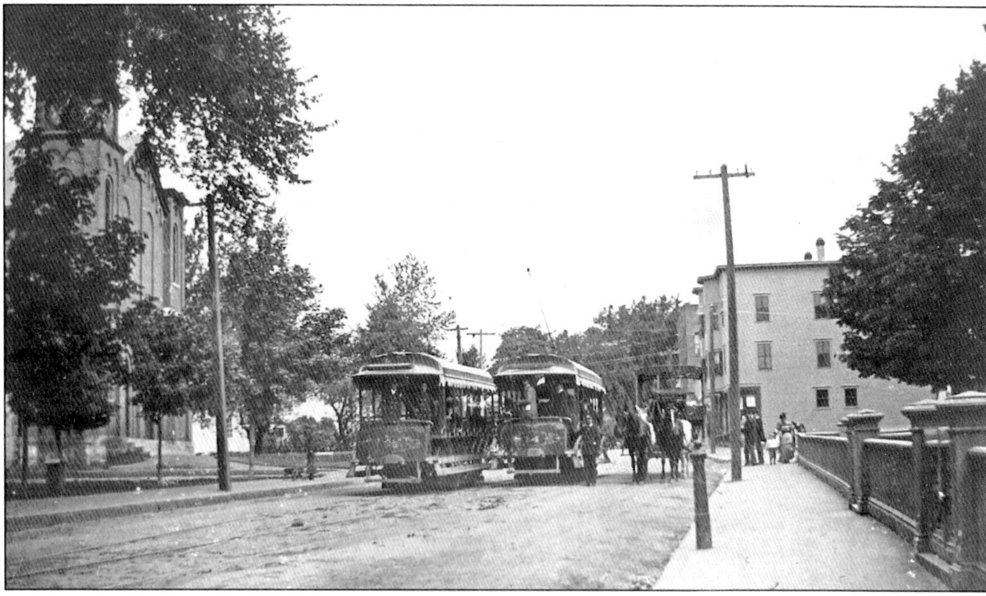

Main Street in 1898 bustled with people drawn by the commercial growth in business blocks such as that owned by Damien Ducharme, visible in the background on the right. Ducharme, a French Canadian immigrant, started working for $5 a week in the Cordis Mill in 1865. By 1888, he was able to buy downtown businesses and in 1892 erected a new brick business block. (Courtesy of Millbury Historical Society.)

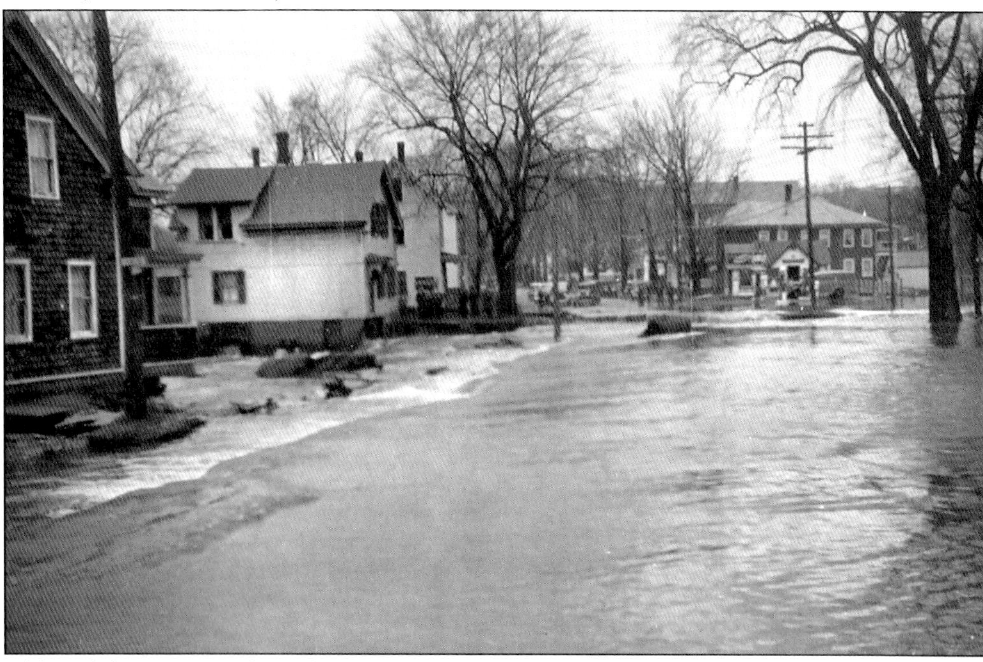

Although business merchants began pressing for an interstate highway as early as 1919, it had not yet been built at the time of the March 1936 flooding. This view looks west along Elm Street from approximately where Route 146 now crosses Elm Street. Both forks in the road take a traveler to West Millbury—the left via Bramanville, the right by way of Old Common. (Courtesy of Millbury Historical Society.)

Five

BRAMANVILLE

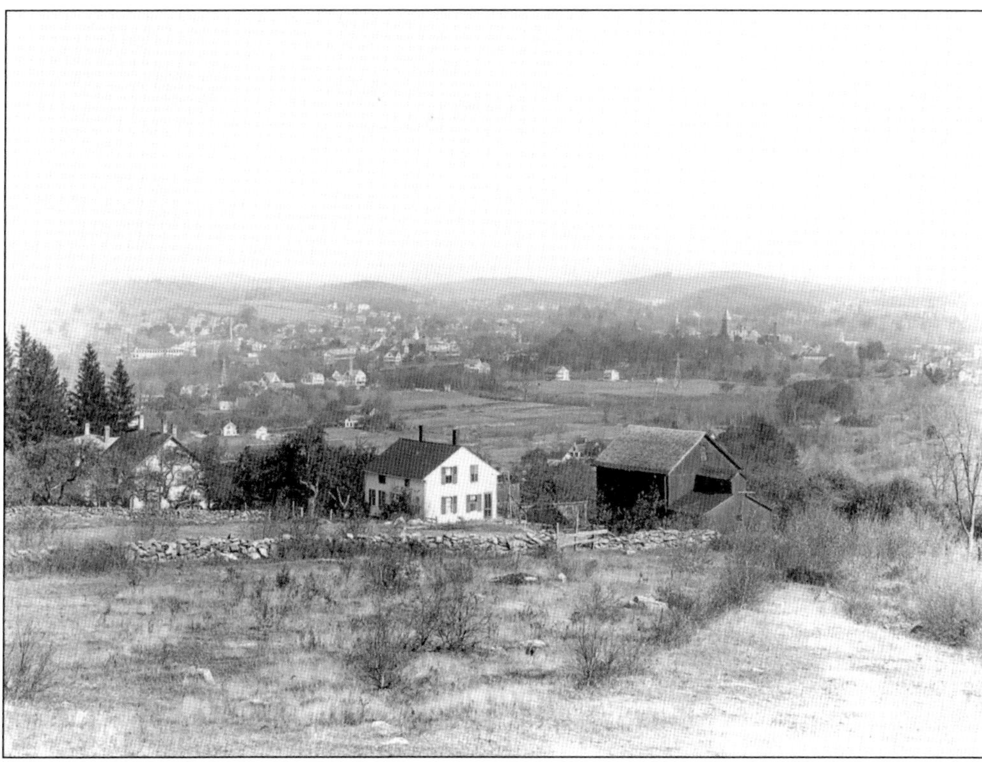

This panoramic view of Millbury was taken from Burbank Hill, looking north and east to the center of town in 1915. Singletary Lake, source of the Singletary Stream, which provided power for the mills of Bramanville, lies about a mile west of the photographer's vantage point. The stream joins the Blackstone River in the middle distance in the center. (Courtesy of Millbury Historical Society.)

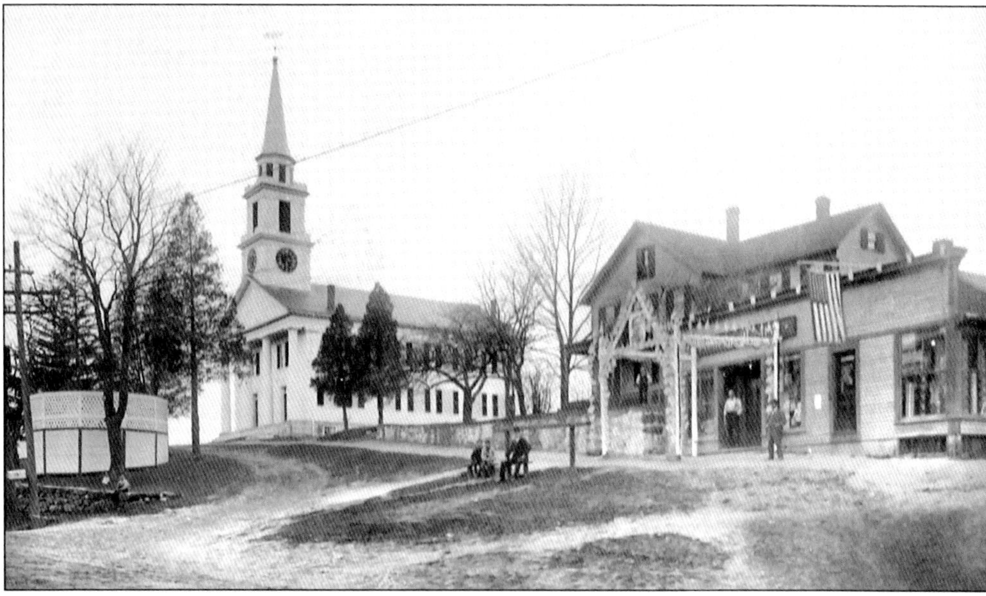

The First Congregational Church in Bramanville was long the center of social and religious life in Millbury, which, like its parent, Sutton, was founded and effectively governed for many years by families of English descent. Charles H. Shaw's store, seen in this view from 1913, was one of many small grocery shops in the village. (Courtesy of Millbury Historical Society.)

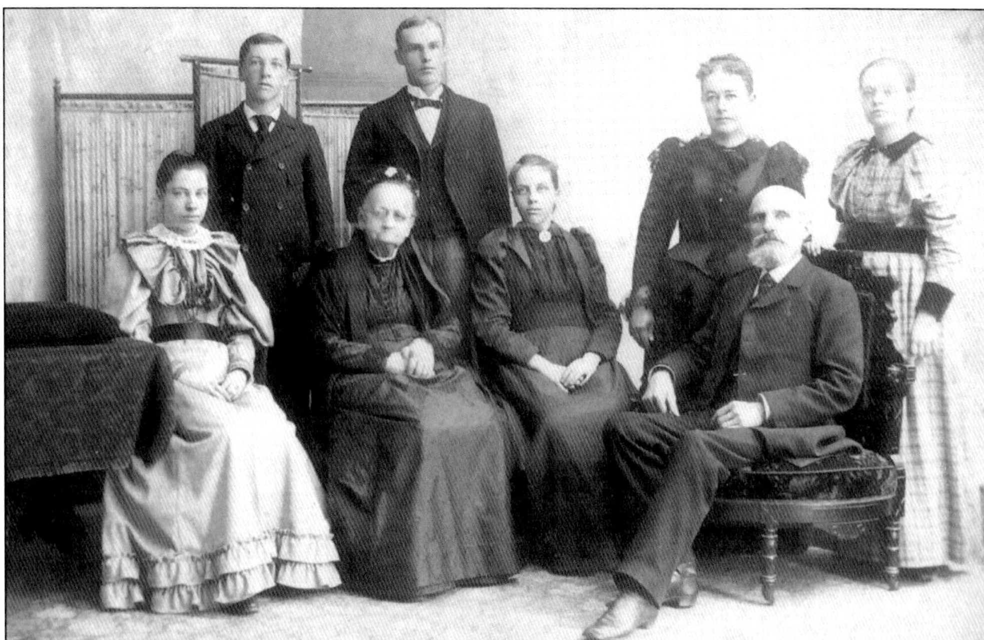

The Rev. George A. Putnam, pastor of Bramanville's First Congregational Church, sits with his family about 1893. They are, from left to right, (first row) Jennie Putnam, born 1867; Hannah Waters Sabin, Putnam's mother-in-law; Fannie May Putnam, born 1873; and Reverend Putnam; (second row) Harry Putnam, born 1878; George Putnam, born 1865; Louisa Sabin Putnam, the pastor's second wife and stepmother to his children; and Florence Putnam, born 1876. (Courtesy of Jerilyn Stead.)

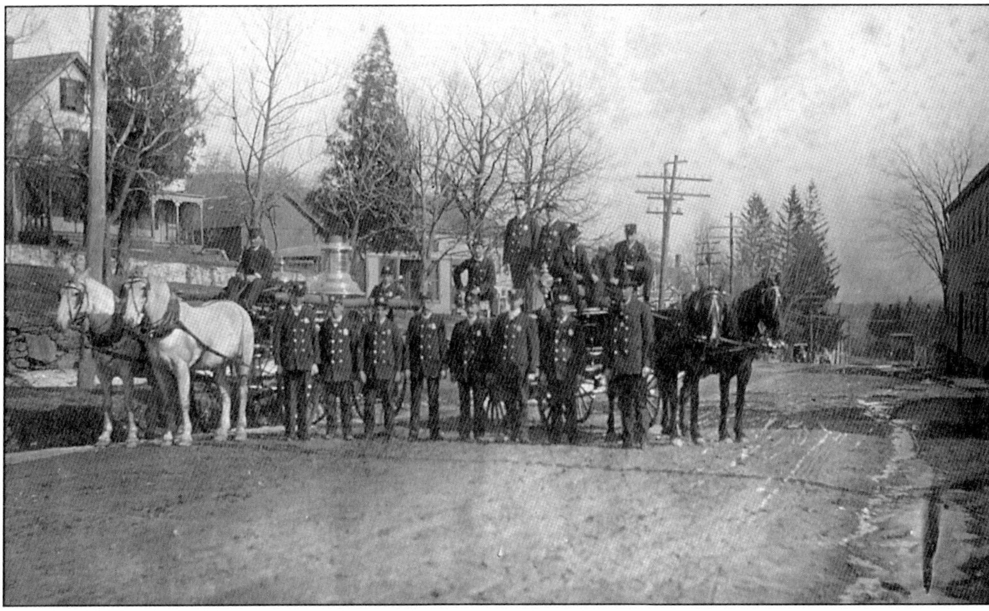

Millbury obtained several fire trucks between 1912 and the late 1920s, but when it came time for the centennial celebration in 1913, members of the William E. Horne Hose Company, Steamer No. 2, of Bramanville put on their uniforms and shined the antique steamer for the occasion. Millbury's fire department began in 1833, and William E. Horne spent 25 years as chief. He died in 1937, by which time his son William D. Horne had been leading the department for more than 15 years. The Hornes were also businessmen and storekeepers at Burbank Square, just down the road from the brick fire station shown in the photograph below. (Both, courtesy of Millbury Historical Society.)

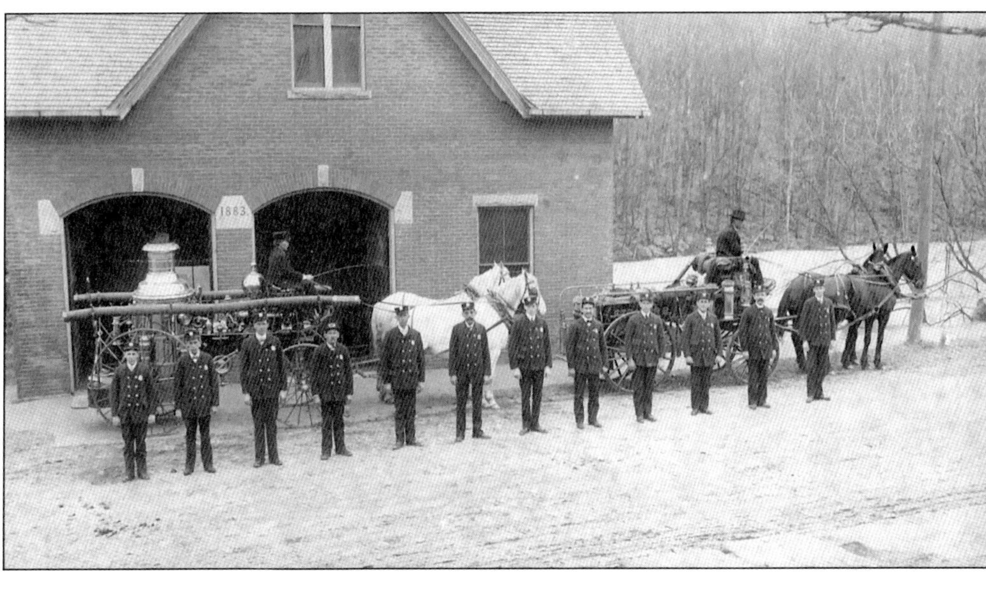

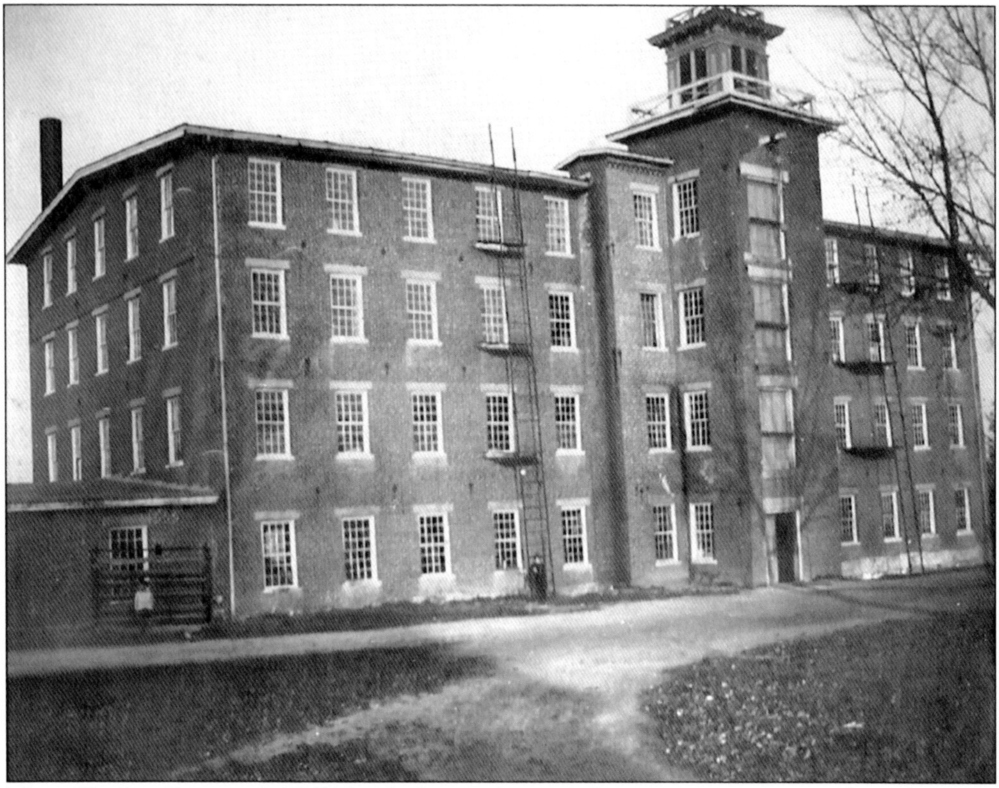

Mayo Woolen Company's Mill No. 2, shown about 1915, occupies a water privilege along the Singletary Stream. It was on the door of a previous mill at this location that the warrant was posted for the town meeting that led to Millbury's separation from Sutton in 1813. The current building was built in the mid-19th century and has been on the town seal since 1900. (Courtesy of Millbury Historical Society.)

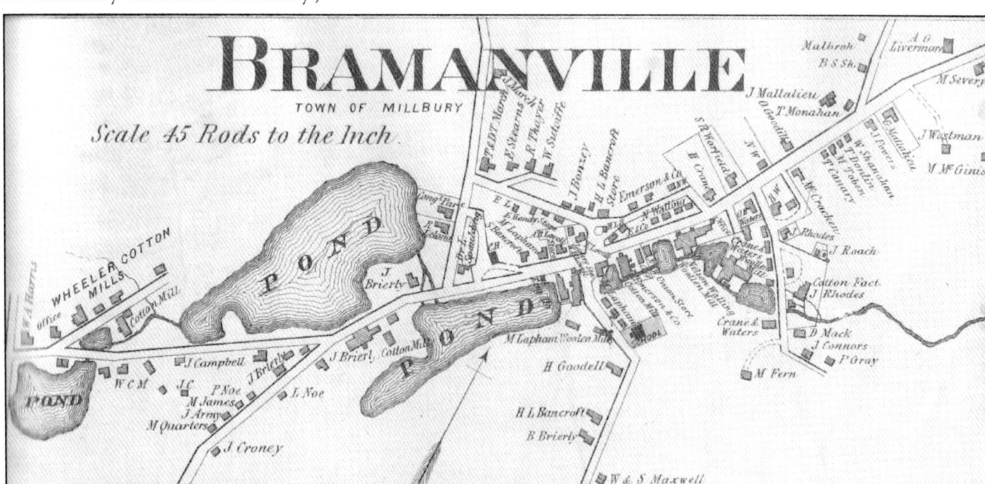

This map of Bramanville from F.W. Beers' 1870 *Atlas of Worcester County Massachusetts* clearly shows how mill owners harnessed waterpower in a series of ponds, dams, and sluiceways flowing west to east from Singletary Lake to the Blackstone River. The largest pond is Brierly, in the center, which flows into the next largest, Mayo Pond. (Courtesy of Chris Sinacola.)

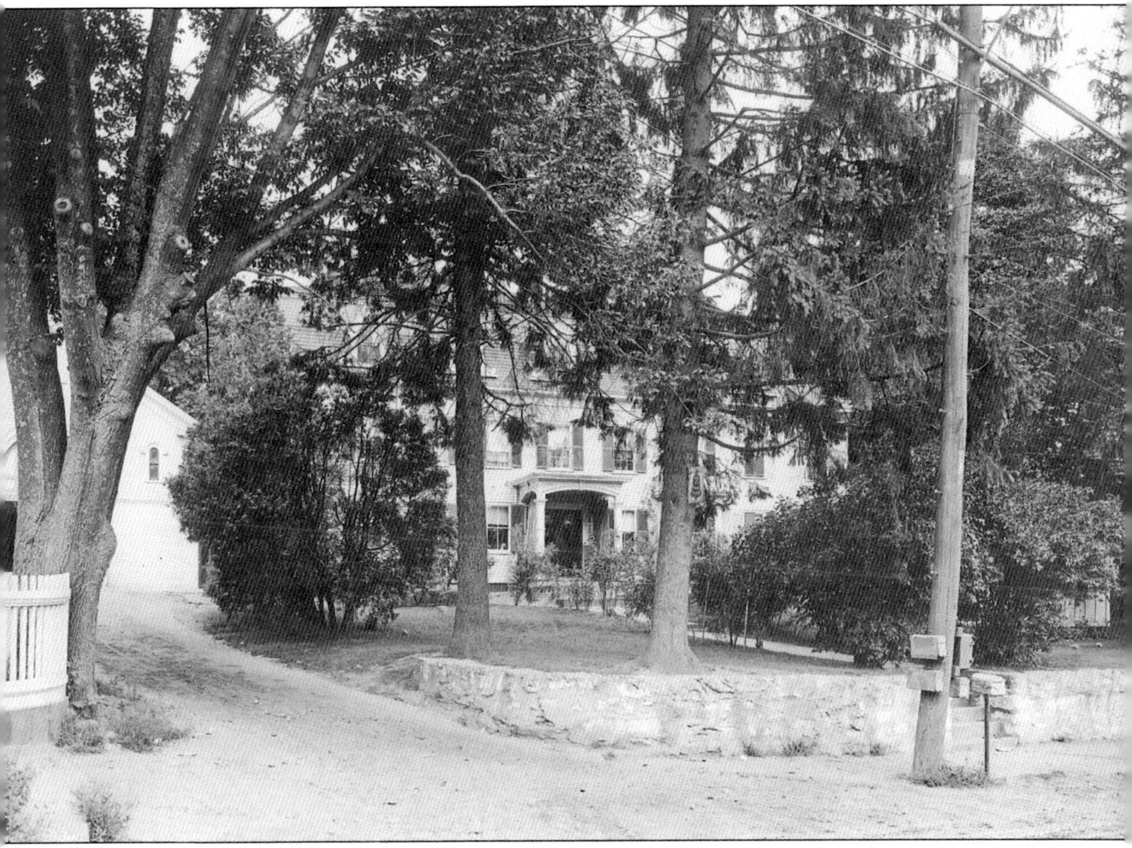

The St. Charles Hotel, located at West Main and High Streets in Bramanville, is a late Second Empire design, built about 1880 by Dr. William Benedict, a prominent Millbury physician and businessman. It is shown here in 1913, and the *Centennial History of the Town of Millbury* reports that "the place was once the residence of Dana A. Braman, and later came into the hands of Elias Lovell, who made some additions to the building and used it for a hotel. In front of this hotel is the terminus of the electric car line at Bramanville, so that it is easy of access from Worcester." Braman was the son of Dr. Amasa Braman, a physician and businessman, one of Millbury's first representatives in the legislature in Boston, and the man for whom Bramanville is named. Dr. Braman kept a home at Old Common and maintained a distillery near the intersection of Elmwood and Beach Streets. The Braman and Benedict families were associated in the cotton industry and shopkeeping. (Courtesy of Millbury Historical Society.)

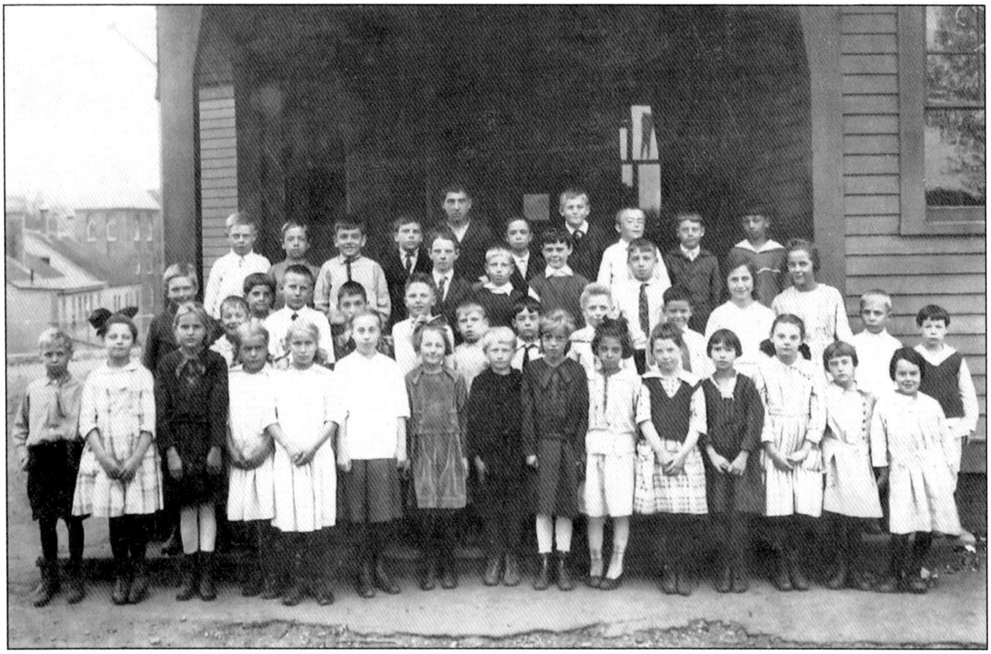

Students from the Burbank School gather on the front step for a c. 1918 group photograph. Like most New England towns, Millbury had a system of neighborhood and village schools. These children, whose parents doubtless worked in the many mills of Bramanville, were largely of Yankee, Irish, and French Canadian heritage. (Courtesy of Millbury Historical Society.)

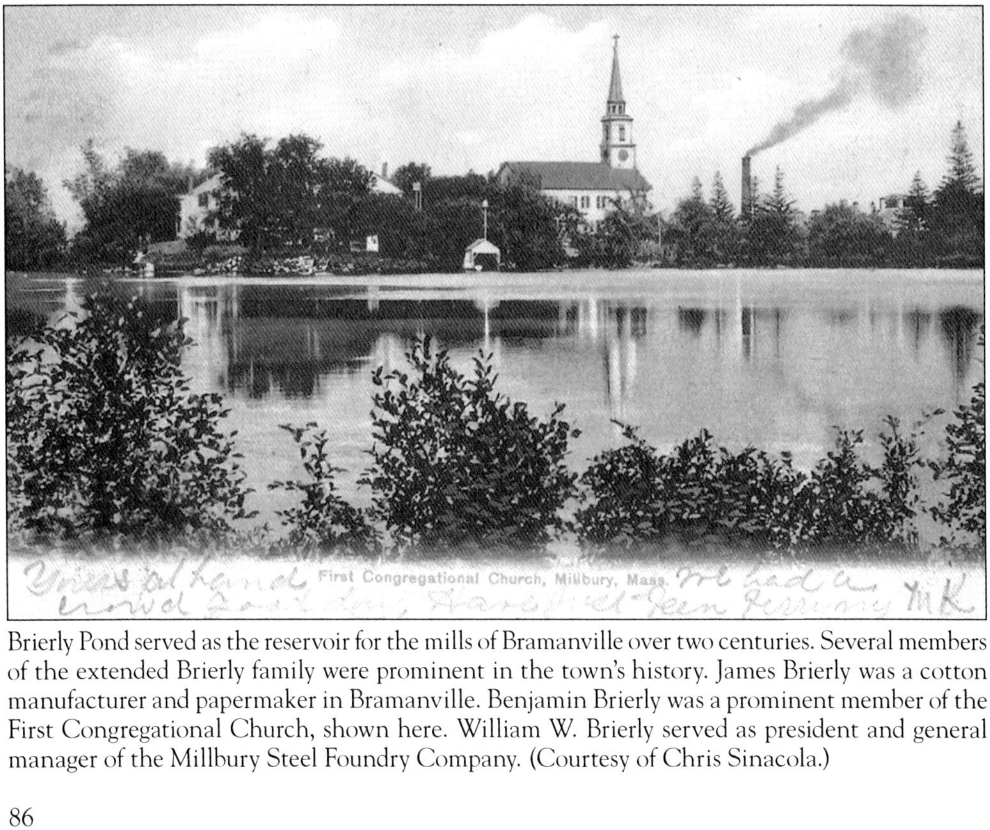

Brierly Pond served as the reservoir for the mills of Bramanville over two centuries. Several members of the extended Brierly family were prominent in the town's history. James Brierly was a cotton manufacturer and papermaker in Bramanville. Benjamin Brierly was a prominent member of the First Congregational Church, shown here. William W. Brierly served as president and general manager of the Millbury Steel Foundry Company. (Courtesy of Chris Sinacola.)

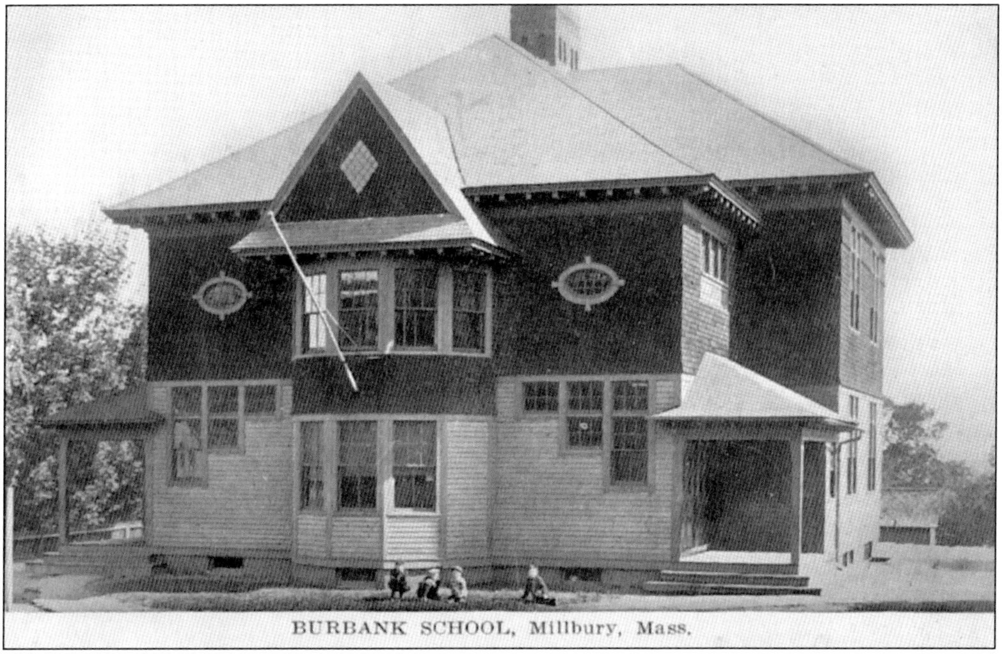

The first school on Burbank Hill was established in the former home of Gen. Caleb Burbank (see page 28), and the town later constructed the Burbank School seen above on a portion of Burbank's lot. It remained open into the 1970s. Miss Mack's first-grade class is seen in the c. 1918 photograph below. On the far left in the classroom stands "The Phonic Chart," reflecting the prevailing reading method in use in American education during that period. A rhyme on the back wall reads: "Come little sparrow, / Fly round and round, / Cover with snow, / The cold bare ground." (Both, courtesy of Millbury Historical Society.)

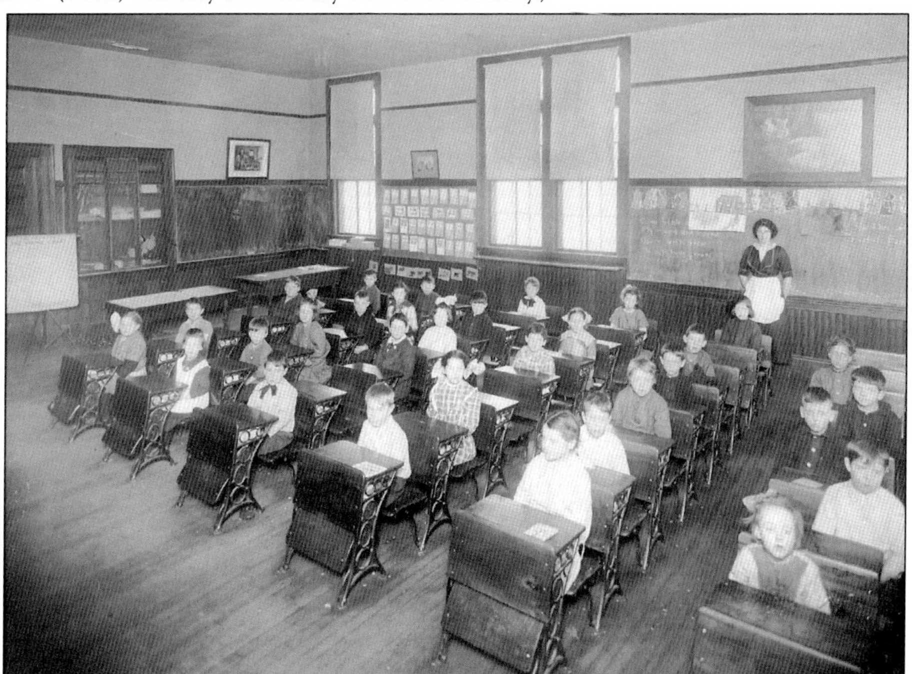

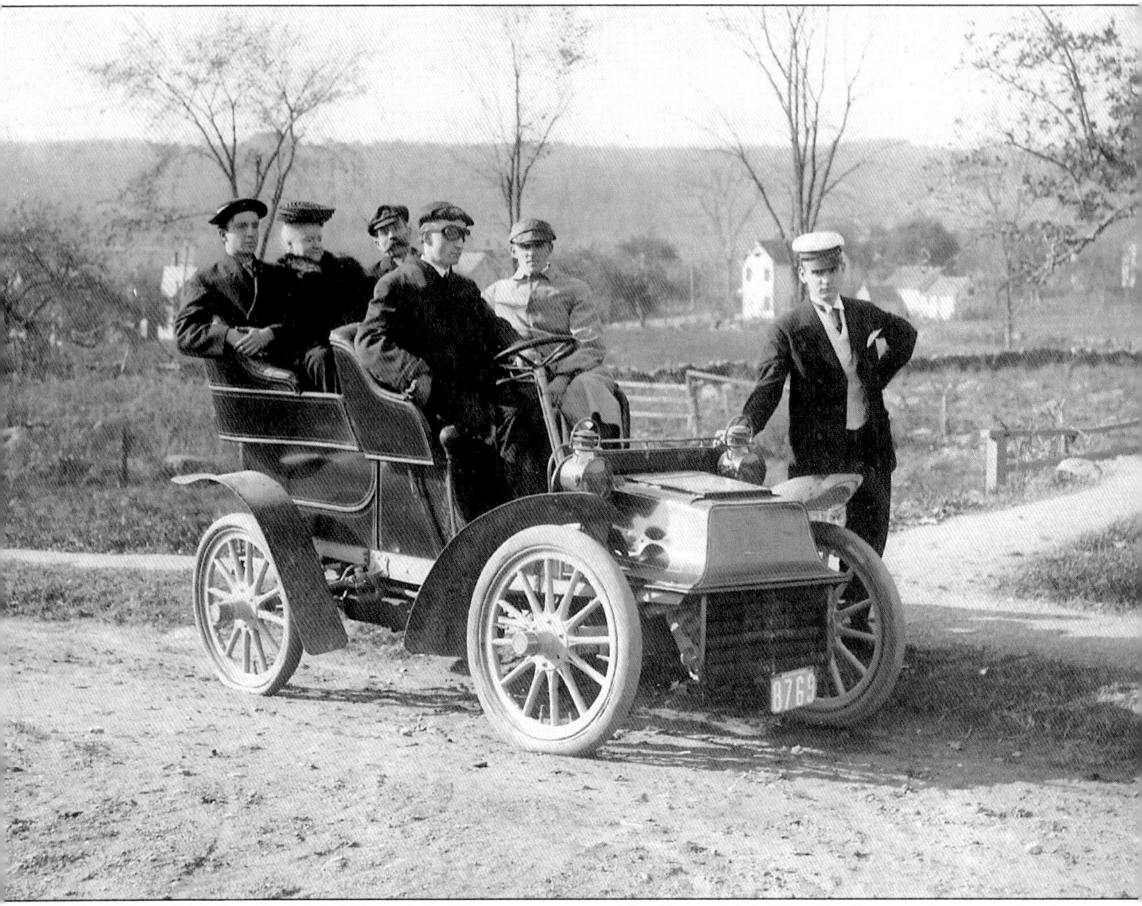

One of the first automobiles in Millbury was owned by Daniel MacDuff, who was born in Airdrie, Scotland, and managed mills in Bridport, England, and North Grafton, Massachusetts, before coming to Millbury. He became general manager of the West End Thread Company in Bramanville village in 1903. Here, MacDuff and his wife Janet are seated in the back seat of their car, on an outing with four of their six sons. Alexander is at the wheel. He was born in 1883 and became a banker and bookkeeper. Charles, born in 1886, is standing beside the car. He was a buyer and advertising manager for Denholm & MacKay Company in Worcester. It is not known which of the couple's other sons are shown here, although it is likely that one is William, who became a foreman in the West End mill. The others were Daniel, who took up civil engineering, James, and Allen. (Courtesy of Millbury Historical Society.)

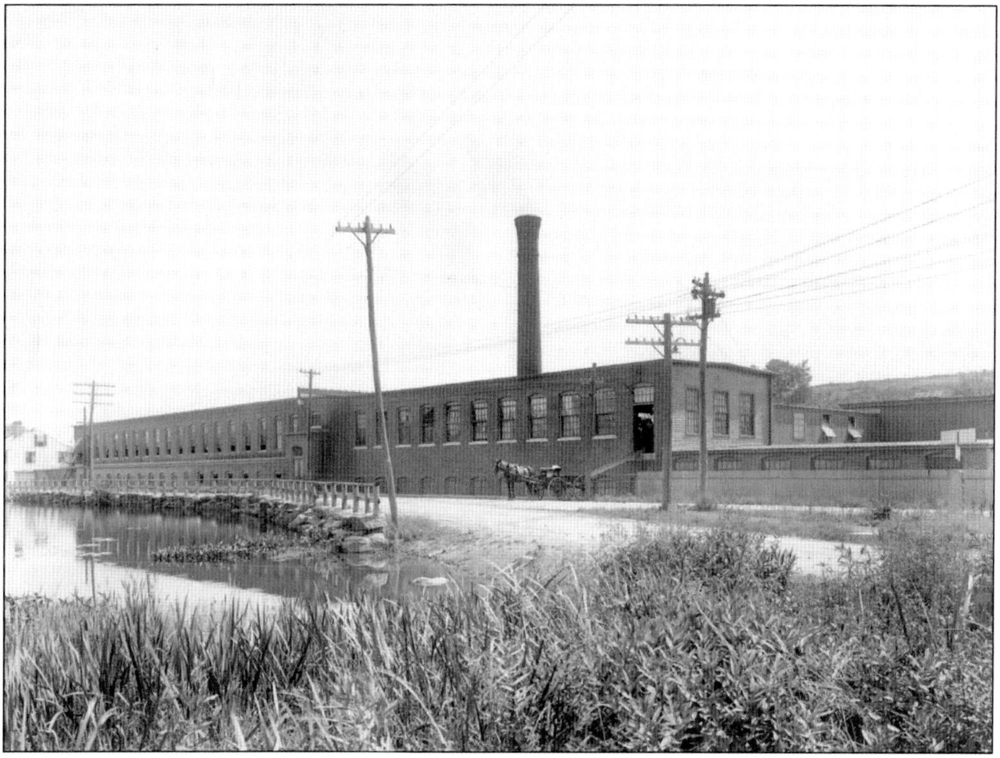

As cotton manufacturing declined in the 19th century, Millbury mill owners converted to the production of woolen goods, napkins, curtains, linen, and other materials that were in growing demand. Nowhere was this process better illustrated than at the West End Thread Company, above, which occupied a spot that had seen a long succession of small mills for cotton and woolen goods. The current mill grew from a brick structure erected in 1886. By 1913, the mill had been expanded several times, West End had become the second-largest taxpayer in town, and additional housing had been built for mill workers, some of whom are pictured below. (Both, courtesy of Millbury Historical Society.)

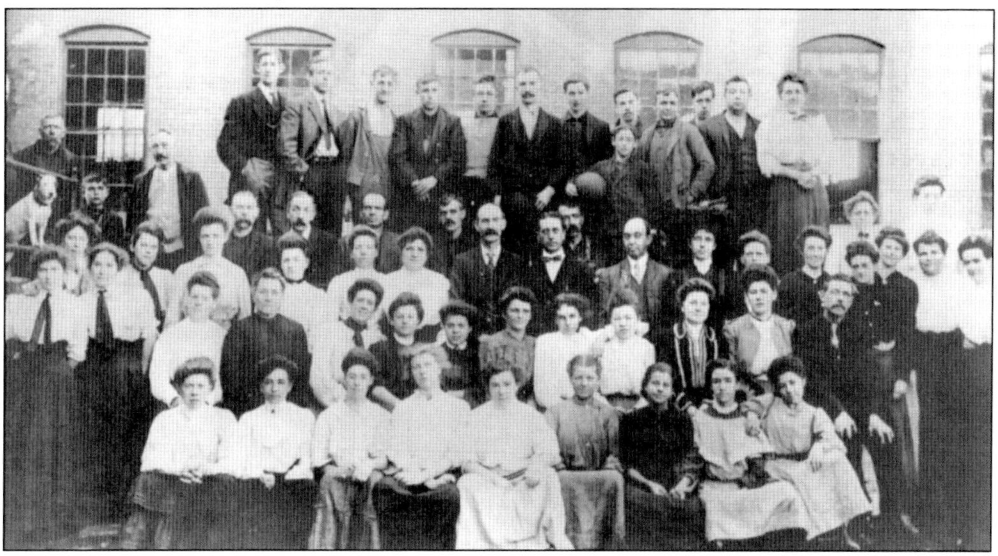

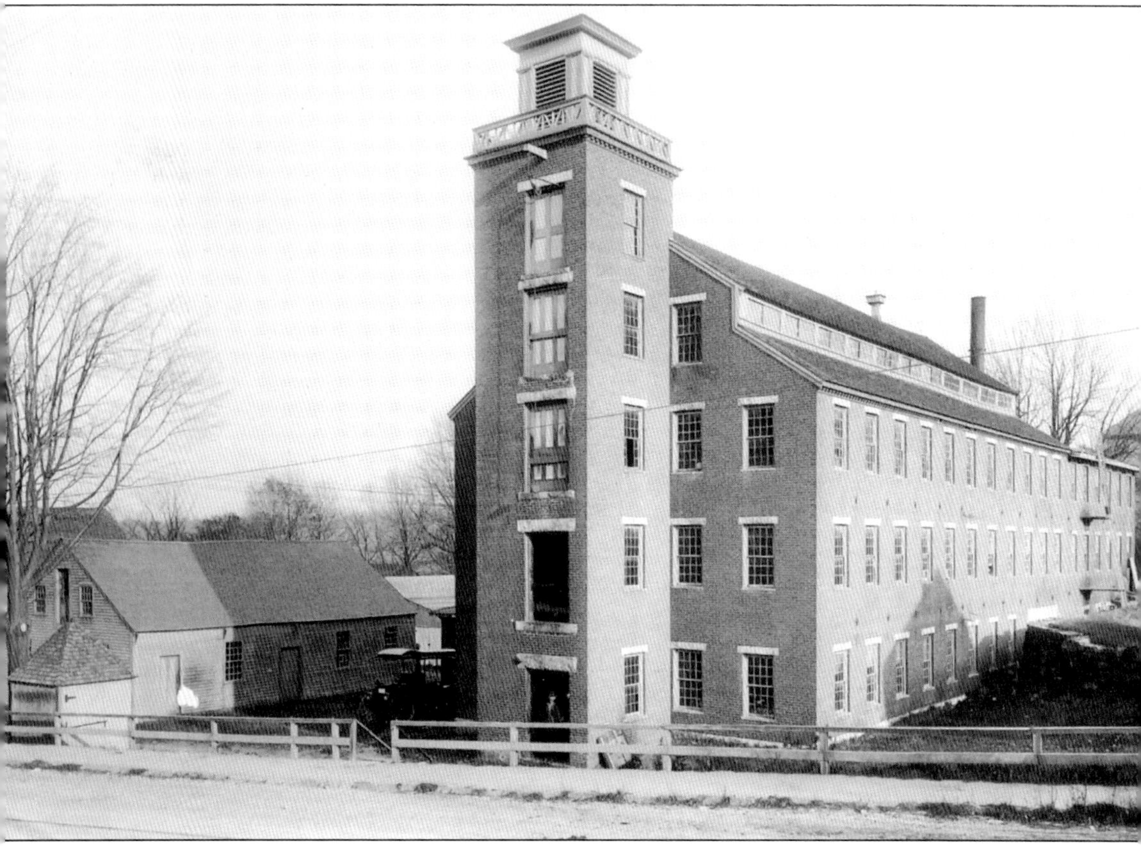

The mill shown here, which is no longer standing, was built in the early 19th century by Dr. Amasa Braman and Dr. William Benedict, on a site where John Waters and Simeon Waters had earlier had a clothing business. Braman and Benedict were both physicians and businessmen—perhaps more of the latter than the former. The mill was located on the north side of the Singletary Stream, just east of Horne's general store at Burbank Square. It passed through several owners before being purchased about 1872 by industrialist John Rhodes, who used it for the manufacture of cotton warp. In 1897, the Mayo Woolen Company was incorporated and acquired four large mills in Bramanville, becoming the leading manufacturer in that area of town. This mill, named Mayo Mill No. 3, was thoroughly renovated and used for preparing stock for the company's other mills. (Courtesy of Millbury Historical Society.)

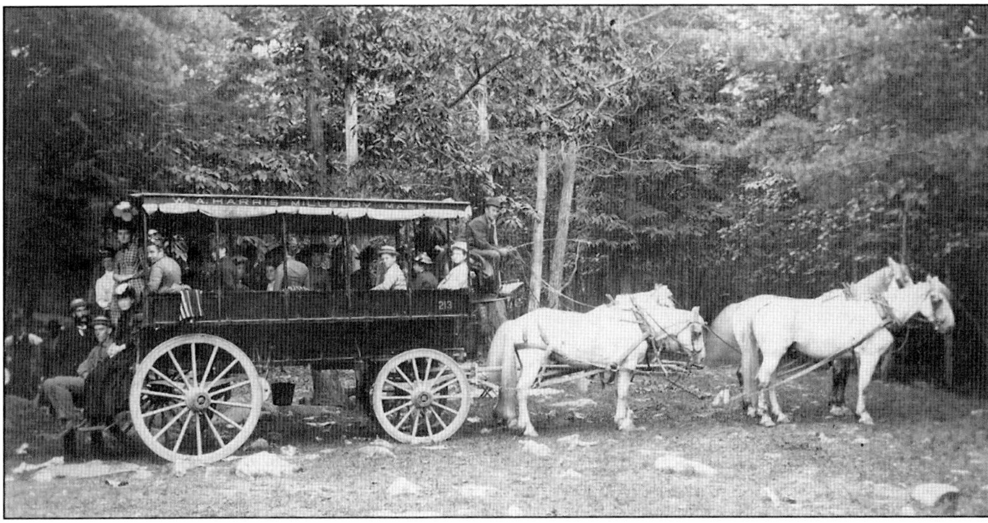

Warren Austin Harris, born in Millbury in 1839, was the son of a Connecticut stoneworker and farmer. Harris became an ice and coal dealer, which he pursued until his death in 1918. This photograph, taken in 1888, shows one of Harris's carriages with a group of Millbury residents enjoying an outing in Purgatory Chasm, a well-known gorge in neighboring Sutton. (Courtesy of Millbury Historical Society.)

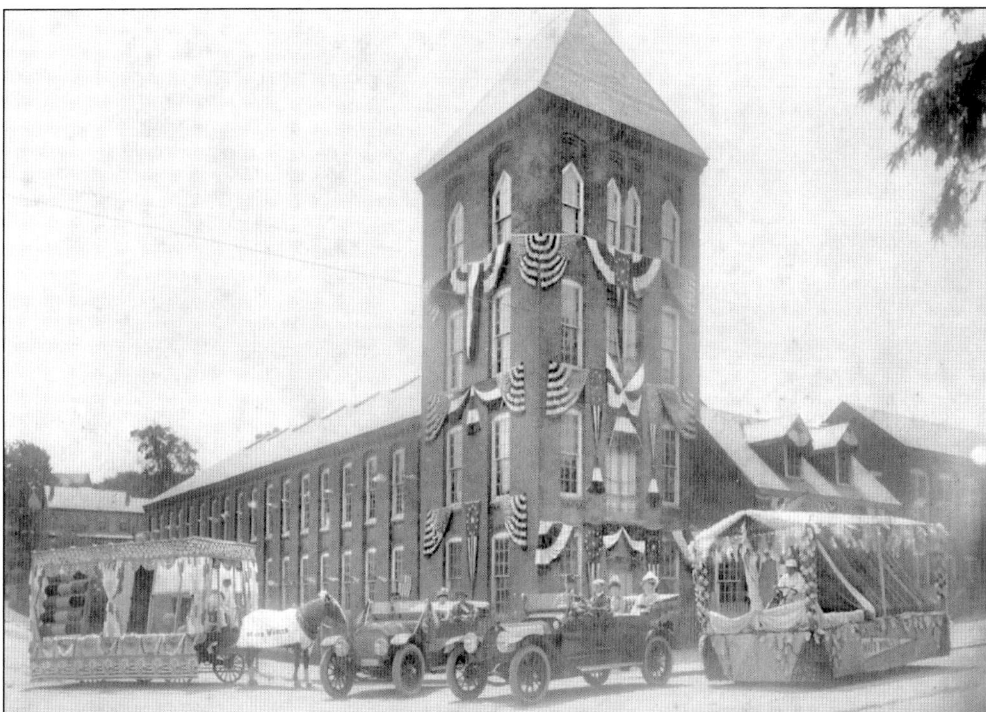

The Mayo Woolen Company was incorporated in 1897 and by 1912 operated four mills in the Bramanville section of town, with 225 employees producing more than half a million yards of woolen cloth each year. This photograph from the centennial celebration shows the Mayo Mill No. 1, which is one of the best preserved mills in town and still houses commercial businesses. (Courtesy of Millbury Historical Society.)

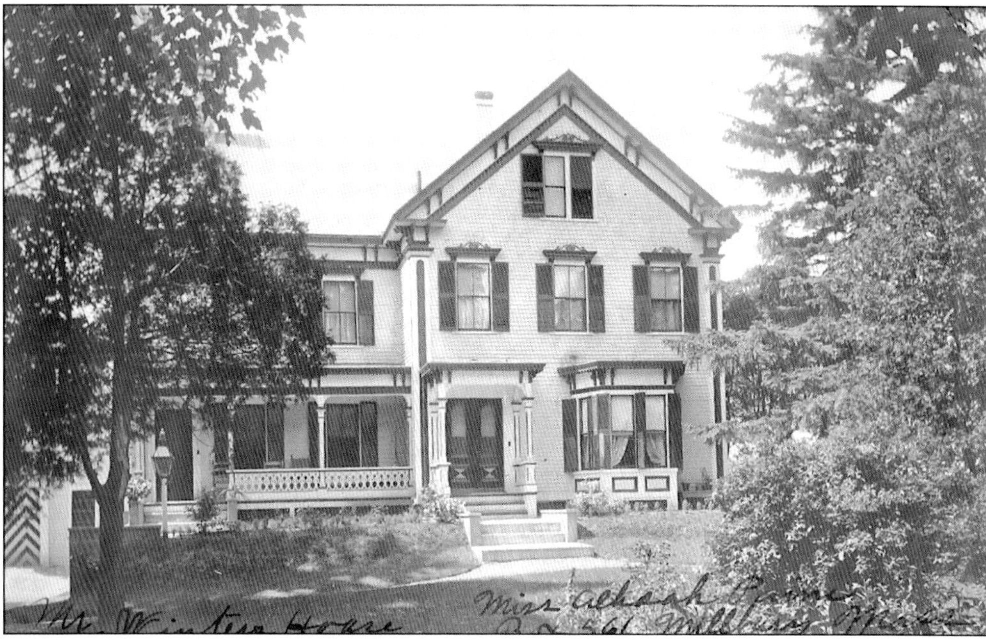

Augustus S. Winter began his career by working for Silas Dunton in the latter's dry goods store in Millbury Center. Years later, he owned the Union Store in Bramanville and became wealthy serving the needs of the many mill workers. He owned the Millbury Grain Company, and served as a trustee of the Millbury Savings Bank and as a director of the Millbury National Bank. About 1890, he was able to build the home shown above on Elmwood Street. The c. 1910 photograph below, shows, from left to right, Achsah Paine, who boarded with the Winter family; Alvan J. Winter, who succeeded his father as proprietor of the Union Store; and Augustus's wife, Sarah. (Both, courtesy of Judy O'Connor, from the Harold C. Kilmer collection.)

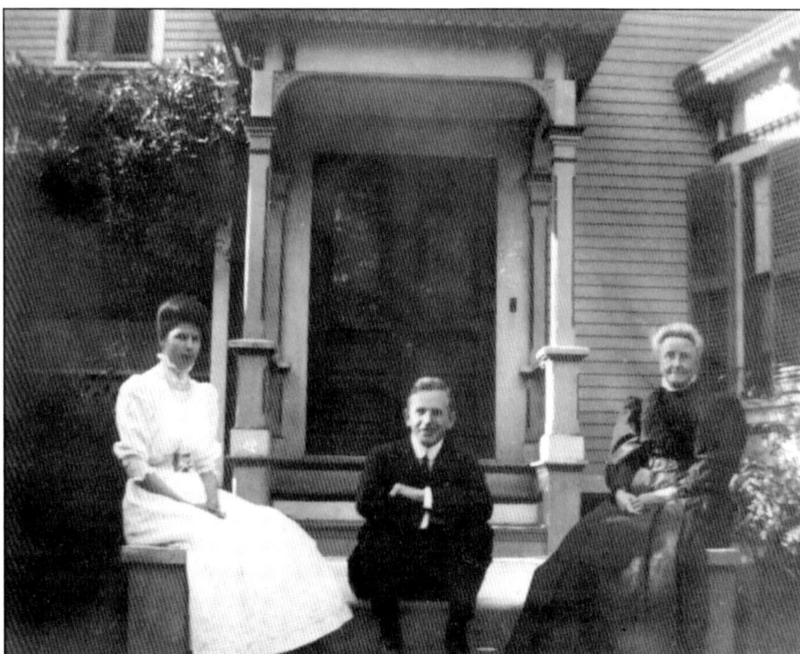

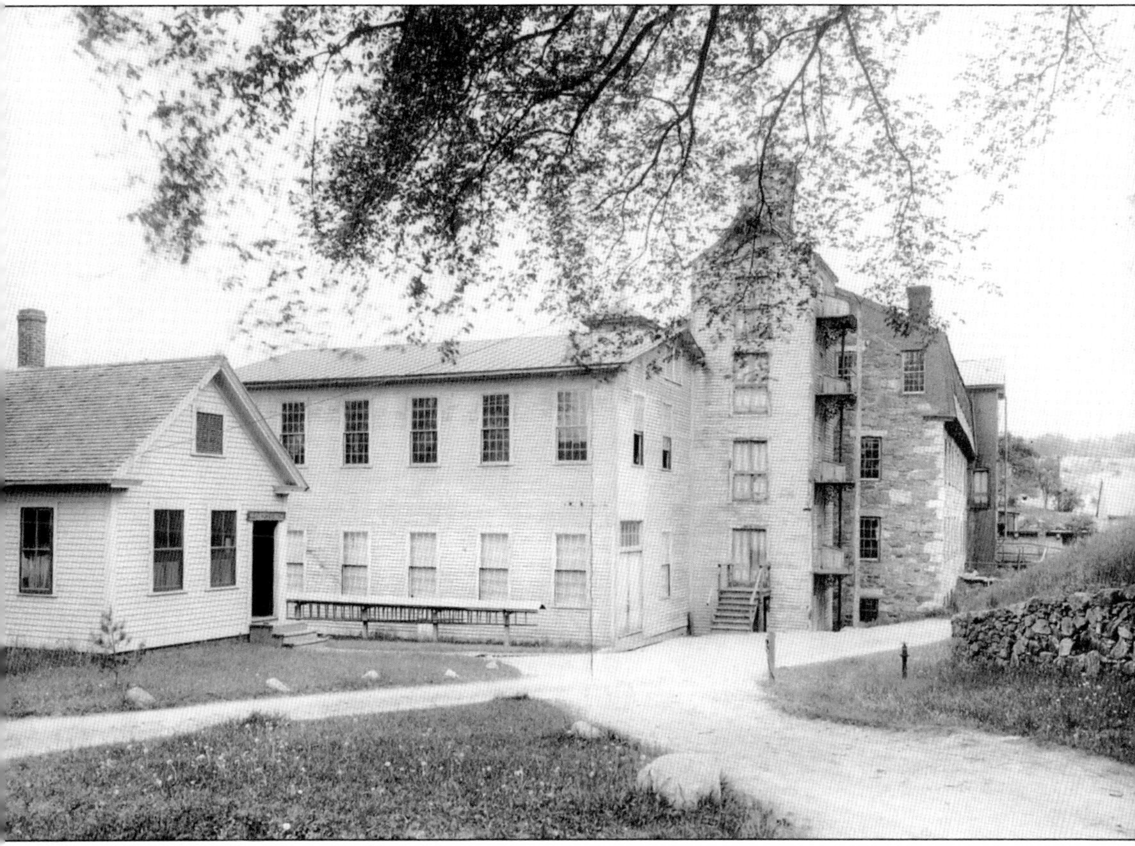

The Edward F. Rice & Co. mill, shown here in 1913, occupied the sixth and final privilege on the Singletary Stream and was located near the present-day intersection of Rhodes and Sycamore Streets in Bramanville. It was close by this mill that the elder Asa Waters maintained a trip-hammer shop associated with his armory at the time of the Revolutionary War. This mill was constructed in 1828 by Samuel Waters for the manufacture of cotton thread. It was producing hosiery about 1850, and John Rhodes produced cotton warp here beginning about 1854. In 1892, it was sold to the Holbrook Manufacturing Company, which sold to Rice, who manufactured cotton napkins. The *Centennial History of the Town of Millbury* surmises that the mill "is almost as old as the town itself, but from all appearances seems capable of witnessing not only the first, but the bicentennial of Millbury." (Courtesy of Millbury Historical Society.)

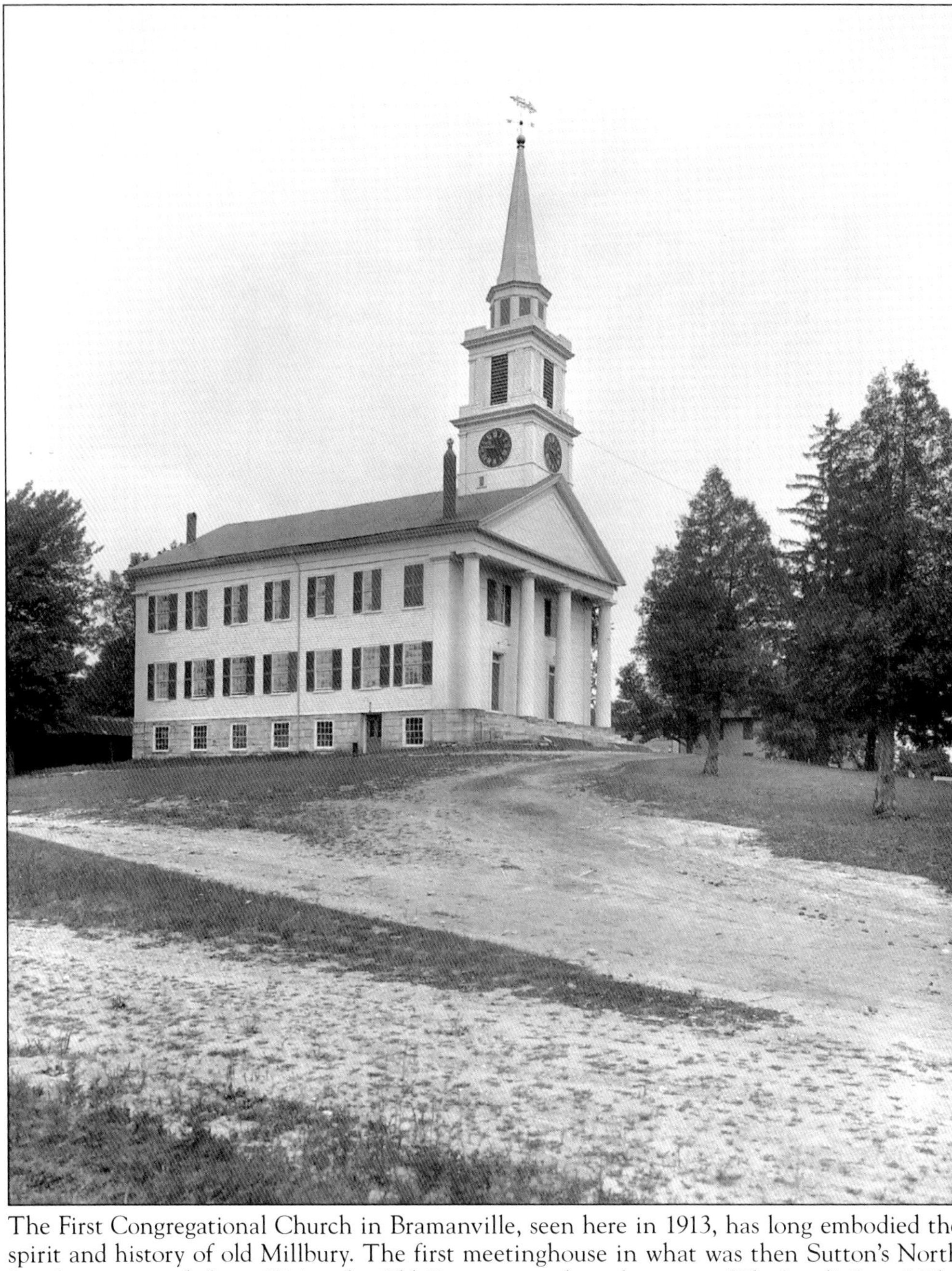

The First Congregational Church in Bramanville, seen here in 1913, has long embodied the spirit and history of old Millbury. The first meetinghouse in what was then Sutton's North Parish was erected about 1744 at the Old Common, and was known as "The Lord's Barn." The congregation was organized in 1747 and included many of the families who would, nearly 70 years later, be instrumental in organizing the new town of Millbury. In 1802, construction of a new church began at Old Common, and it was dedicated two years later. After Millbury became a town in 1813, its growth, particularly along the Singletary Stream, suggested that the church be moved to Bramanville. In 1835, this church was taken down and moved in pieces to its new site, where it was reassembled, with a rededication ceremony in January 1836. (Courtesy of Millbury Historical Society.)

Six

West Millbury

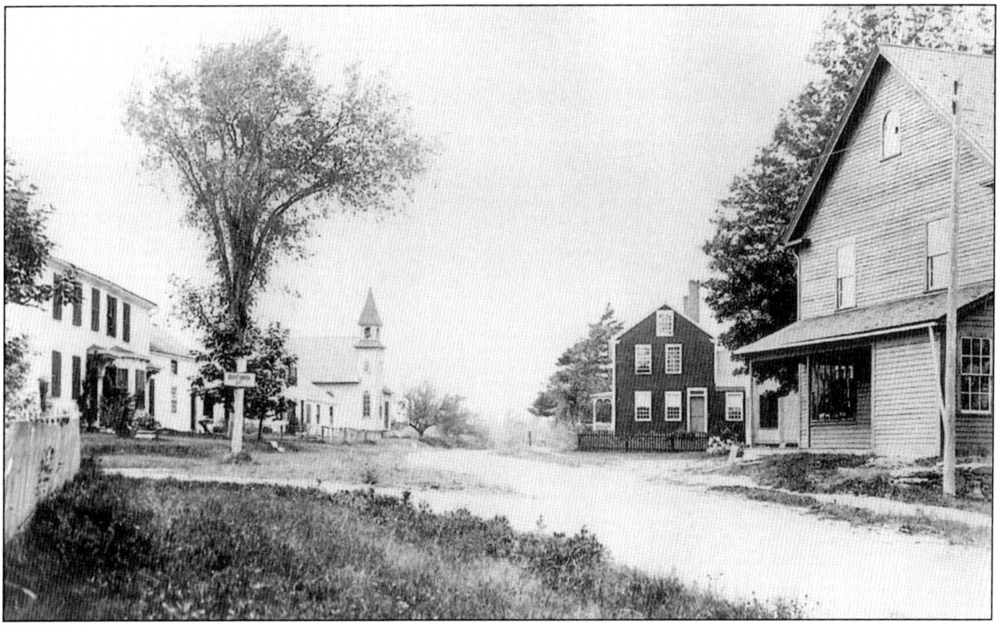

West Millbury has always maintained a distinct identity, with its farms, mills along the Ramshorn Stream, a church, and the West Millbury Cemetery, where many early settlers are buried. This is the intersection of West Main Street and South Oxford Road as it appeared about 1910. The building at far right, now gone, was for many years a community meeting hall. (Courtesy of Millbury Historical Society.)

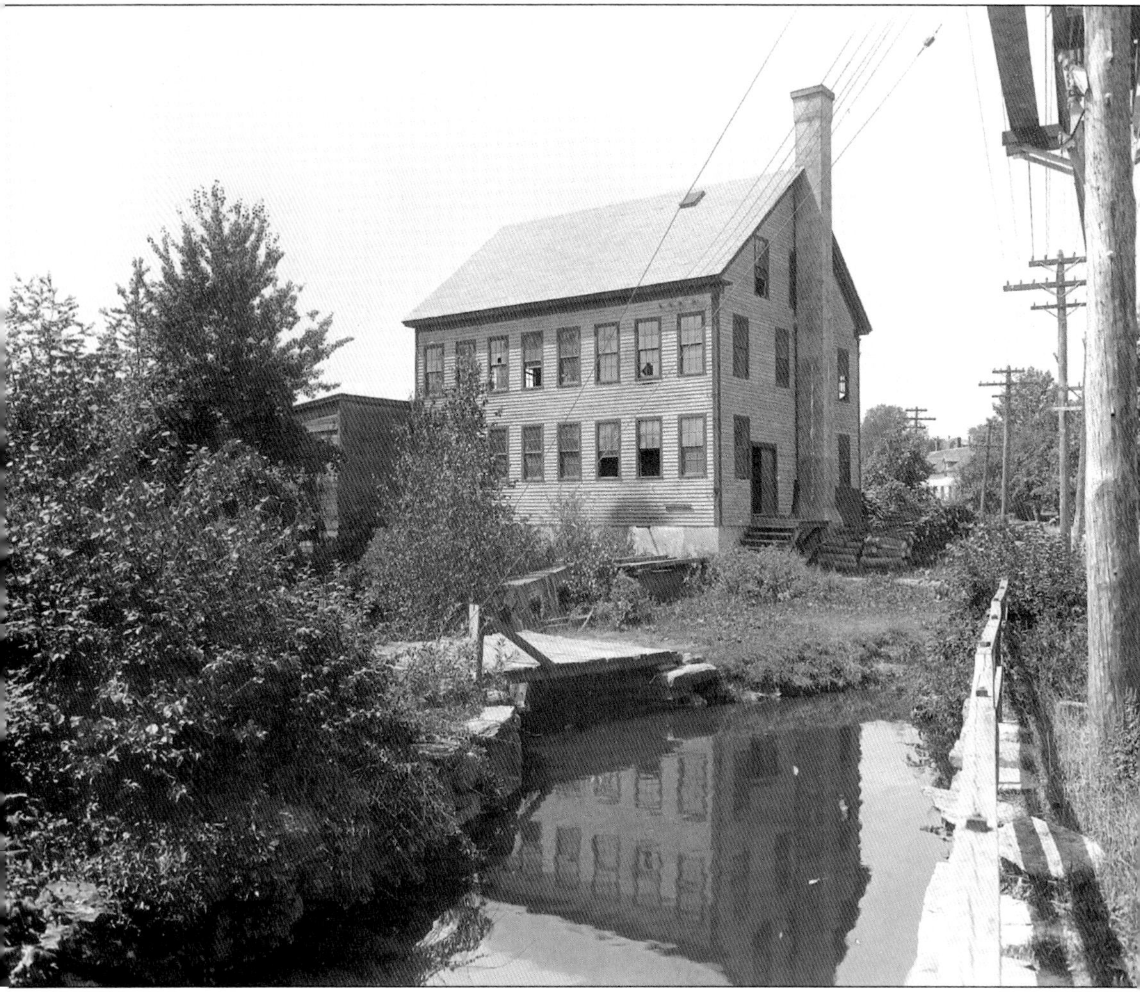

The Henry W. Glover shop stood for many years on the Ramshorn Stream, where it runs underneath West Main Street in West Millbury. On this site, in the early 19th century, stood a complex of buildings owned by Solomon Marble, including a blacksmith shop, scythe shop, and tannery. Later activities included grinding of black lead or graphite for use in polishing stoves and painting the hulls of ships. It was also at this site that the inventor Thomas Blanchard worked on the development of his eccentric lathe. A series of disasters in the late 19th century, including a dam break in 1873 that caused extensive damage, interrupted commerce along the Ramshorn Stream. The last of the old mills at this site was taken down in 1899 and replaced by a new structure, which in turn was destroyed by fire. Sometime after 1900, the structure shown here was built by Henry W. Glover, who was born in Worcester in 1862 and came to Millbury as a young man. Glover manufactured handles for edge tools. (Courtesy of Millbury Historical Society.)

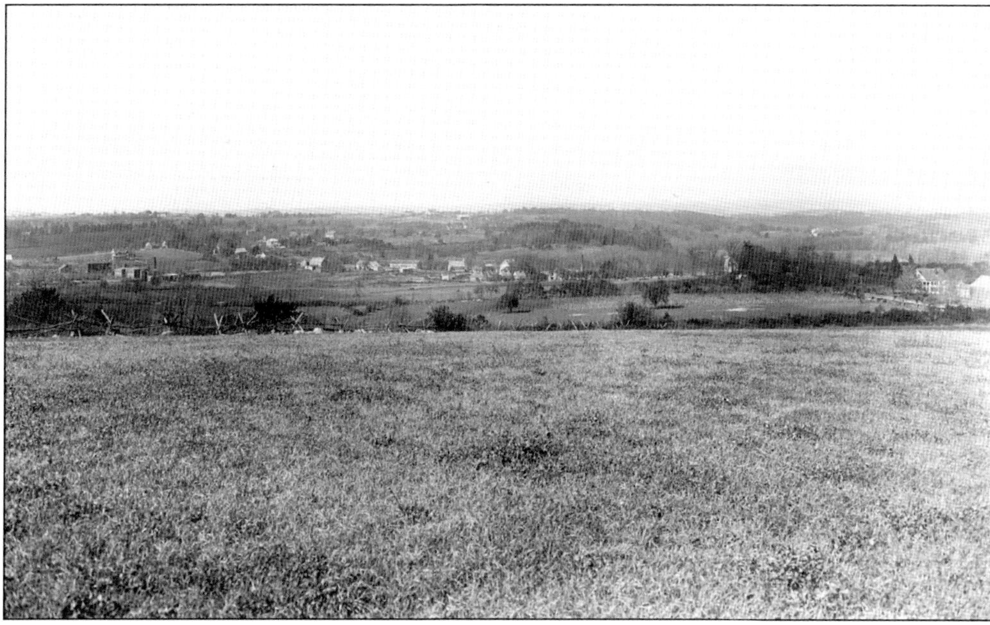

This view of West Millbury village was taken from Harris' Hill near Lake Singletary, looking northwest, about 1913. The Ramshorn Stream flows left to right in the middle distance, its course marked by the Hoyle Mill on the left, Henry W. Glover shop on the right, and the house, barn, and shops belonging to Charles Soule, located in the clump of dark trees on the right. (Courtesy of Millbury Historical Society.)

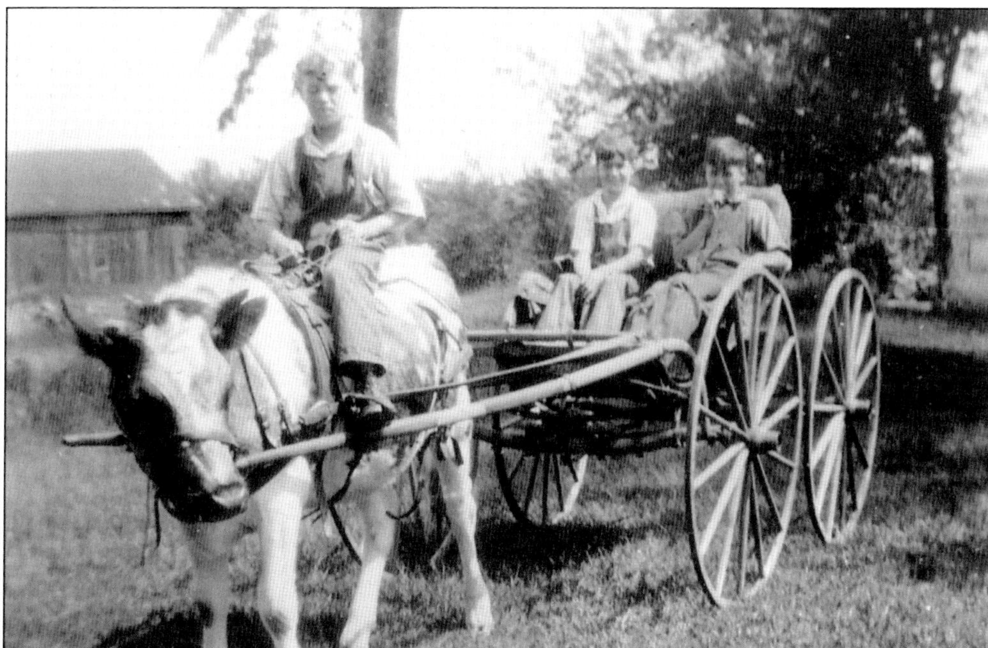

A trio of friends enjoys an outing at the John Pierce farm in West Millbury in the summer of 1926. They are, from left to right, Herbert Davidson riding the heifer, Freeman Davidson, and Harold C. Kilmer. (Courtesy of Judy O'Connor, from the Harold C. Kilmer collection.)

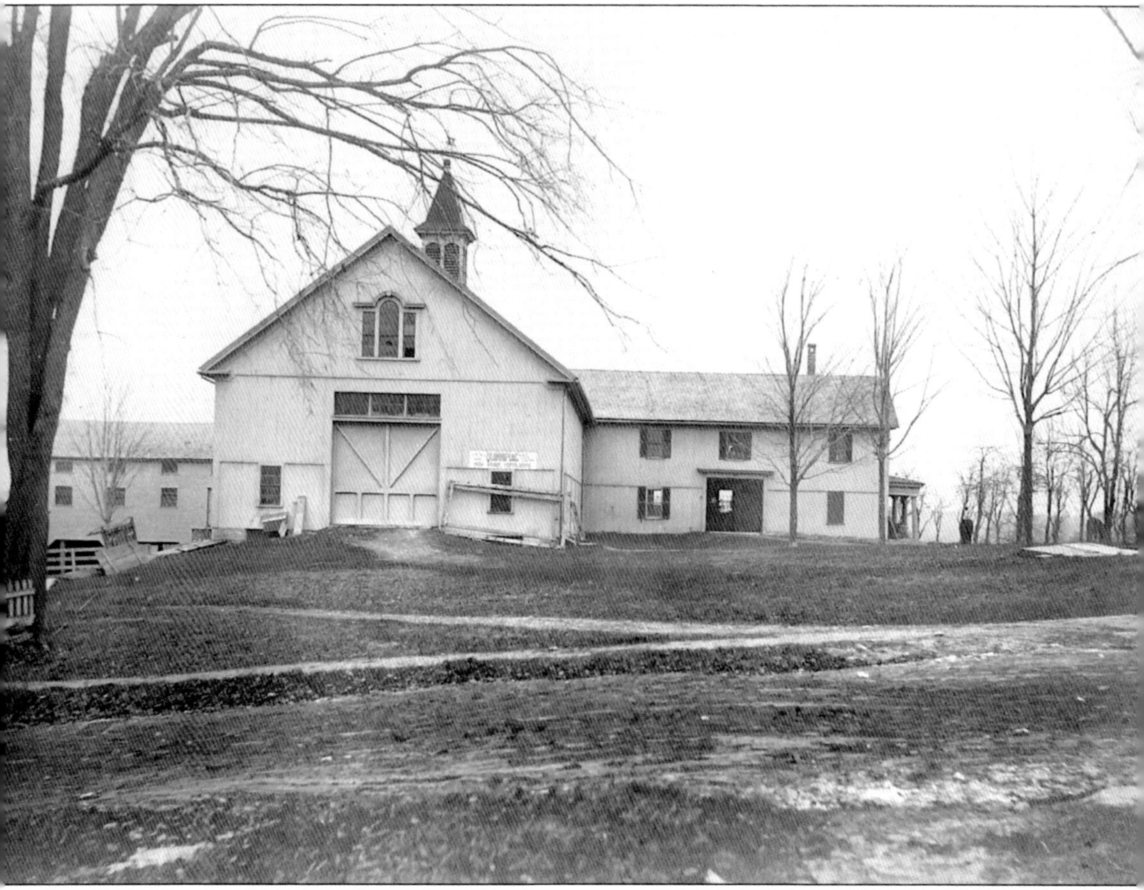

Capt. Amasa Wood was born in Upton, Massachusetts, in 1784 and moved to Sutton about 1808, settling on the farm shown on these pages, which was located in what is now West Millbury. Wood was a farmer and shoe manufacturer. The *Centennial History of the Town of Millbury* notes that the shoes "were carried in saddle-bags upon horse-back to Boston and Providence. . . . The fatigue of these journeys was somewhat relieved by the numerous taverns along the routes." A leather tannery business was begun, but burned in 1833, and the financial panic of 1837 dealt Wood further losses. But the family persevered, employing many residents of Millbury, and even expanding to a tannery in Halifax, Vermont. The family's shoes were distributed throughout the nation, and, as the *Centennial History of the Town of Millbury* notes, "shoes bearing the name of 'A. Woods & Son' were looked upon as *ne plus ultra*." The barn in this photograph was located on the north side of West Main Street, between the house and Ramshorn Stream. It burned down in 1977. (Courtesy of Millbury Historical Society.)

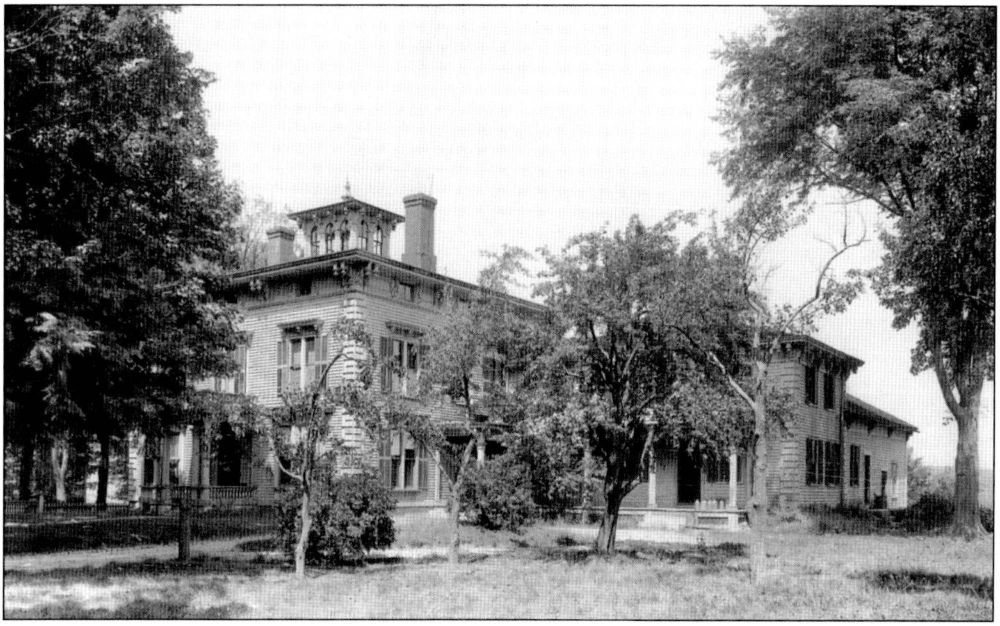

The Capt. Amasa Wood mansion in West Millbury, shown in these photographs at the time of the 1913 centennial, was built in the Italianate style. Shoe manufacturing was originally done in a first-floor room on the west side of the house, and many of the family's shoes were sold in the South, where they were purchased by plantation owners for use by slaves. Wood died in 1856. The property was purchased in 1892 by Charles F. Soule, a native of Brimfield, Massachusetts, who developed a large and successful dairy farm here. Time, fire, and neglect took their toll in later years, and the house is now gone. (Above, courtesy of Millbury Historical Society; below, courtesy of Kay and Roland Lachance.)

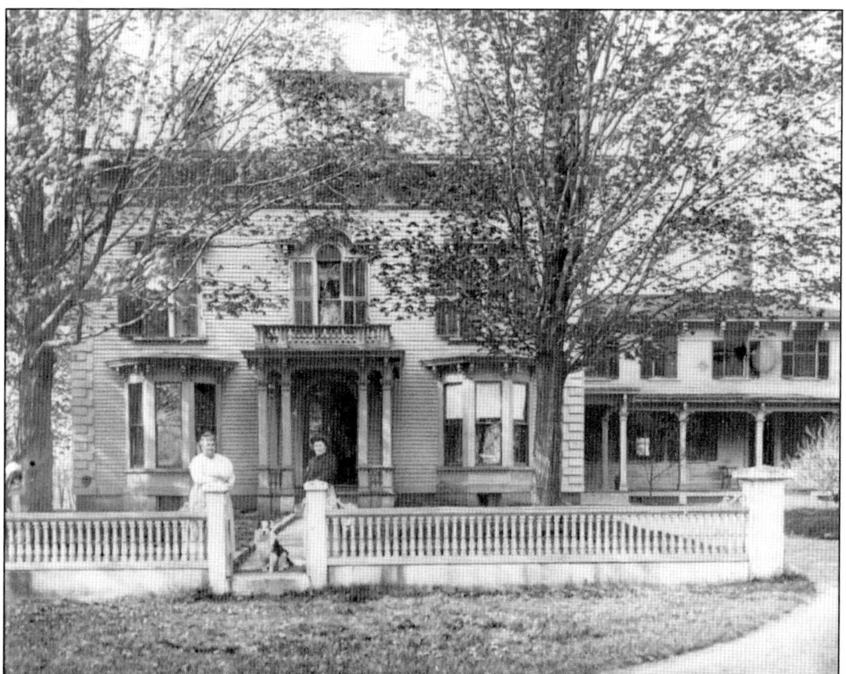

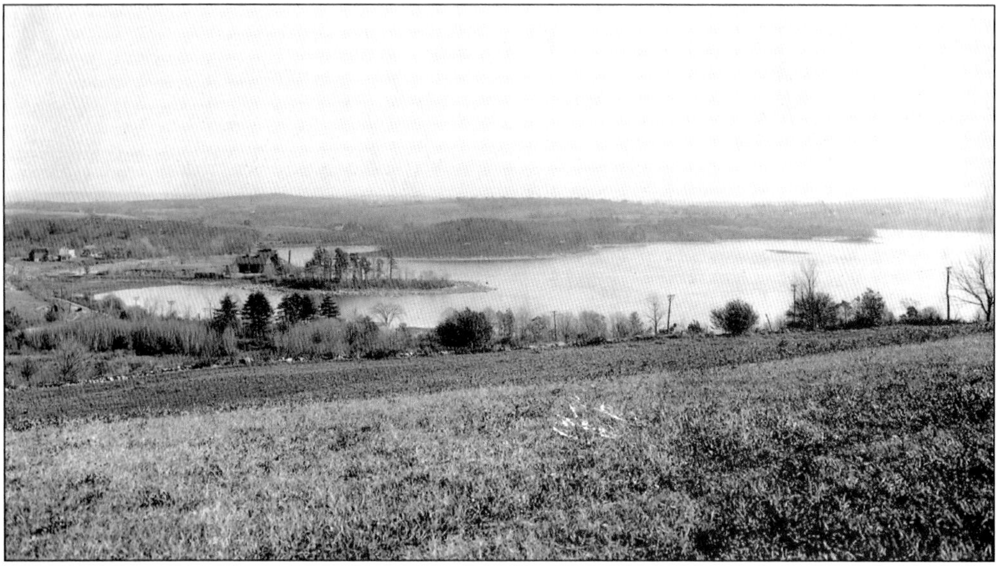

This 1913 view of Singletary Lake from Harris Hill shows the Harris family's icehouse in the center on the left. Burbank Hill is in the distance on the left; to the right is Sutton Center. There are fewer trees during this period and relatively few houses along the shoes of the lake, which teems with activity today. (Courtesy of Millbury Historical Society.)

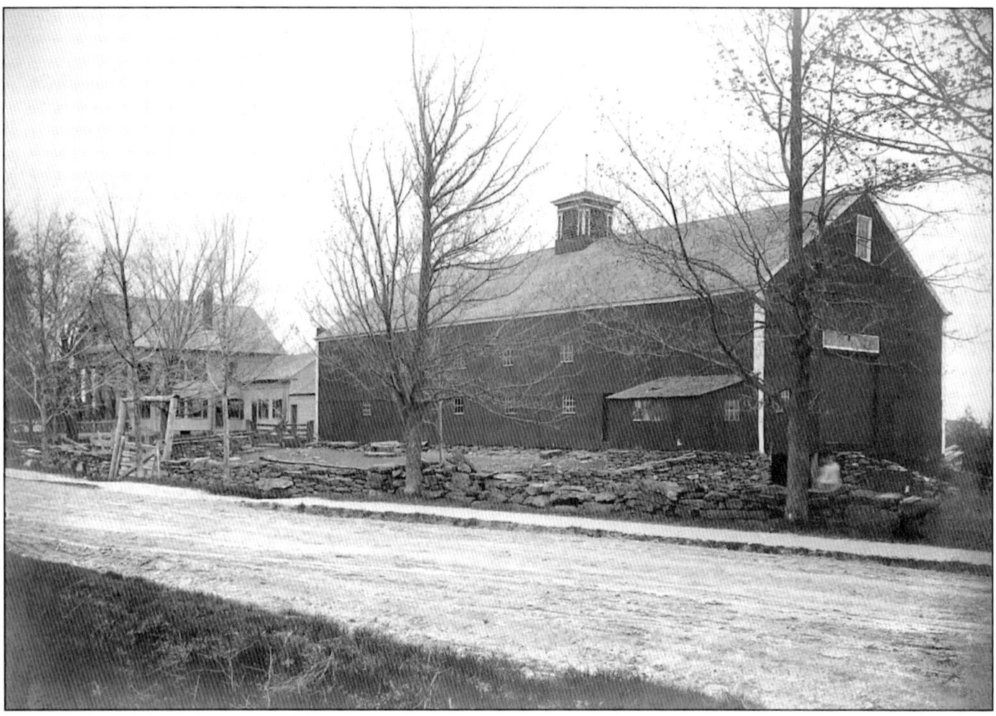

Located at 272 West Main Street, this home and barn was built about 1850 and was the residence of Charles R. Harris at the time this photograph was taken in 1915. The property was formerly the homestead of Jonathan Waters, who settled in what was then Sutton in the early 18th century. His son Asa Waters Sr. (1742–1813), who pioneered gun-making efforts in Armory Village, was born on this property. (Courtesy of Millbury Historical Society.)

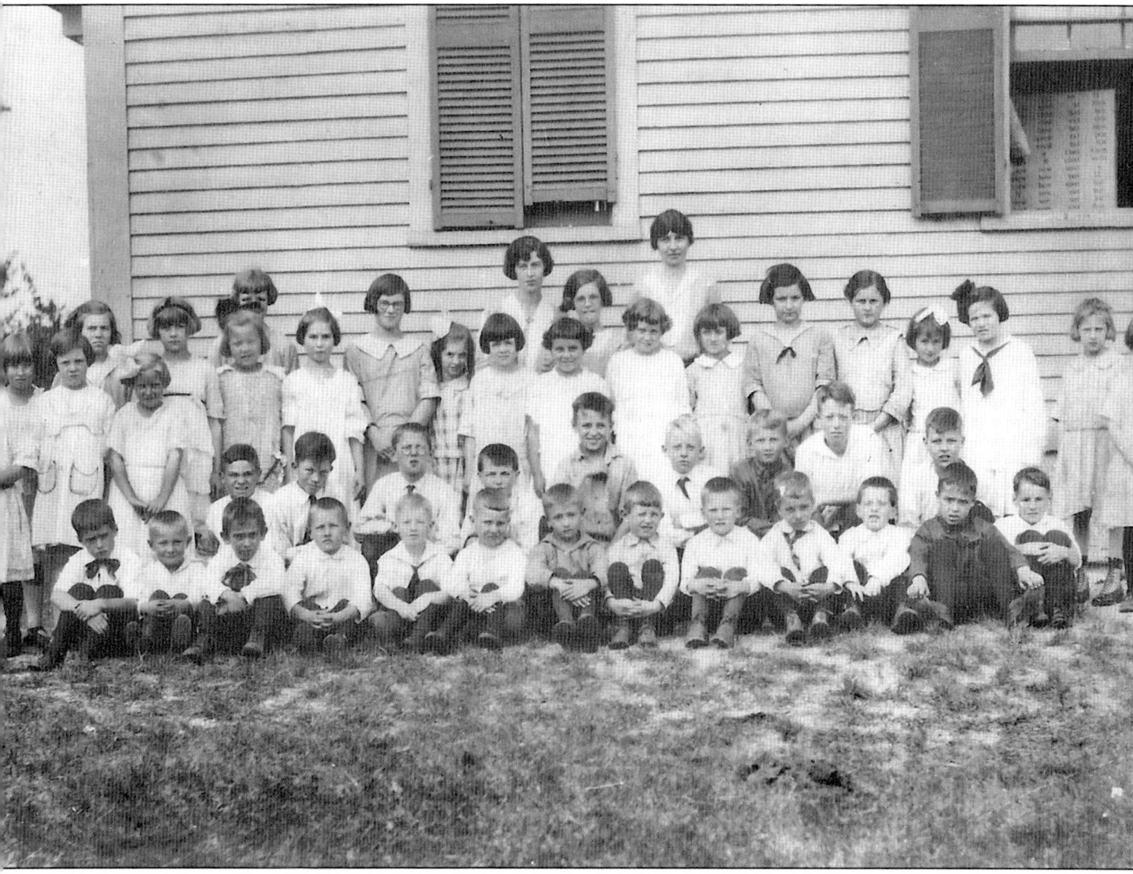

The first Grass Hill School in West Millbury was a brick structure built in the early 19th century on the west side of the West Main Street, where the Union Church now stands. After it was destroyed by fire, a new, two-story wooden school was built in 1861 opposite it. This photograph shows the students of the Grass Hill School in 1923. The boys are, from left to right (front row), Freeman Davidson, George Cullina, Everett Fairbanks, Vincent Kersulis, Kenneth Culver, Raymond Greenwood, John Cullina, Charles Whitten, Everett Glover, Francis Stockwell, ? Kemp, Harold Kilmer, and George Stowe; (second row) Everette Gilbert, Frederick Stockwell, Frank Kersulis, Harold Frasier, James Cullina, Newell Culver, David Watkins, Clarence Culver, and Warren Greenwood. Girls, from left to right, are Signe Berg, unidentified, Gertrude Glover, Helen Paine, Gertrude Broberg, unidentified, Arlene Day, Eva Backstrom, Ida Davidson, Josie Gilbert, Beatrice Blanchette, Gladys Paine, teacher Hazel Woodman, Ruth Reavy, Carolyn Stowe, Dorothy Reavy, teacher Agnes Faron, Genevieve Kersulis, ? Frasier, Florence Lee, Nellie ?, Helen Kemp, unidentified, and Anna Paine. (Courtesy of Judy O'Connor, from the Harold C. Kilmer collection.)

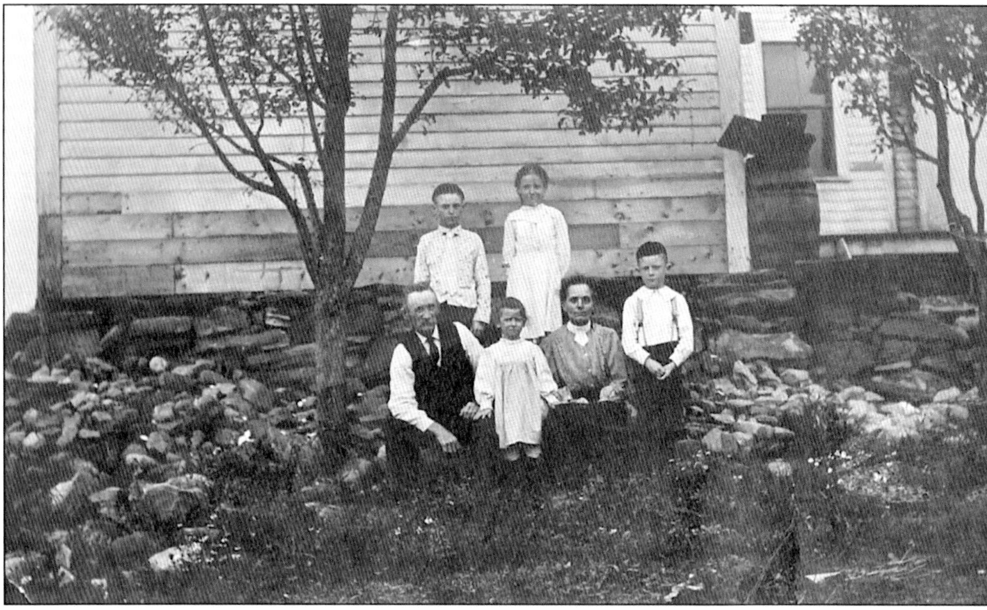

The Jacques family is gathered about 1902 at their farm, originally the Richard Bartlett farmstead, on Grass Hill in West Millbury. The house was built sometime between 1750 and 1780, and in 1820 was sold to Abijah Davis of Oxford, who left it to his son Erastus. It was sold again in 1879 to the Jacques family, whose descendants have lived there since. Pictured above, from left to right, are (first row) Mark Jacques, daughter Sarah, wife Ida, and son Joseph; (second row) son Luke and daughter Agnes. Below, the Jacques children are seated on the porch. The eldest to youngest and from left to right are Luke, Agnes, Joseph, and Sarah. (Both, courtesy of Kay and Roland Lachance.)

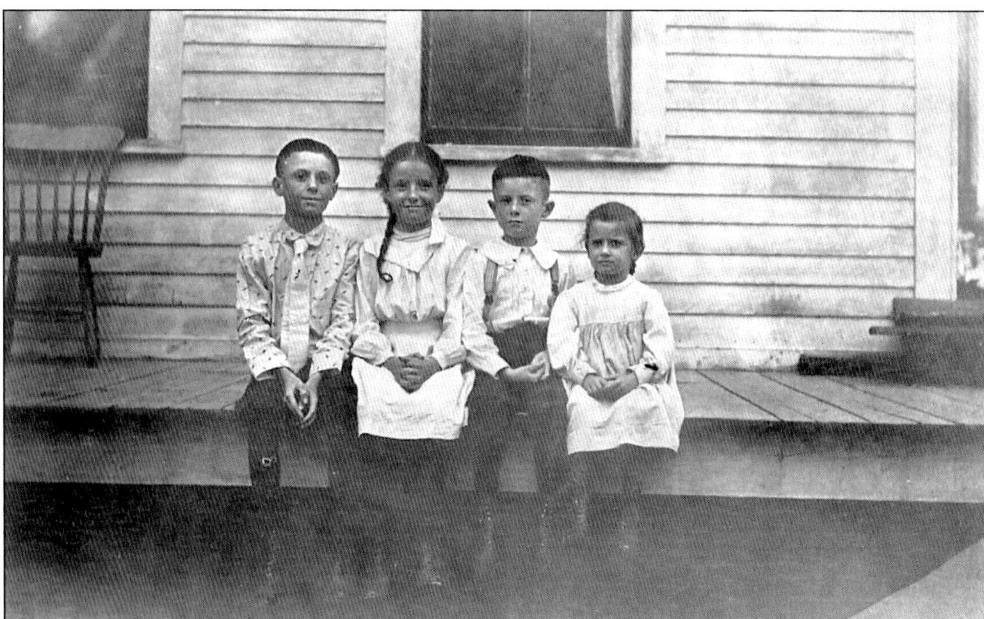

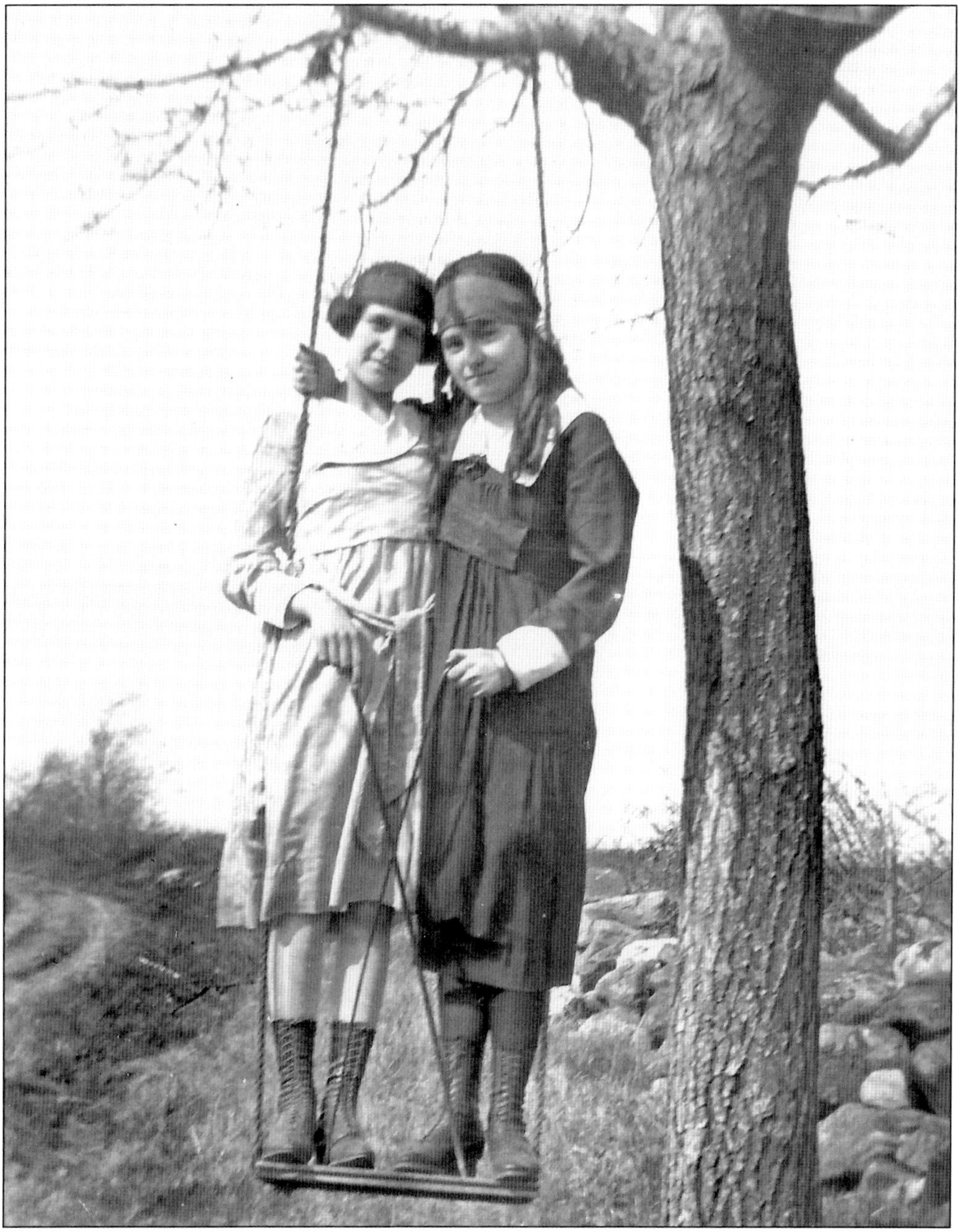

Sisters Sarah, left, and Agnes Jacques pose for the camera in the early 1920s near their home on Grass Hill in West Millbury. Sarah and Agnes, like their mother, Ida, and brothers, Luke and Joseph, were deaf-mutes and inseparable friends. After their father, Mark, died in a fall from the roof of the house, Ida rented the family house and moved to Southbridge with her four children, all of whom were enrolled in the American School for the Deaf in West Hartford, Connecticut. Eventually, the family returned to Millbury and reoccupied the farmhouse. Sarah married a member of the Mercer & Dunbar Armored Car company and settled in Avon, Connecticut. Agnes married Lucien Lachance and had four children, including one son, Roland, who recalls that as a child he learned sign language before he could speak. (Courtesy of Kay and Roland Lachance.)

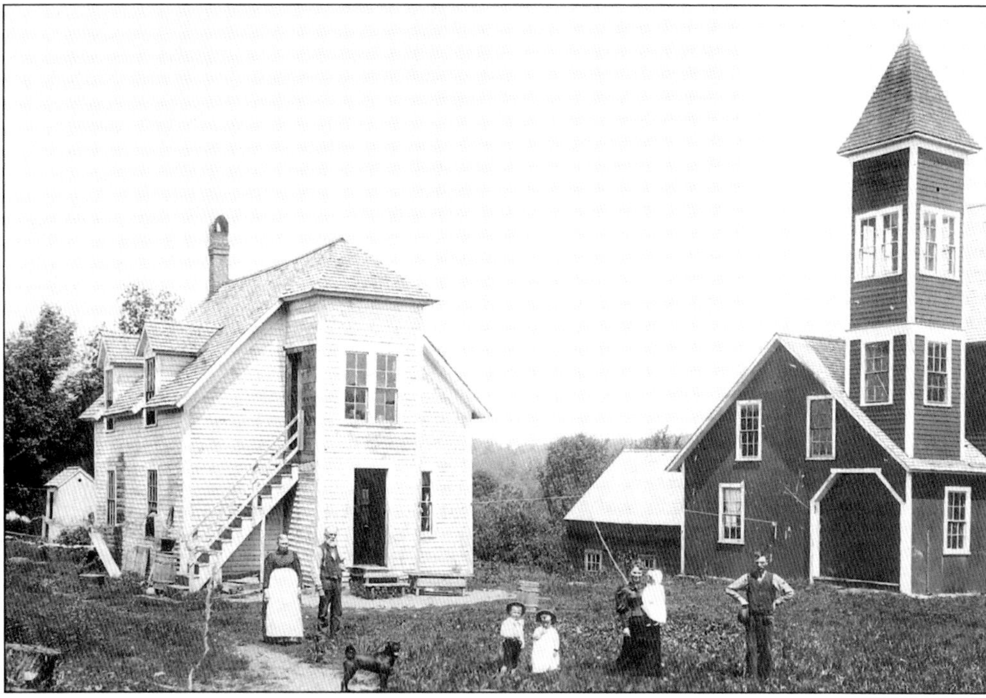

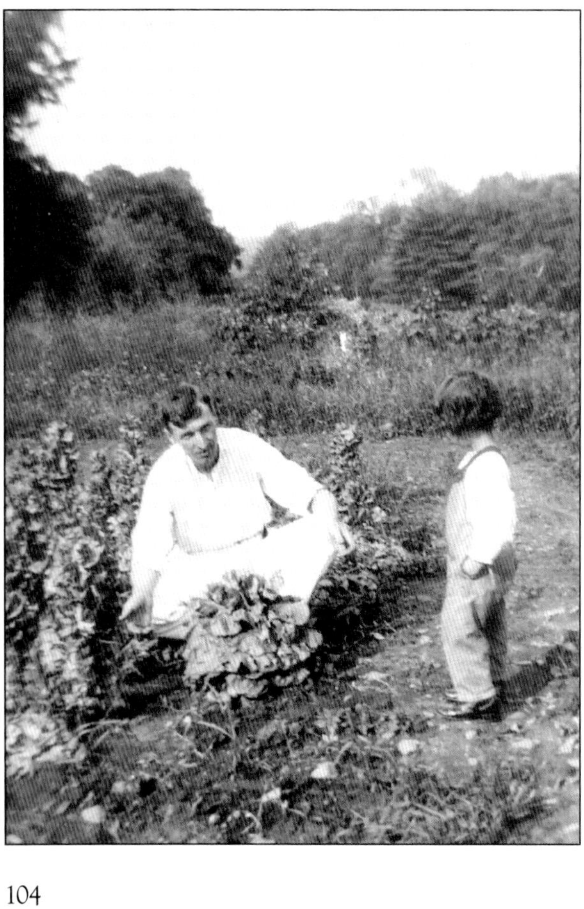

The John Rich grist and shingle mill was located on the Ramshorn Stream at Carleton Road. John G. Wood, son of Capt. Amasa Wood, earlier moved two buildings from West Main Street to this site, including the former West Congregational Church, for use as mills. One burned in 1876. This 1895 photograph shows the Rich family and buildings they constructed after acquiring the site. (Courtesy of Millbury Historical Society.)

Charles M. Kilmer and his son, Harold, work in their garden at the Balcom House on West Main Street, West Millbury, in the early 1920s. Father and son shared a lifelong love of horticulture. Years later, the two kept a large garden on Beach Street. Charles was known for cultivating cactus, and Harold kept careful records of his annual crop yields. (Courtesy of Judy O'Connor, from the Harold C. Kilmer collection.)

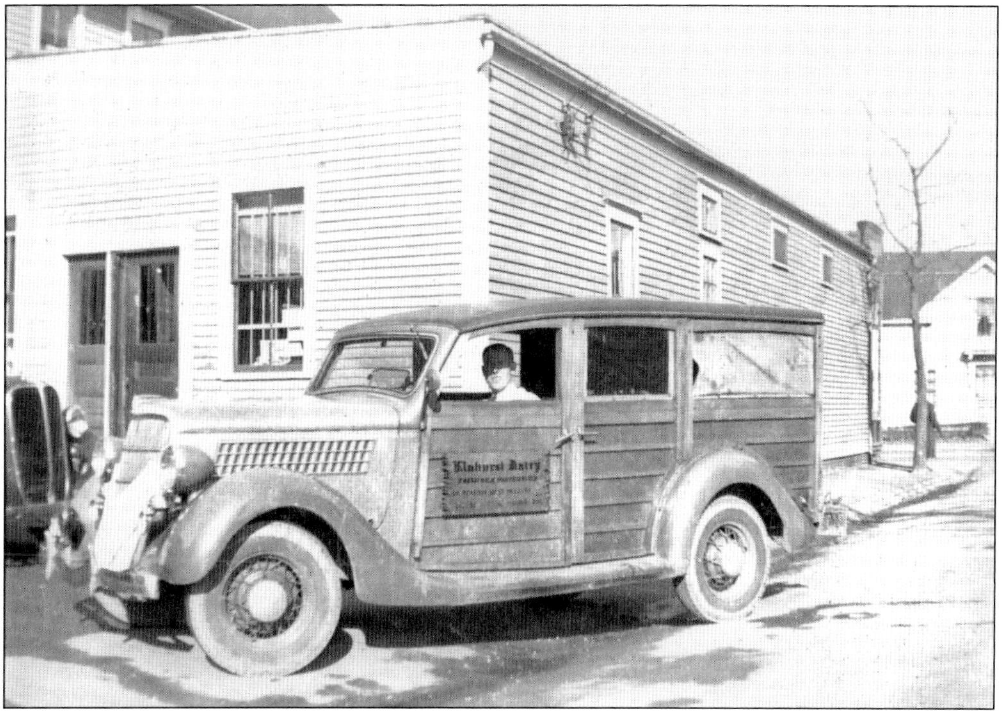

The Pearson family has run a dairy in West Millbury for more than a century and remains one of a very few in Worcester County that continues to control its entire production cycle—land, cows, milk production, and distribution—including home delivery. Above, Oscar Pearson makes a delivery to the Anderson & Sunquist store in Worcester's Quinsigamond Village about 1940. In the photograph below, his son Robert is shown standing on the running board of one of the family's milk trucks about 1935. Robert and his family continue to run the dairy today. (Both, courtesy of Robert and Barbara Pearson.)

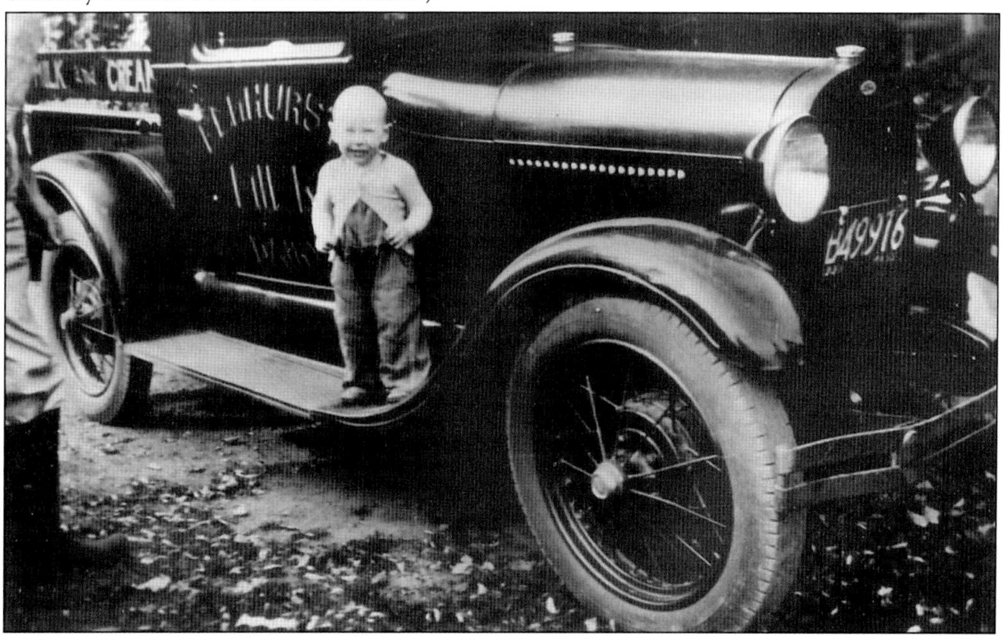

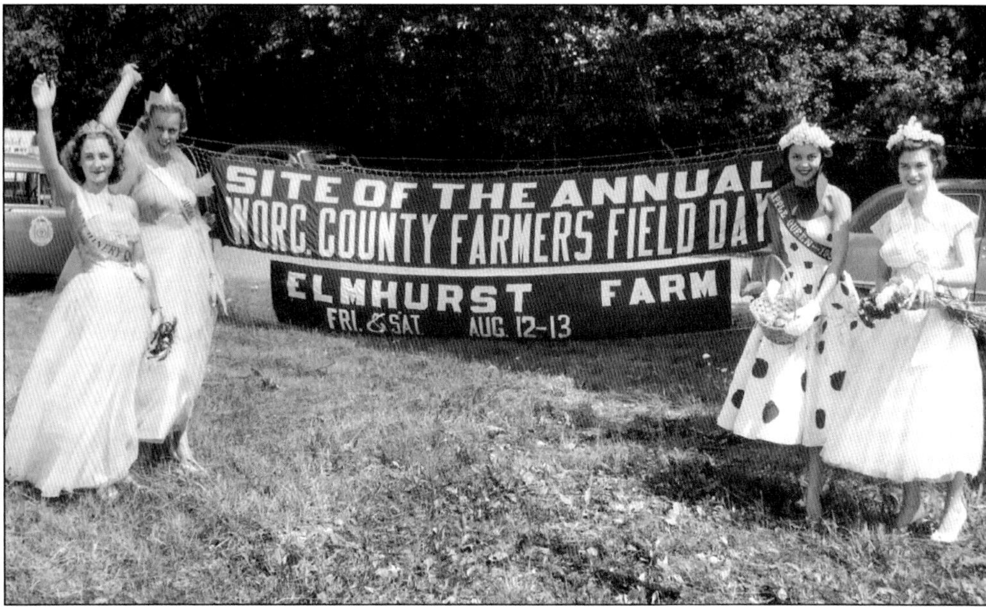

Farmers from throughout Worcester County gathered in the summers of 1955 and 1956 for their annual field days at West Millbury's Elmhurst Farm, owned and operated by Edward and Albert Fjellman. Events included horse and cattle shows, an oxen pull, and exhibits of fruits and vegetables. Above, the fair's four queens don their finery and broad smiles. Below, the Worcester County Electric Company has adopted a campy sales pitch to push its products and services, with "Chief Kil-O-Watt-Um" declaring: "Indian like 'lectric blanket 'specially for fall and winter nights ahead. Always safe, warm and comfortable . . . costs little wampum!" (Both, courtesy of Robert and Barbara Pearson.)

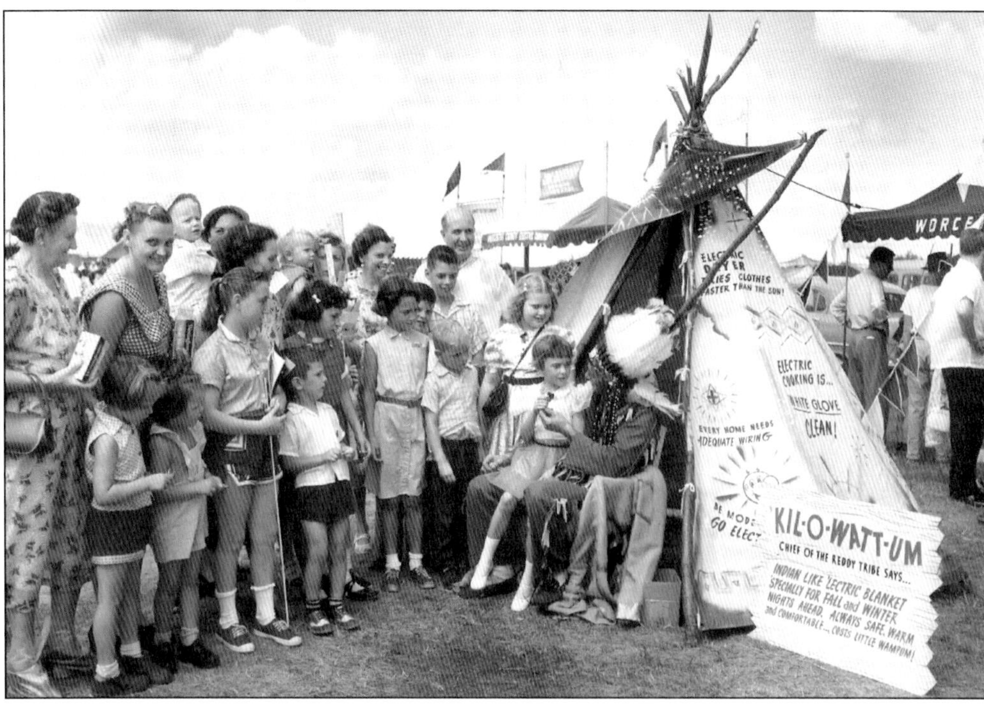

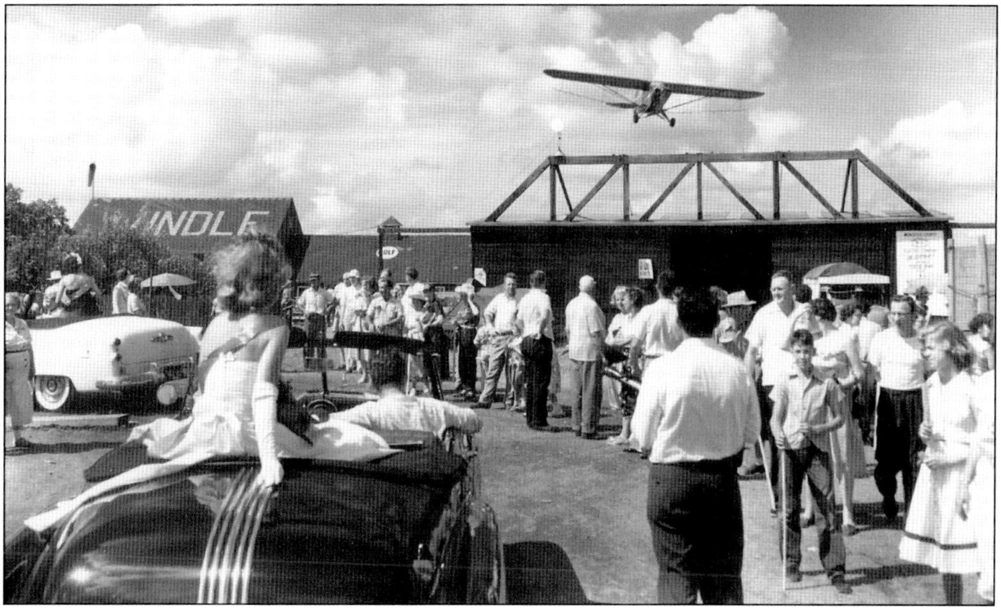

Countywide field days required lots of open space, and West Millbury offered plenty of that, given its rolling farmland. In 1955 and 1956, the event was held at the Windle Airport, which meant that crop-dusting demonstrations, above, could be held. Other events including water dowsing, a machinery parade, an ox pull, a horse parade, beekeeping demonstrations, a barnyard circus, a firemen's muster, a chainsaw contest, and sheepdog demonstrations. After dark, the crowds could enjoy a band concert, with dancing "on the green." Below, children are gathered around a man-made pond for some fishing fun. (Both, courtesy of Robert and Barbara Pearson.)

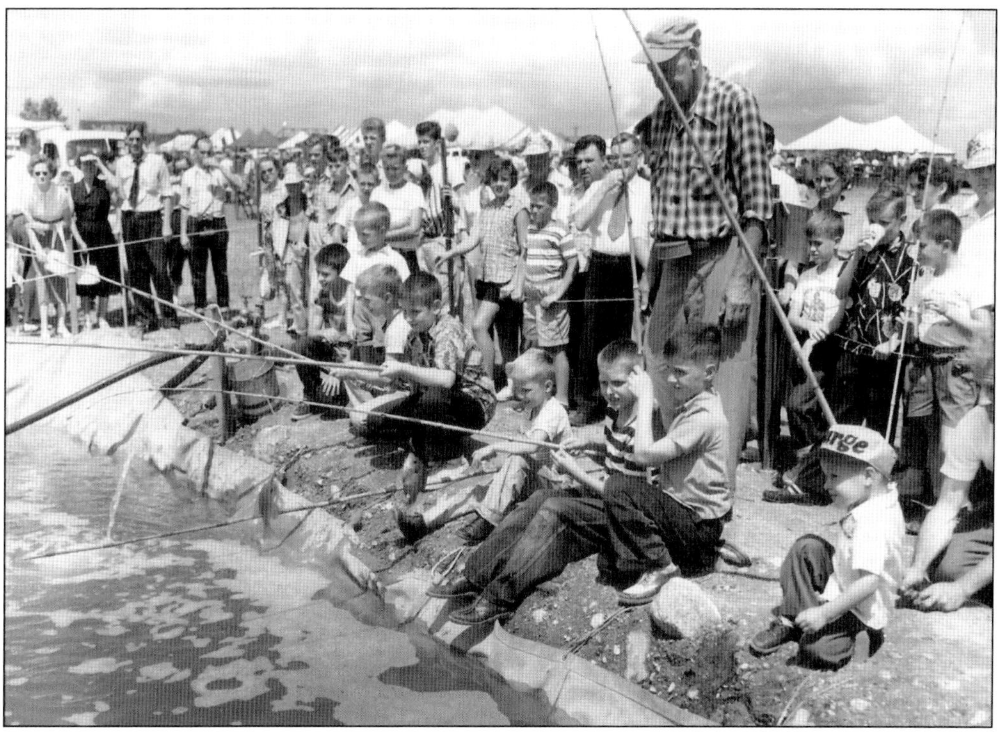

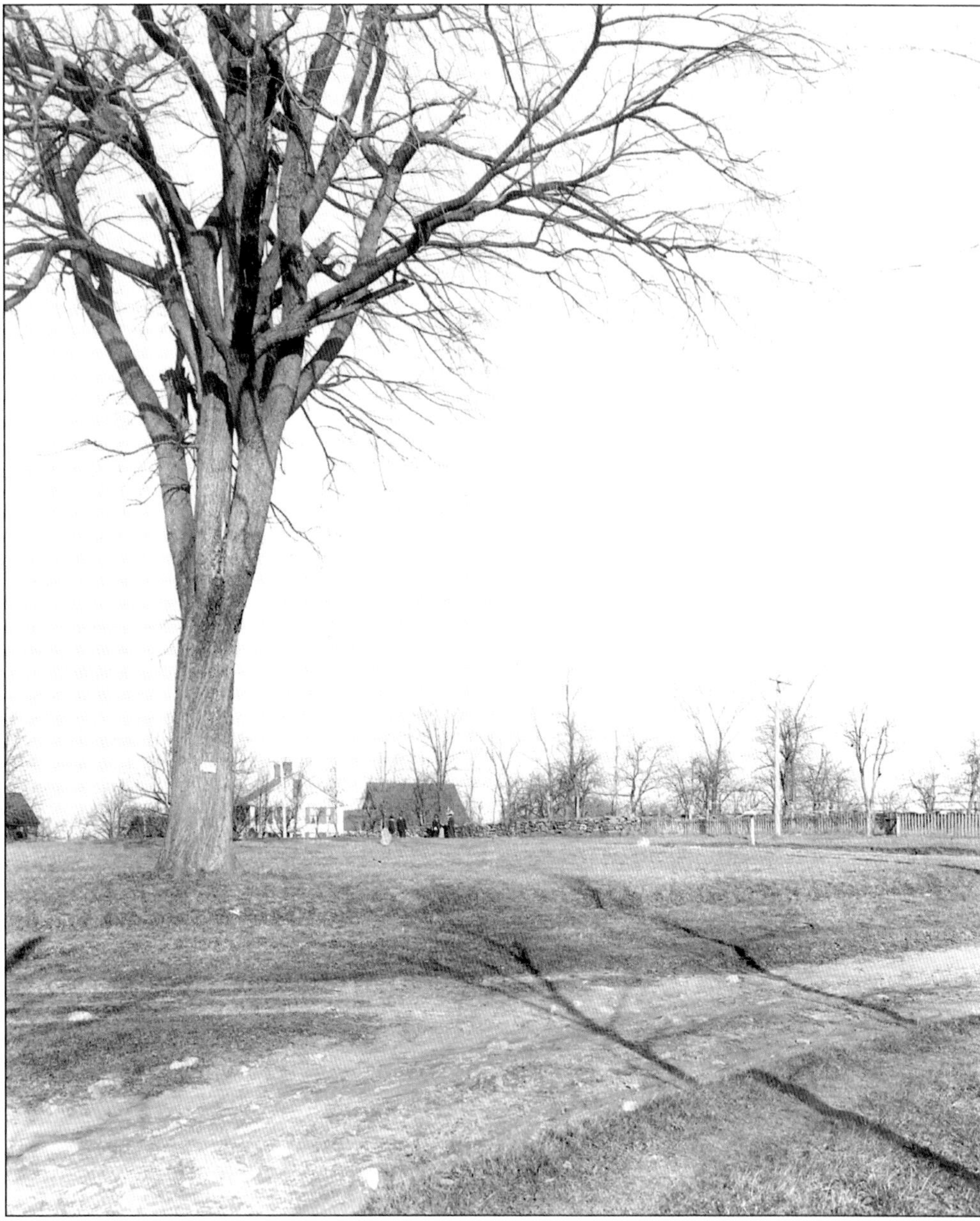

Isaac Barnard of Sutton granted the land now known as the Old Common "unto the Inhabitants of the Second Parish" on August 19, 1746, "in the 19th year of the Reign of our Sovereign Lord George the Second of Great Britain." At its birth in 1813, this land was the center of the town, with a meetinghouse, store, and several homes clustered around it. Later, the First Congregational Church was built on the lot at the right in this photograph, just beyond the stone wall and fence. In the mid-19th century, some small industries were carried on here, including carpet-making, a potash works, and the production of porcelain shuttle eyes vital to the textile industry during the Civil War. But the town's commerce migrated to more favorable sites along its watercourses, and Old Common is today, as it was when this photograph was taken in 1913, a quiet and beautiful residential area, a reminder of the past in the midst of a town that continues to grow. (Courtesy of Millbury Historical Society.)

Seven

SCHOOL AND SOCIETY

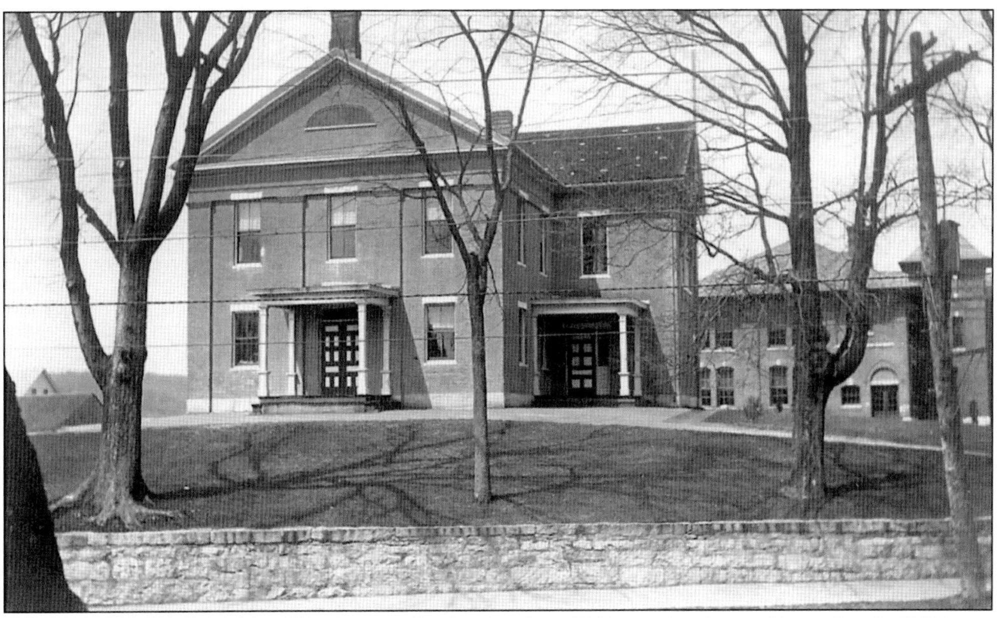

Millbury Academy, replaced by the new high school in 1914, was built in 1832 on land off Waters Street donated by Asa Waters. It was one of five such schools in Worcester County at that time, when Millbury's population was just 1,600. The first teachers were William Hall from Dartmouth College and Charlotte Spooner from Troy, New York, with 91 pupils enrolled the first year. (Courtesy of Millbury Historical Society.)

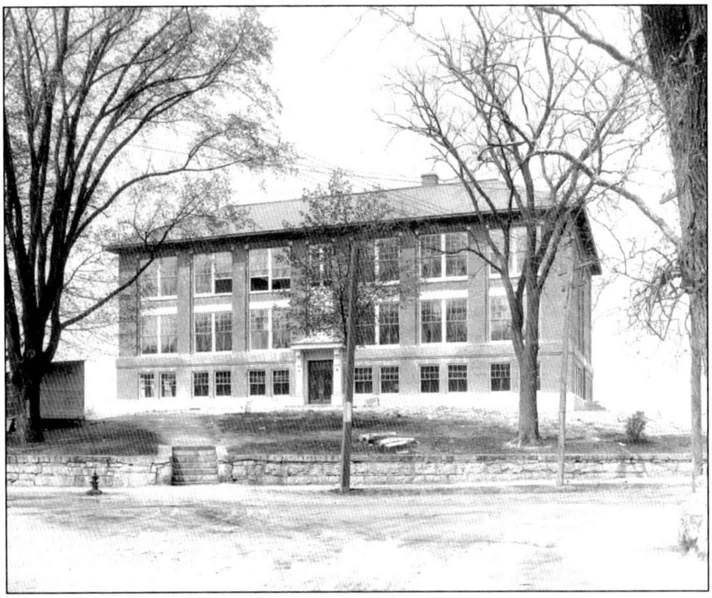

In 1851, a committee chosen the previous year to report on the feasibility of establishing a public high school recommended that the town purchase the Millbury Academy building (see page 109). As the town grew over the next 60 years, the need for a larger building became clear, and the new high school replaced Millbury Academy. The new school is shown under construction in 1913. (Courtesy of Millbury Historical Society.)

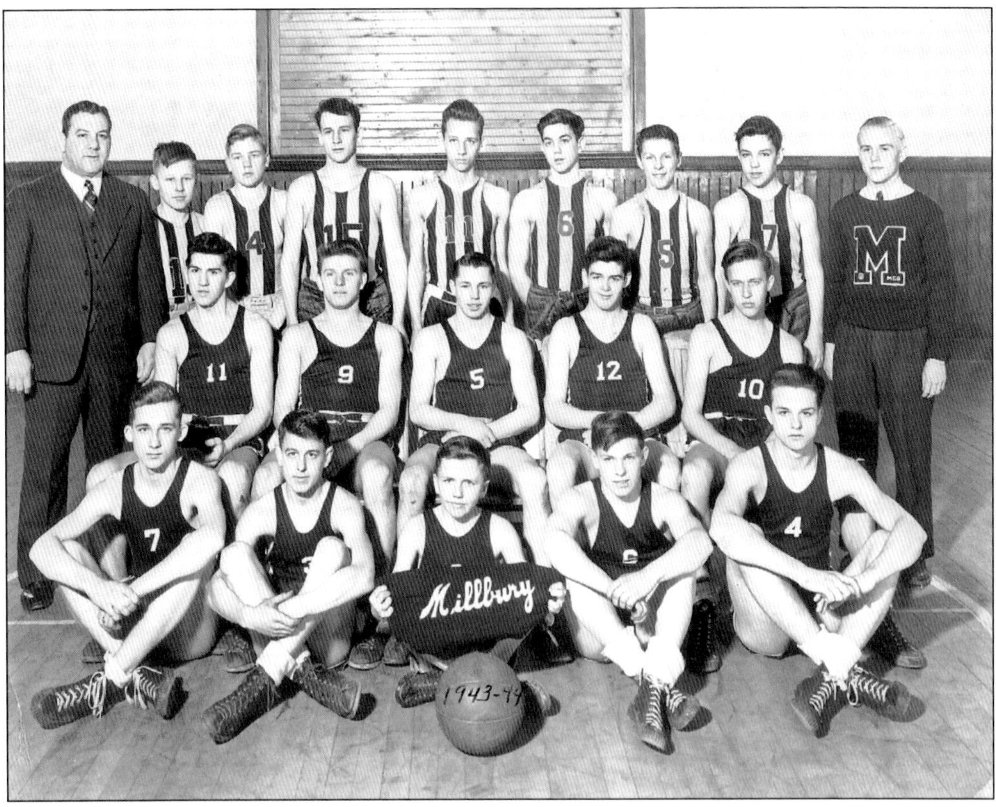

In this photograph of the Millbury High School basketball team in 1943–1944 are, from left to right, (first row) Donald Lucas, Eugene Perron, George Gallacher, Paul Aubin, and Dave Lynch; (second row) Roger Vayo, Rudy Pinsky, Russ Lachapelle, Roland Shepard, and Richard Brady; (third row) Mike Favulli, coach; Alan Ojerholm, Donald Moe, Ben Miles, Bob Lucas, John Barron, Bill LeClaire, Bill Murphy, and Charles Lindeberg. (Courtesy of Millbury Historical Society.)

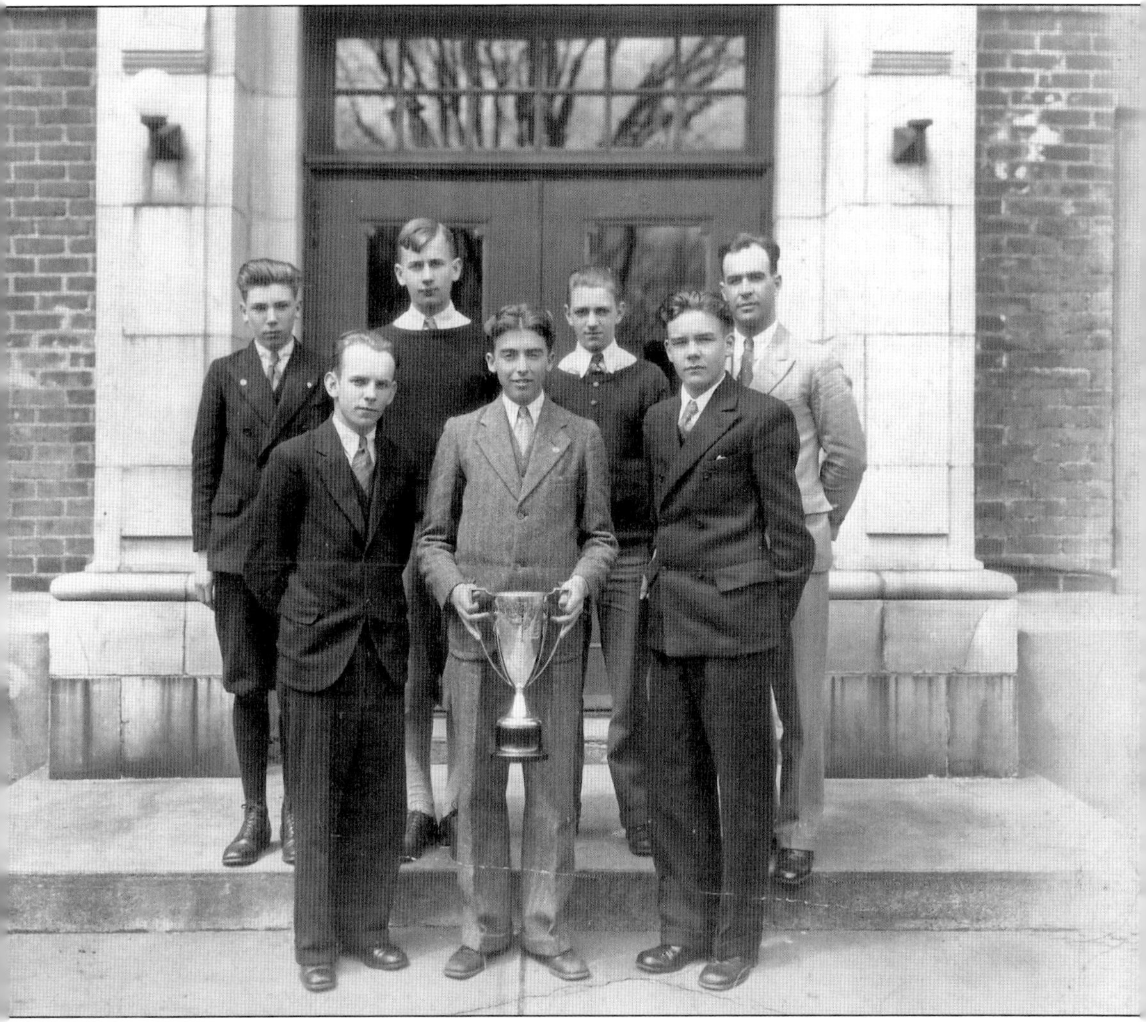

The public schools of Millbury have always struck a balance between academics and athletics. The athletic traditions were strengthened by the existence of the highly competitive Blackstone Valley League in baseball, which drew on the brawn of the mill workers and gave the town's high school players role models to emulate. The same was true for the town's intellectual traditions, for Millbury was the birthplace of the American lyceum movement, forerunner of adult and continuing education. In this early-1930s photograph, members of the Millbury High School Debating Team have gathered at the main entrance to the high school on Waters Street to display the championship trophy they won at an event held at Clark University in Worcester. Pictured are, from left to right, (first row) team members Chester Ethier, Alphonse Beauregard, and Joseph Stead; (second row) William O'Connell, Richard Montague, Lawrence Bertrand, and coach Raymond Shaw. Shaw was a longtime instructor in the schools; the Raymond Shaw School was named after him. (Courtesy of Millbury Historical Society.)

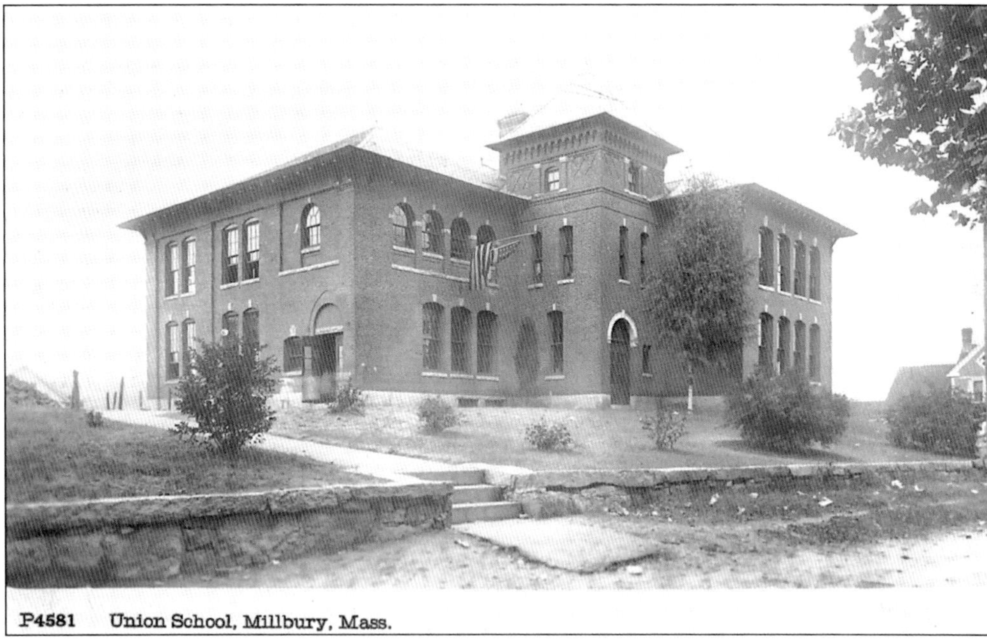

The Union Grammar School, shown here in 1913, was built on Waters Street, north of the original Millbury Academy. It served in tandem with that building and the new high school that replaced it in 1914. Years later, after the new Millbury Memorial High School was opened on Martin Street, this building fell into disuse. It was destroyed by arson in the 1970s. (Courtesy of Rich Hamilton.)

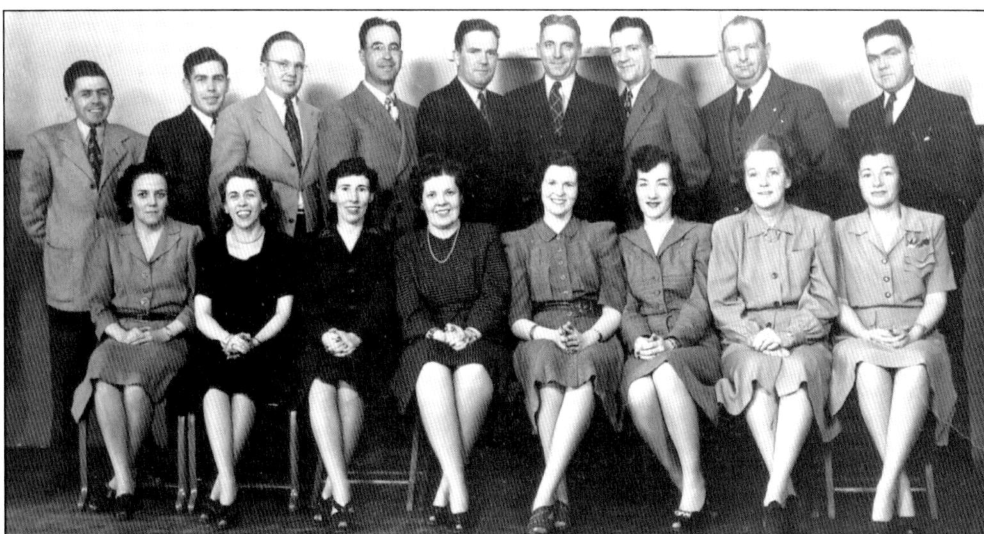

The faculty of Millbury High School in 1947 includes, from left to right (first row) Mary Grogan, Kathleen Burns, Margaret Donovan, Marie Walsh, Helen Brown, Margaret Marlborough, Alice Donohue, and Rose Massei; (second row) Harold Jannery, Richard Kenary, Paul Lacouture, Raymond Shaw, Martin Roach, Stephen Beaton, William Kinniery, Wilmar Ela, and Thomas McGinn. (Courtesy of Millbury Historical Society.)

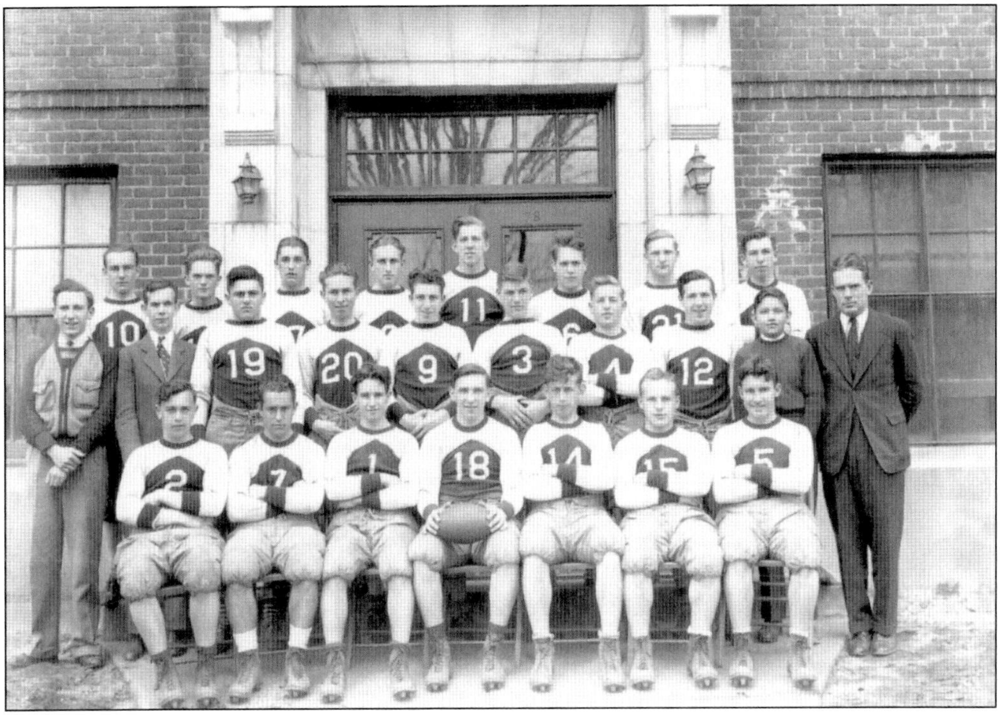

The Millbury High School football team of 1938 was the first that the school had fielded in some 30 years. Under the direction of coach Martin Roach, the team had a record of 1-5-1 when it inaugurated an annual series of Thanksgiving Day games with Douglas High School. The Millbury squad played hard but gave up a safety early and, after losing a fumble in the second quarter, surrendered a touchdown, enabling Douglas to record an 8-0 victory. (Courtesy of Millbury Historical Society.)

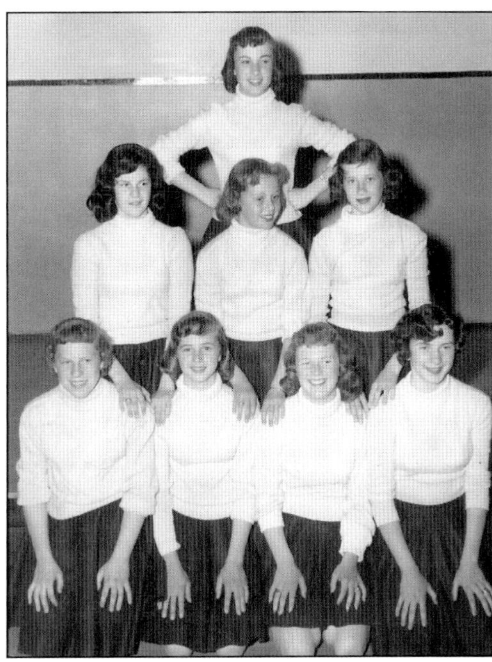

Millbury has a long and proud tradition of excellence in athletics and never lacked for spirited support for its teams. This photograph from 1956 shows members of the eighth-grade cheerleading squad. From left to right are (first row) Joy Gustafson, Susan Falk, Carol Healey, and Carol O'Lesky; (second row) Maxine Grenier, Ann Rutherford, and Jean Krumsick; (third row) Carol Cullina. (Courtesy of Millbury Historical Society.)

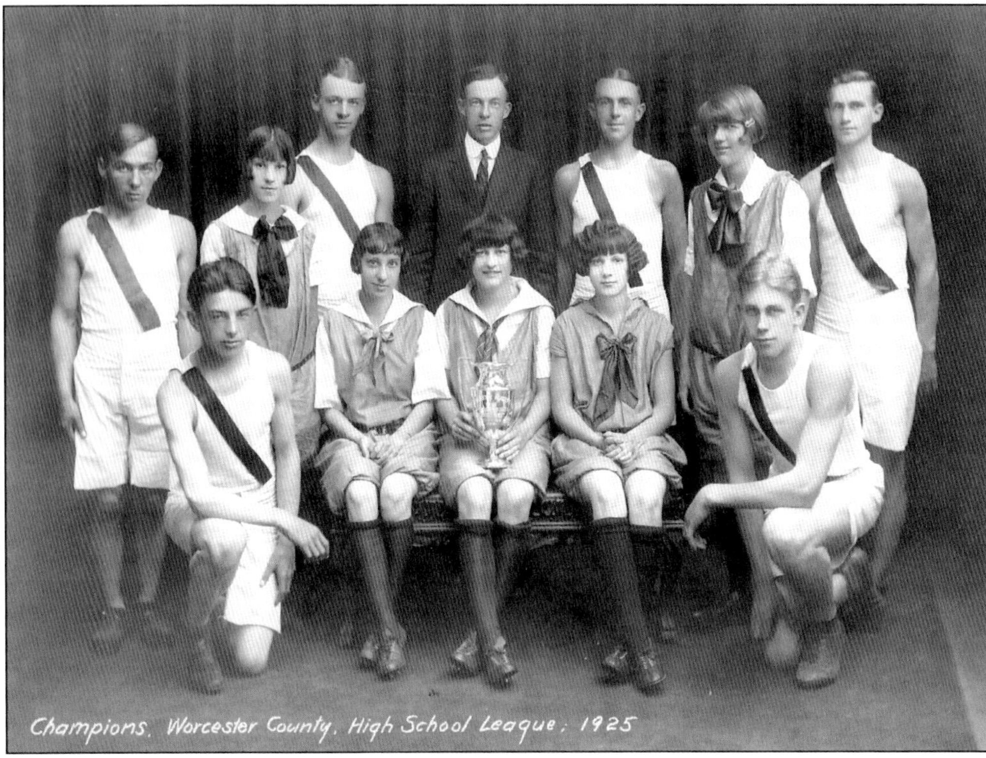

In 1925, runners from Millbury High School proved to be fleetest of foot, winning the Worcester County High School League track championship. Pictured, from left to right, are (first row) Daniel Murray, Claudia Cofske, Alice Shaw, Carmen Phillips, and Kendall Crane; (second row) Fred Fox, Hazel Hildreth, Russell Whitworth, Coach Pratt, Everett Crouch, Helga Jacobson, and Walter Brierly. (Courtesy of Millbury Historical Society.)

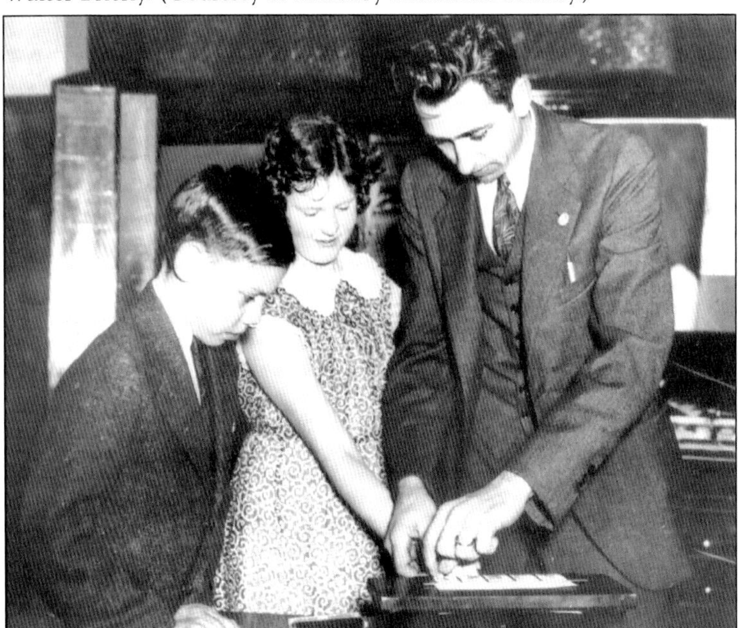

In 1934, schoolchildren in Millbury were among the first in the nation to be fingerprinted, a program undertaken in response to a wave of kidnappings in the United States. The *Worcester Telegram* newspaper ran this photograph of fingerprint expert Ralph Horne taking the prints of two eighth-grade pupils, William Tatro and Helen Brown. (Courtesy of Millbury Historical Society.)

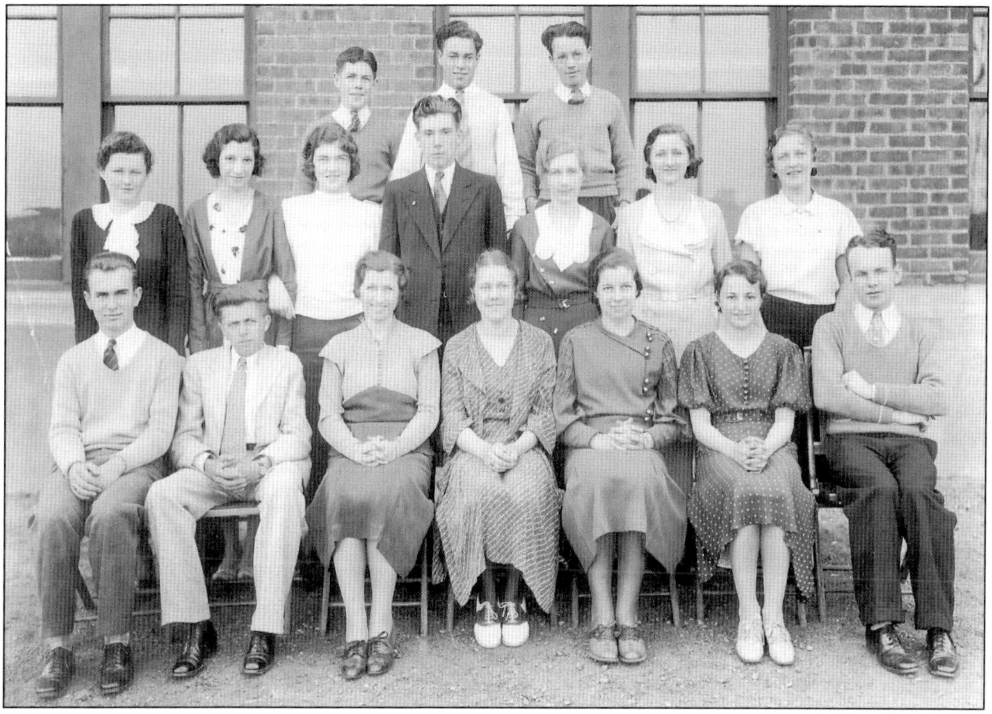

The staff and advisor of the 1931–1932 Millbury High School *Reflector* are, from left to right, (first row) Leo Gravel, Harold Jannery, Catherine Reardon, Alice Johnson (faculty advisor), Ruth Mannix, Elvira Paletta, and Chester Ethier; (second row) Ruth Higginson, Annette Fontaine, Marion McGill, William O'Connell, Helen Bacon, Genevieve Kersulis, and Olga Dalida; (third row) Richard Kenary, William Gibson, and John Sibilio. (Courtesy of Millbury Historical Society.)

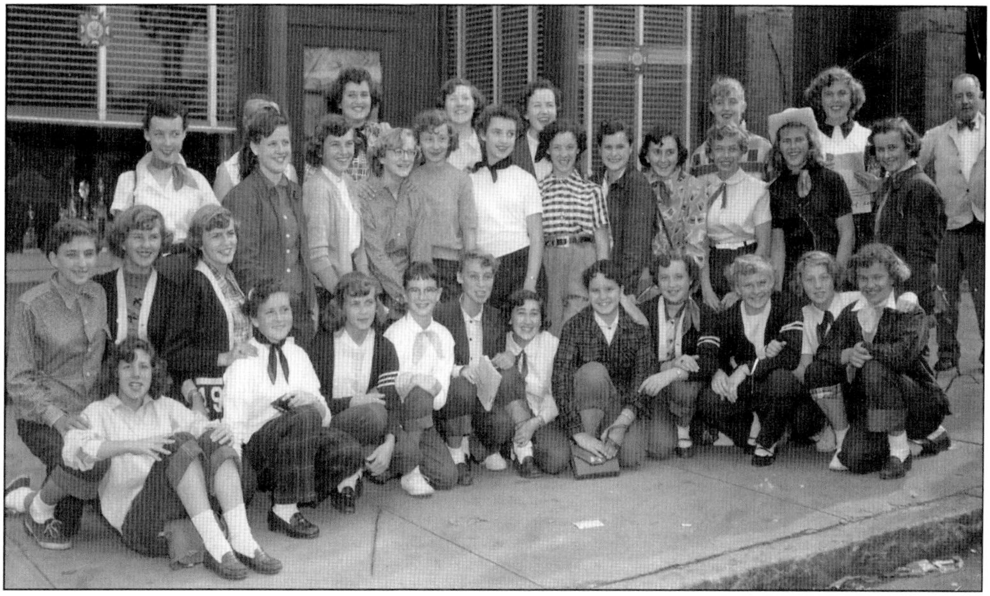

The Millbury Girls Fife, Drum & Bugle Corps won the Massachusetts state championship in 1955. Here, the girls are assembled outside the Veterans of Foreign Wars post prior to their bus trip to defend their title. (Courtesy of Millbury Historical Society.)

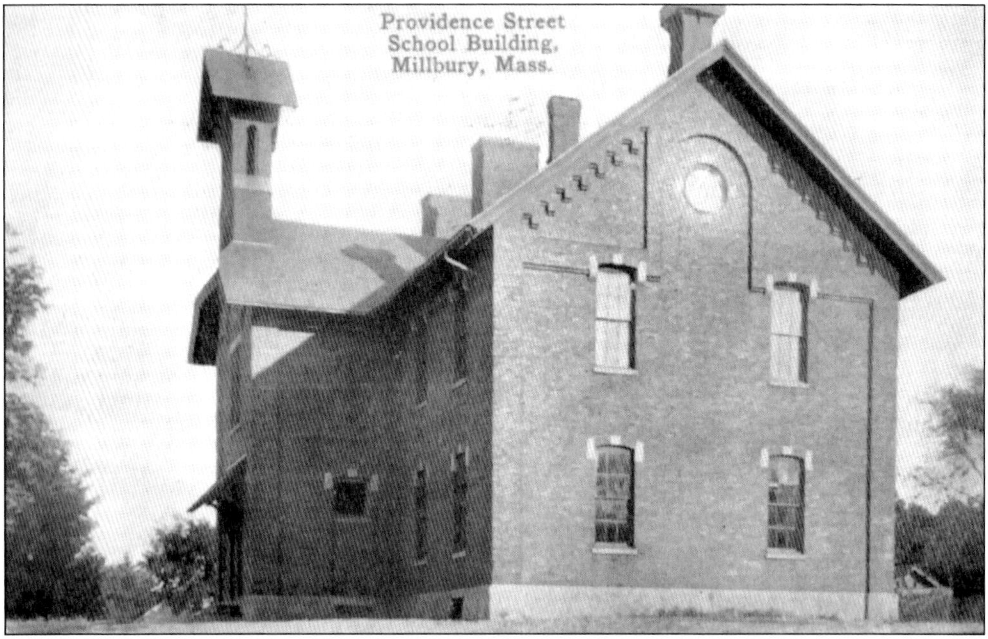

Today, educational expenses account for more than half the municipal budget in Millbury and many other communities. A century and two ago, however, school buildings, teachers, and curriculum commanded much less attention. Millbury's first schools were modest buildings and scattered about town, in Bramanville, Old Common, West Millbury, and on the road to Wilkinsonville. As the town's population grew, the need for larger and more centralized buildings became apparent. The Providence Street School, above, was built in 1869 and served generations of children, such as those pictured below, during the next century. By the late 1960s, the town laid plans to close these now outmoded schools and embarked on the construction of the new elementary, middle, and high schools that continue to serve the town today. (Above, courtesy of Chris Sinacola; below, courtesy of Millbury Historical Society.)

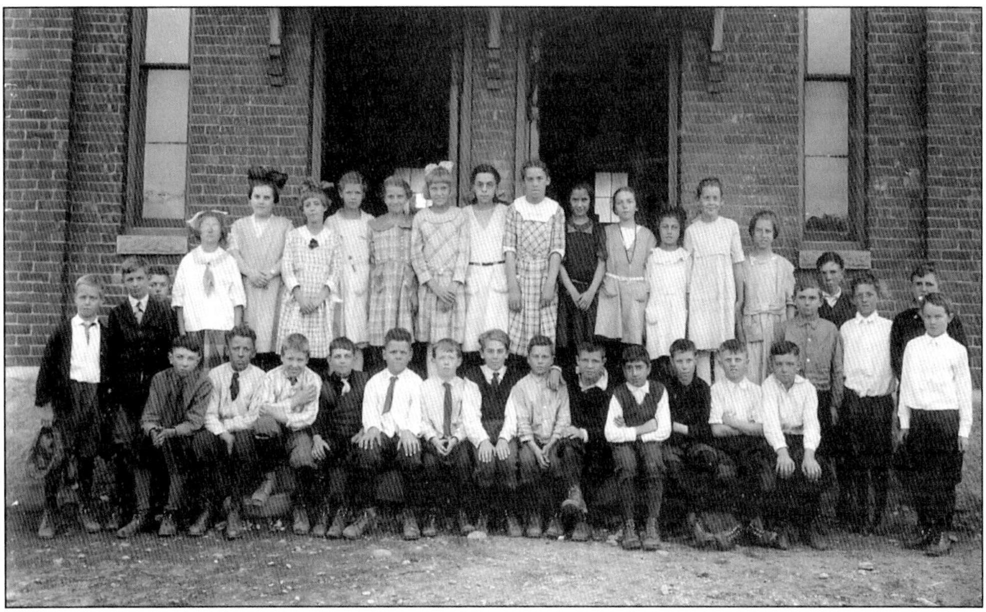

Eight

Church and Home

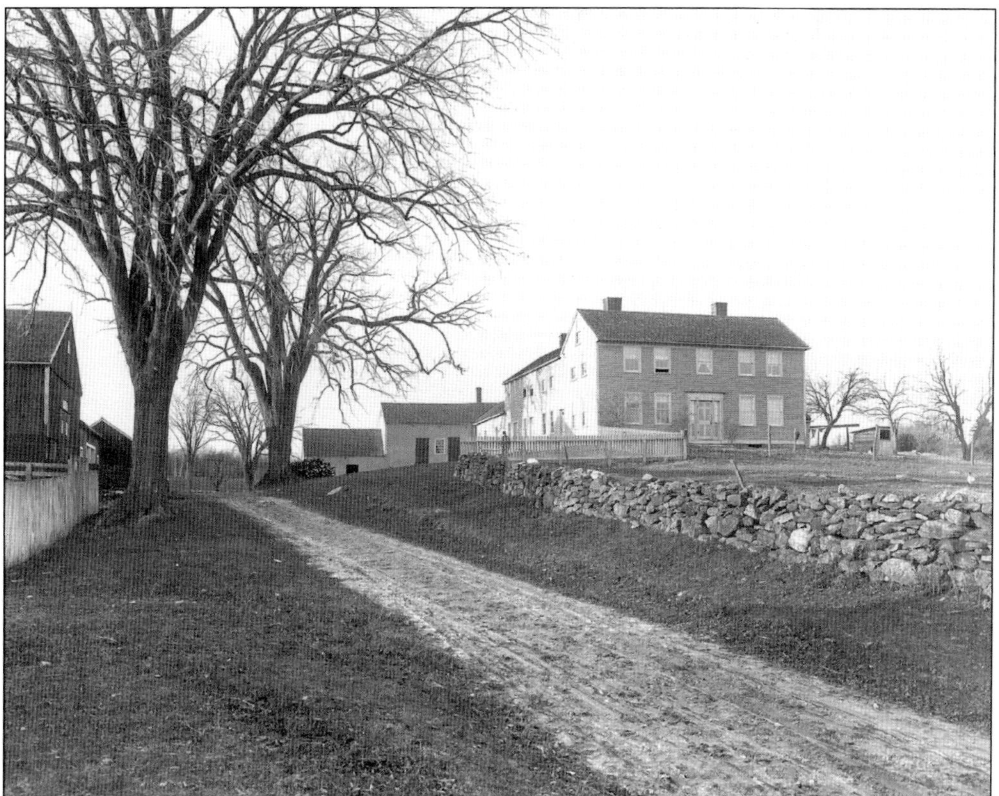

This house, formerly on Stowe Road, was the home and office of Millbury's first town clerk, Aaron Pierce. The *Centennial History of the Town of Millbury* notes, "Although at present [1913] this place seems to be too far removed to serve as the town clerk's office, at that time the Old Common was the center of town." (Courtesy of Millbury Historical Society.)

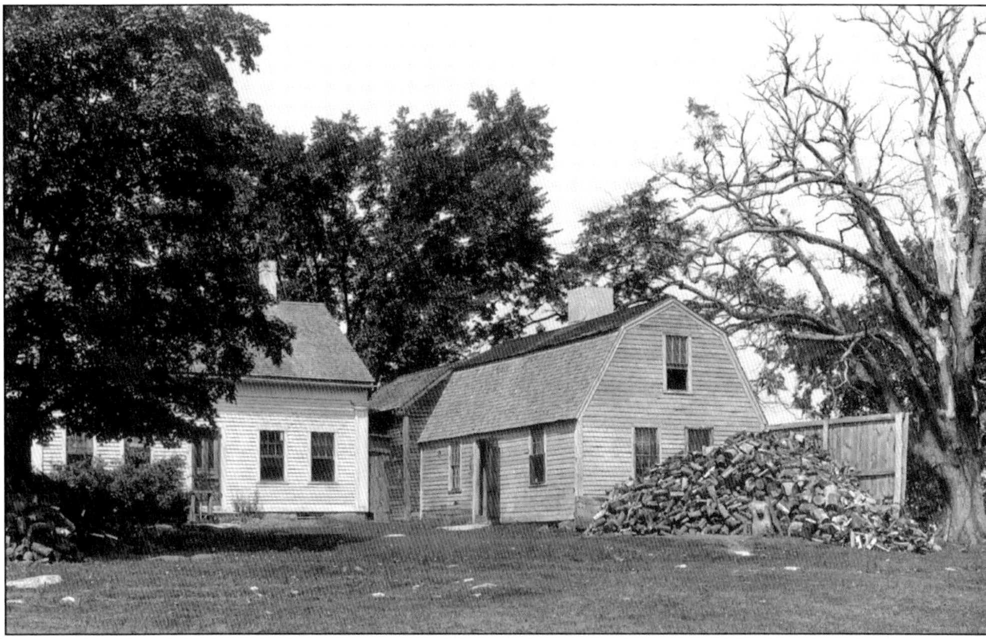

Josiah Bond moved from the Boston area and established a farm on Auburn Road in 1740. The Bond family grew and prospered, and Josiah and his descendants served their community and nation over the next five generations and beyond. His son Jonas served in 1779 on a town committee to work with the colony's committee of correspondence, coordinating efforts against the British during the Revolutionary War. (Courtesy of Millbury Historical Society.)

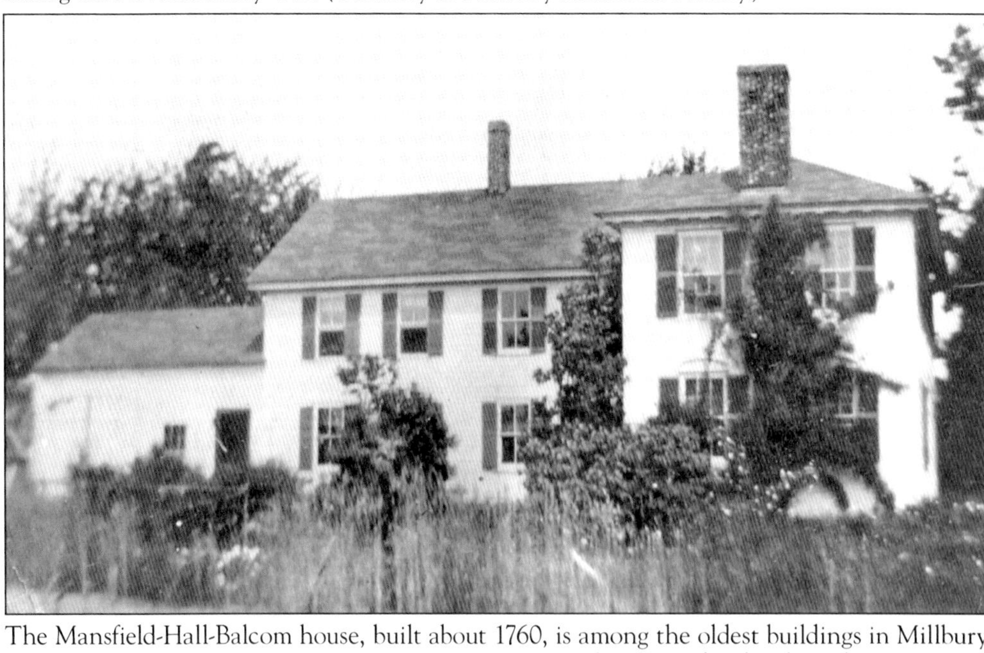

The Mansfield-Hall-Balcom house, built about 1760, is among the oldest buildings in Millbury. Located at the intersection of West Main Street and Carleton Road, it has been home to many families over the years, including, prior to the Civil War, that of Thaddeus Hall and his son Orson, who was at one time proprietor of the St. Charles Hotel in New Orleans. (Courtesy of the Hagstrom family.)

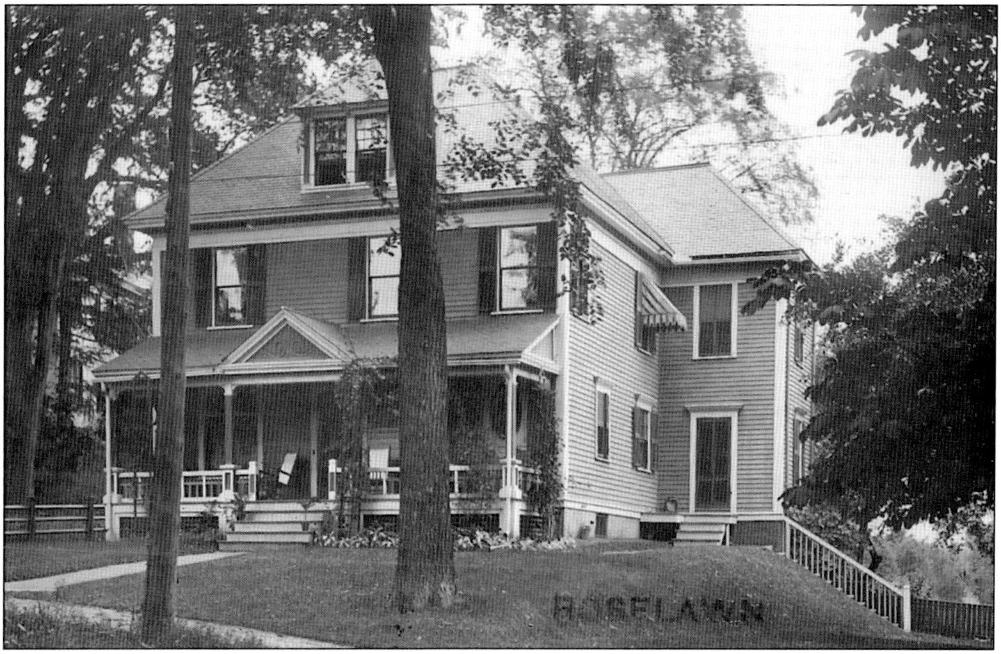

This house on Canal Street was home to Charles B. Perry, who served 25 years as town clerk and was a lawyer in Worcester, keeping an office with former US representative John Alden Thayer. According to the *Centennial History of the Town of Millbury*, Perry "is recognized as an authority on the laws and the rules of procedure governing town meeting." He also served briefly as a selectman and member of the school committee. (Courtesy of Rich Hamilton.)

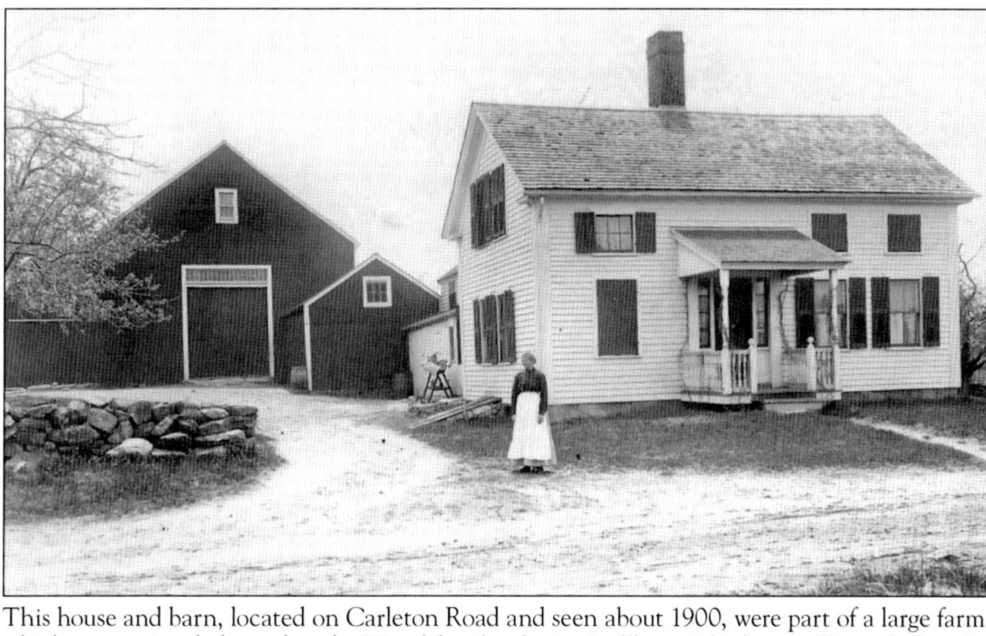

This house and barn, located on Carleton Road and seen about 1900, were part of a large farm, which at one time belonged to the Wood family of West Millbury. The barn still stands, but the house shown here was replaced about 1926. Reforestation has given this property, like many in New England, a much less open appearance, particularly as so many families turned away from farming. (Courtesy of the Hagstrom family.)

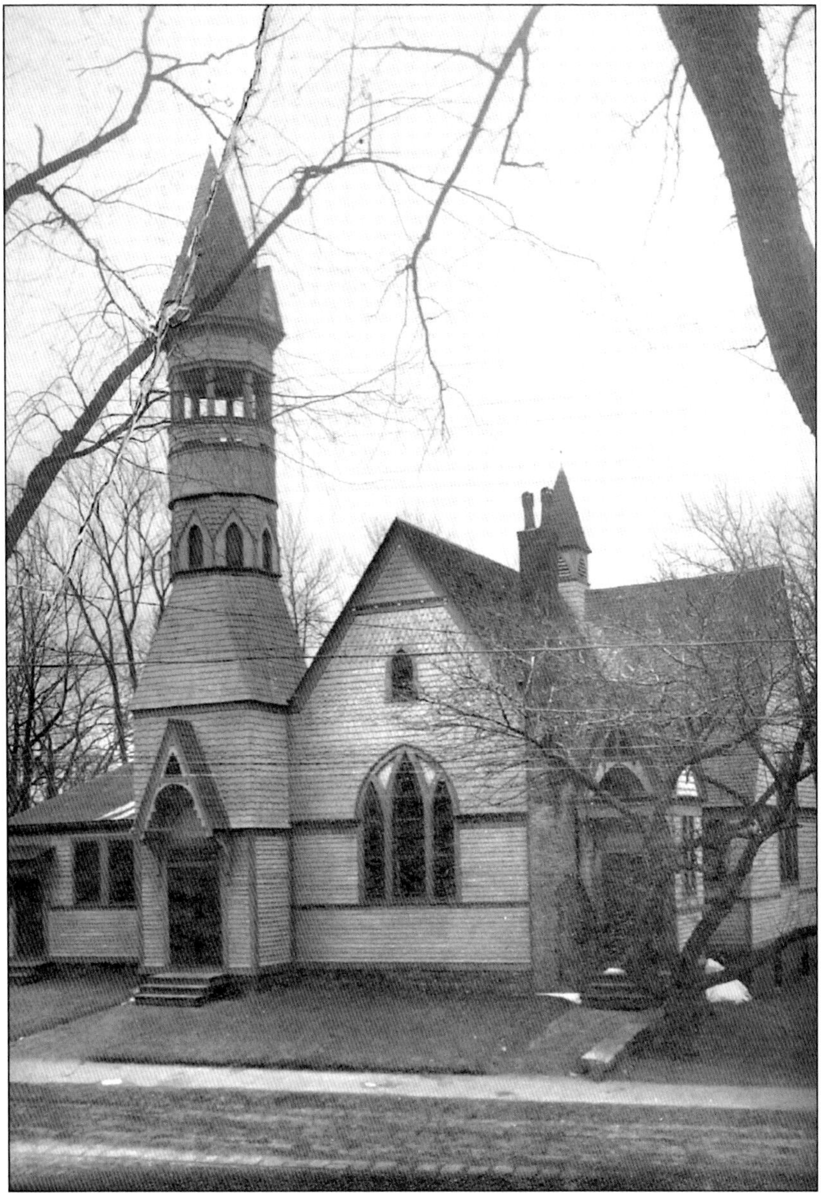

Like its parent town, Sutton, Millbury's early history was dominated by Congregationalism, and it was for largely religious reasons—a desire for their own identity, centered around their meetinghouse at Old Common—that residents petitioned for a new town in 1813. With the arrival of Irish Catholic canal workers in the 1820s and the ongoing migration of French Canadian and European peoples to work in the town's mills, religious diversity grew throughout the 19th century. By 1879, according to the *Centennial History of the Town of Millbury*, "at different homes meetings were held, presided over by various Unitarian clergymen." In March 1884, a group of citizens instituted the First Unitarian Church of Millbury, and a building committee was appointed three years later. That church, shown here, was constructed in the Victorian Gothic style and was dedicated on September 20, 1888. It was torn down in 1922. Located on Elm Street, across from Waters Street, the site today is occupied by the town's war memorials and also serves as entrance to the municipal office building. (Courtesy of Millbury Historical Society.)

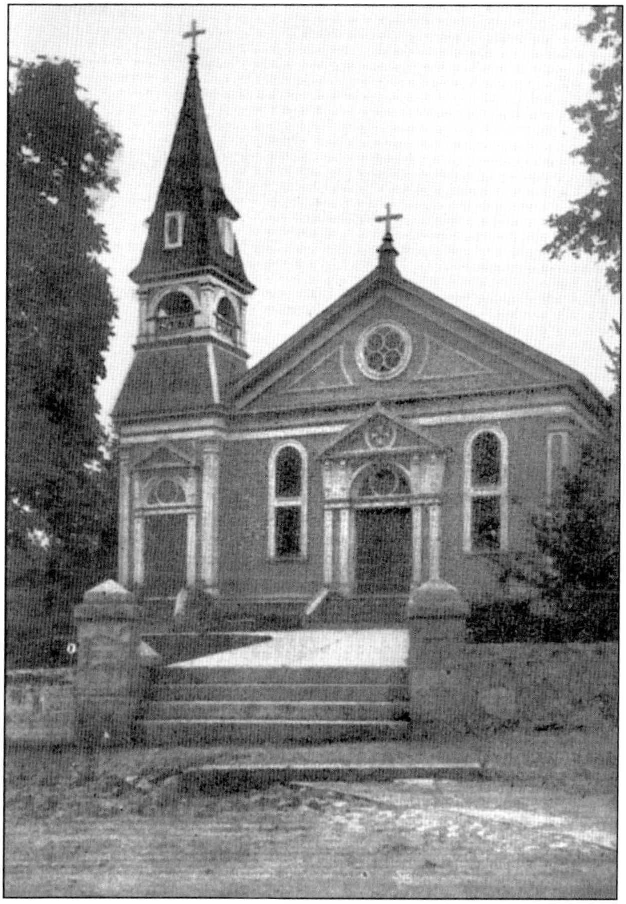

Millbury has long had two Roman Catholic parishes. The first, shown above in a view from the early 20th century, was St. Brigid's Roman Catholic Church, built in the fall of 1850 at the corner of Providence Road and what was then known as Dublin Street (now Pearl Street). A new St. Brigid's was built on Main Street between 1954 and 1955. The view below is from Our Lady of the Assumption Church, built on Waters Street in 1886. It shows the elaborate altar typical of Catholic churches prior to the reforms of the Second Vatican Council in the early 1960s. (Both, courtesy of Rich Hamilton.)

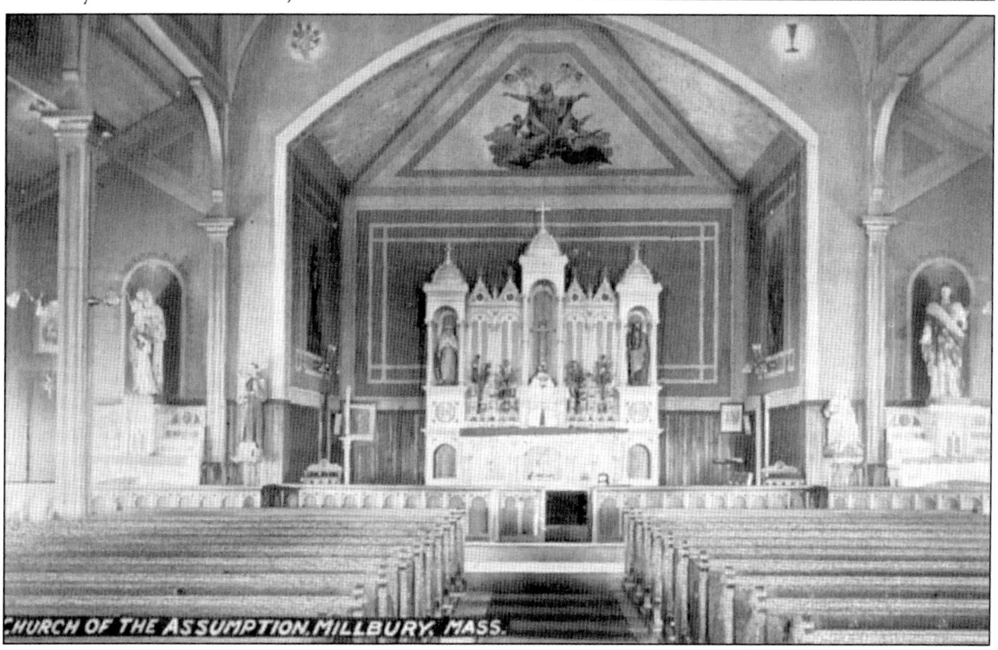

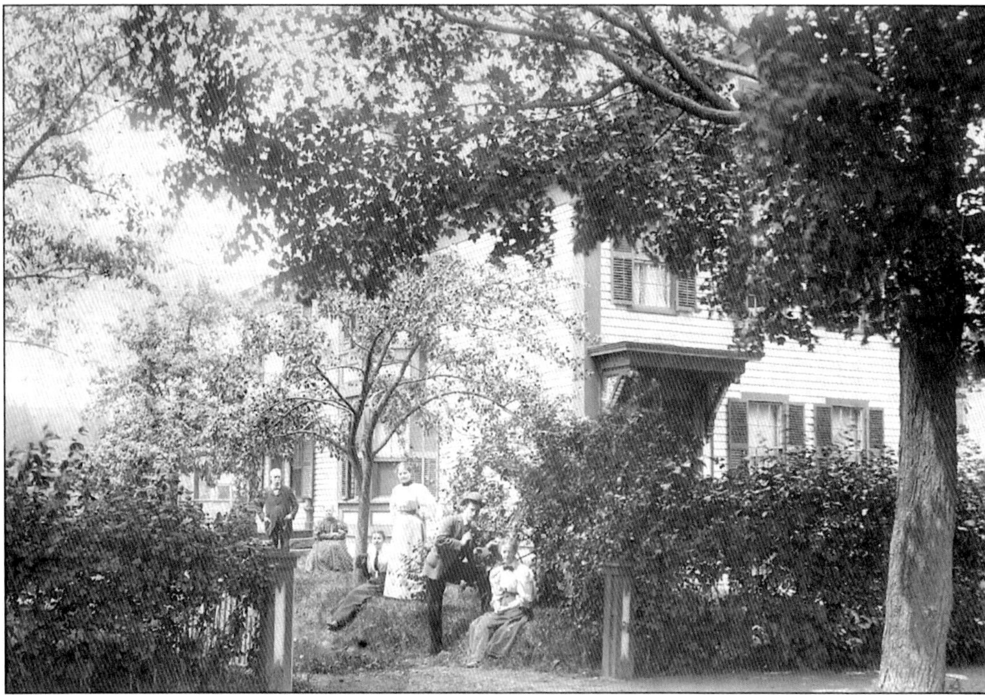

The Mulhane family has run an undertaking business in Millbury for five generations, beginning with Dennis Mulhane. The photograph above, taken in 1895, shows Mulhane in the background at left, with members of his family at their home on Maple Street. In times past, it was common for families to hold wakes in their own homes, often in the front parlor. Gradually, such services were held in funeral homes. The Mulhane family later purchased the property shown below, which continues to serve as the family business today. (Both, courtesy of Mary Lou Mulhane.)

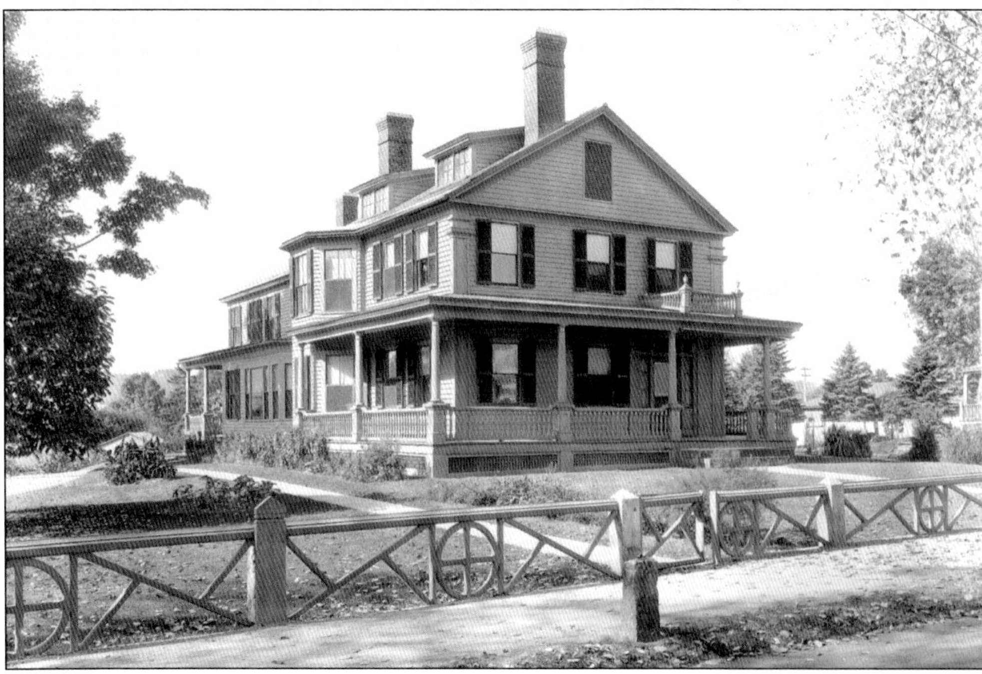

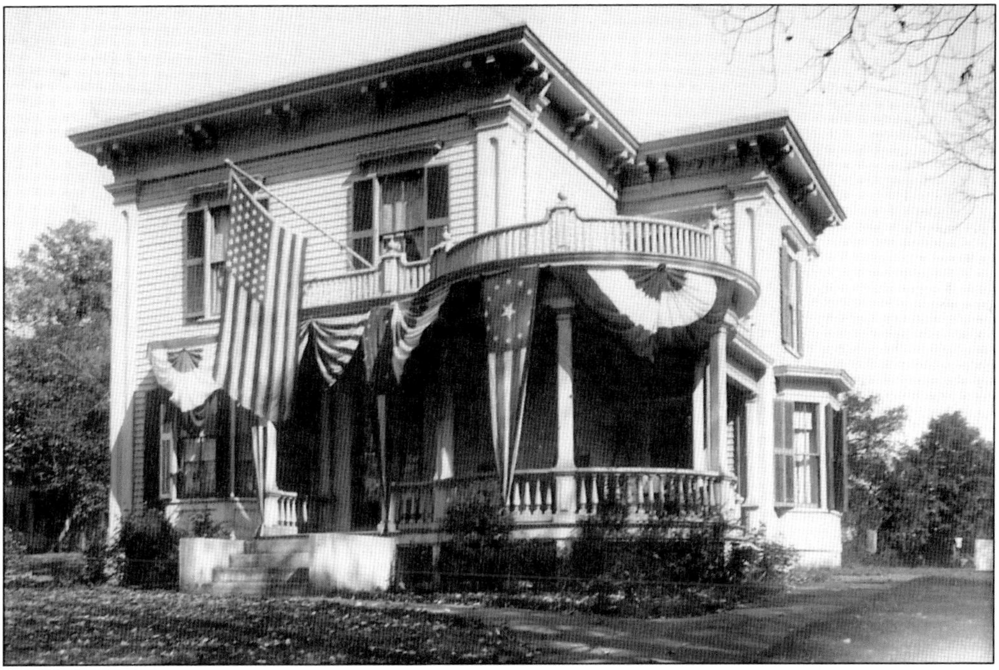

Built in 1860, the house at 74 North Main Street is a beautiful example of Italianate architecture. It was long home to the family of shopkeeper Daniel J. Dempsey, who ran the corner store at Main and Elm Streets. This photograph was taken on or about October 12, 1919, on the occasion of the town-wide celebration to welcome Millbury's veterans home from World War I. (Courtesy of Millbury Historical Society.)

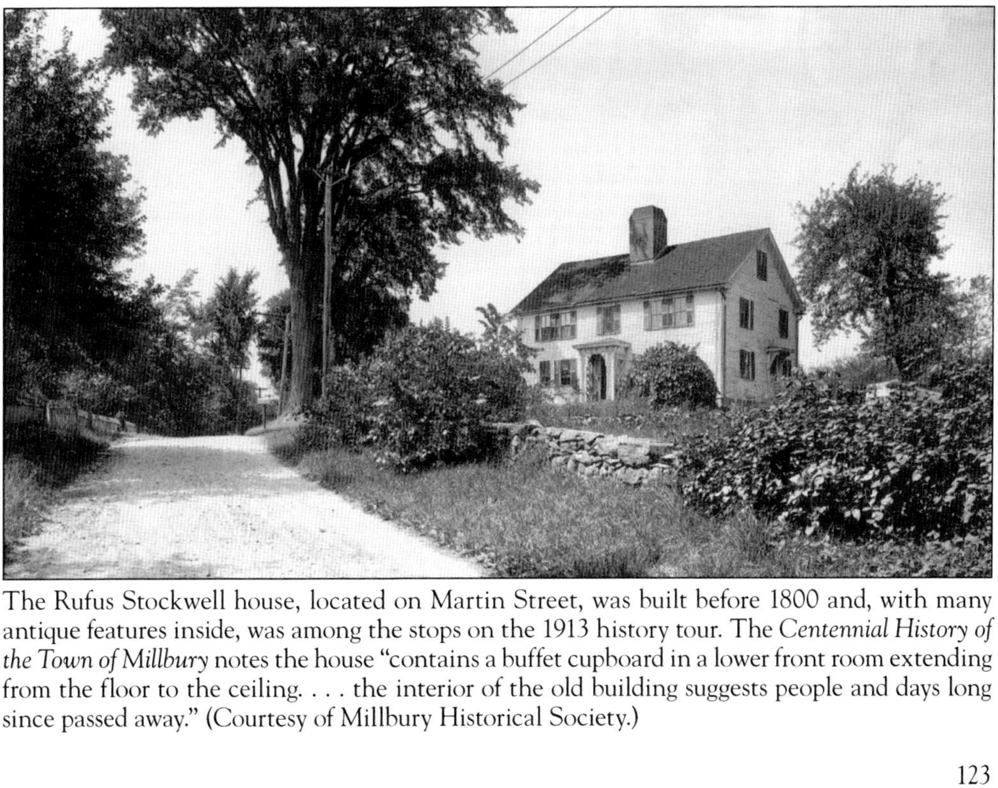

The Rufus Stockwell house, located on Martin Street, was built before 1800 and, with many antique features inside, was among the stops on the 1913 history tour. The *Centennial History of the Town of Millbury* notes the house "contains a buffet cupboard in a lower front room extending from the floor to the ceiling. . . . the interior of the old building suggests people and days long since passed away." (Courtesy of Millbury Historical Society.)

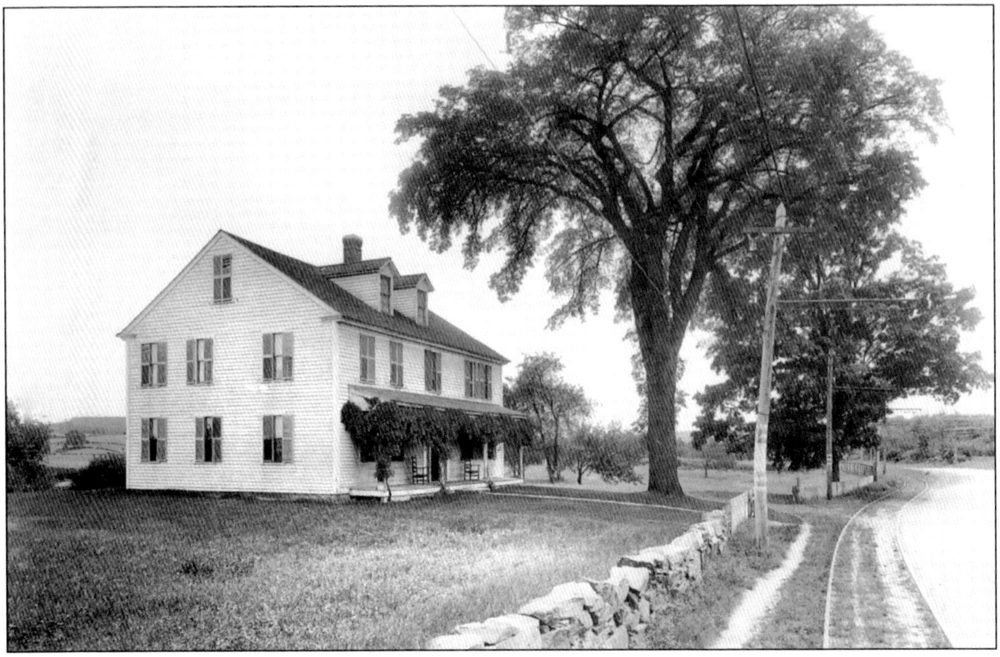

Samuel Chase of Newbury came to what was then Sutton in 1733, along with his father, Daniel "Miller" Chase, who owned a mill on the Blackstone River. Later generations of the Chase family lived in this home on Providence Street, along the Blackstone River. (Courtesy of Millbury Historical Society.)

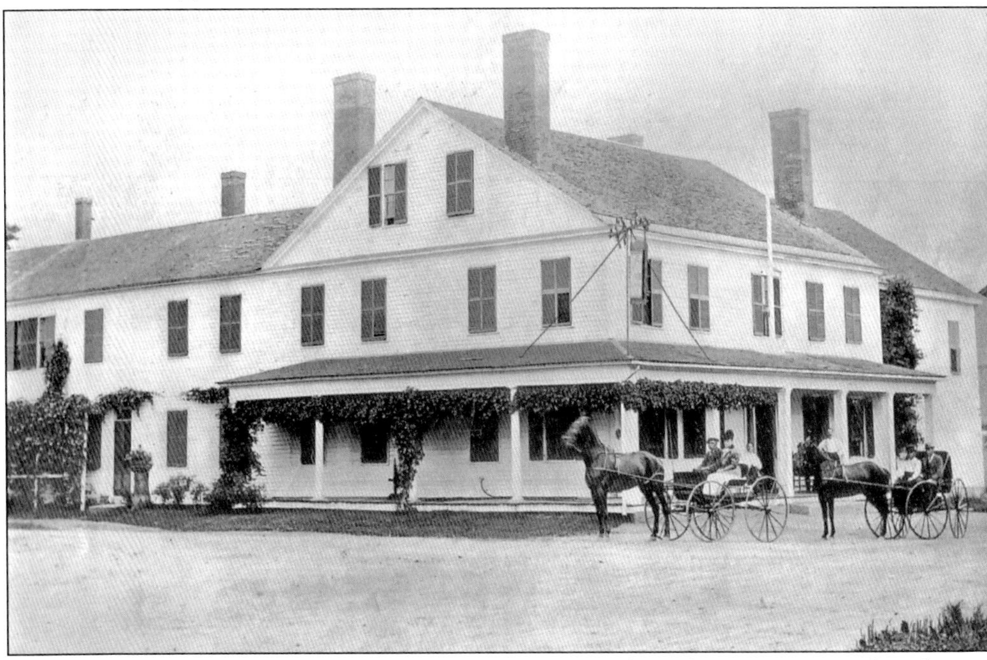

This house, which still stands at the corner of Riverlin and Grafton Streets, was long known as "The Lower Tavern." It was known a century ago as the Tourtellotte House, after proprietor Charles Tourtellotte, and was popular for dancing parties and game bird suppers. (Courtesy of Millbury Historical Society.)

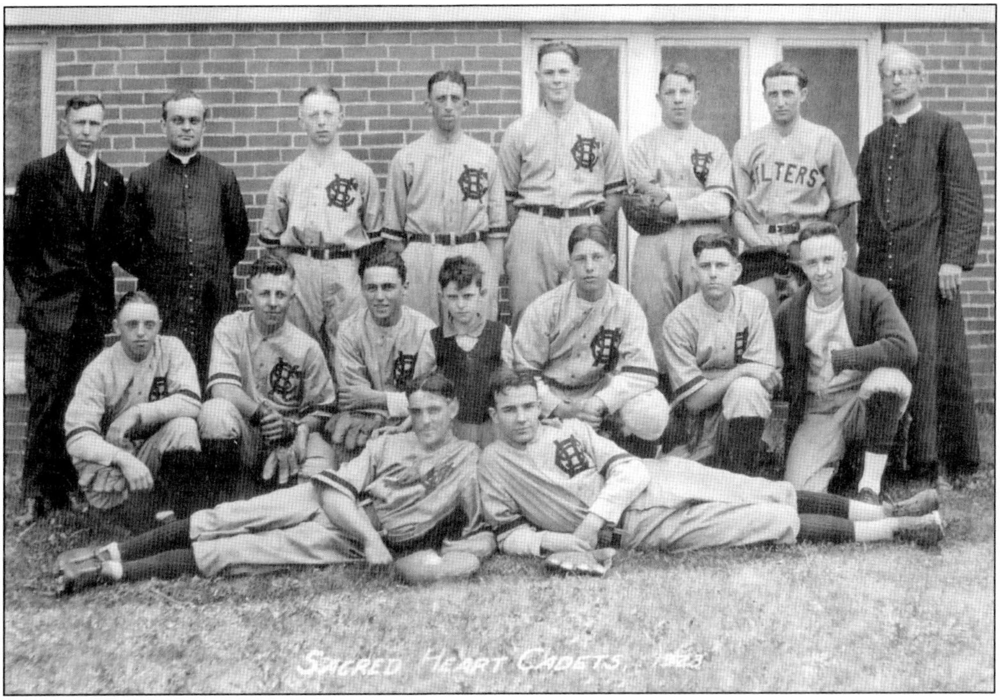

Baseball has been a part of the athletic scene in Millbury for as long as the sport has existed. Teams sponsored by mill owners composed the Blackstone Valley League, which flourished from the 1920s through the mid-1950s and counts numerous major league players among its alumni. Other teams, of all ages, were often sponsored by community organizations and churches. Above, members of the Sacred Heart Cadets team are shown in a 1923 team photograph. Little League Baseball, below, arrived in Millbury in 1953. Players and coaches of the Catholic Men's Club team are, from left to right, (first row) Wayne Bergeron, Terry Riley, Bobby Bernier, Bernie Holland, Larry Bernard, Richie Gonyea, and Joey Krumsiek; (second row) Paul Sweet, Jimmy Graves, Richie Jacobson, Coach Bill Caron, Phil Hodgman, Coach Mickey Aubin, Roy Pella, Gordon Modig, and Bobby Carrignan. (Both, courtesy of Millbury Historical Society.)

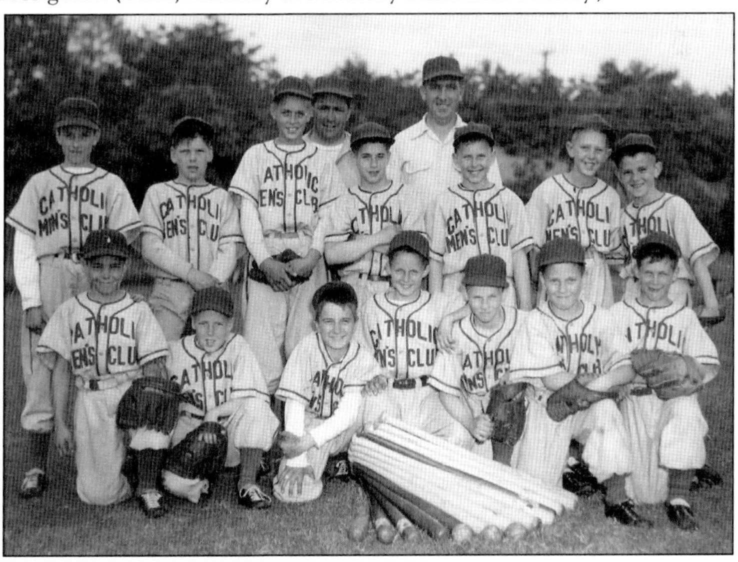

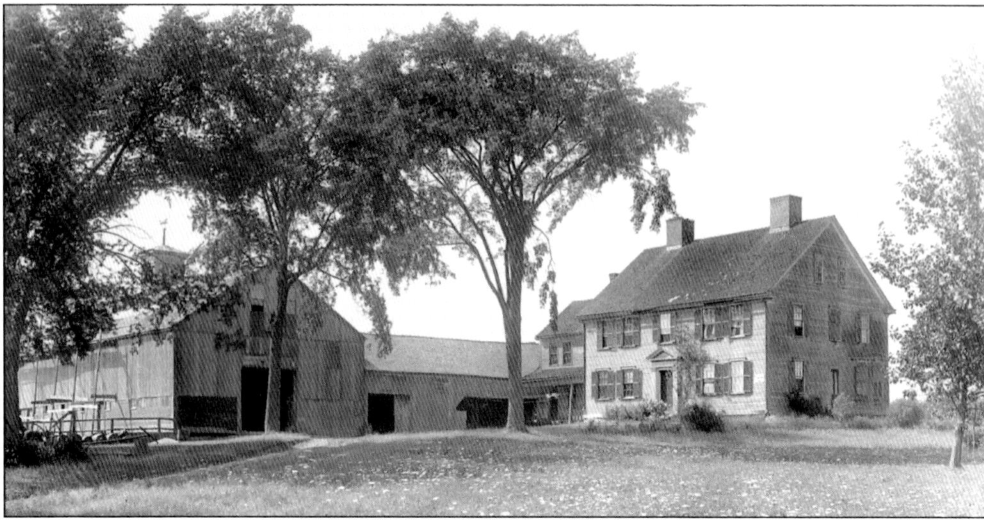

Born in 1732, Jonathan Holman became a colonel in the cause of American independence. He led a regiment that fought at the battles of White Plains, Bennington, and Saratoga during the Revolutionary War, and retired to his 3,000-acre farm and house in West Millbury, shown here in 1913. Holman, an ancestor of Pres. William Howard Taft, remained active in town affairs. (Courtesy of Millbury Historical Society.)

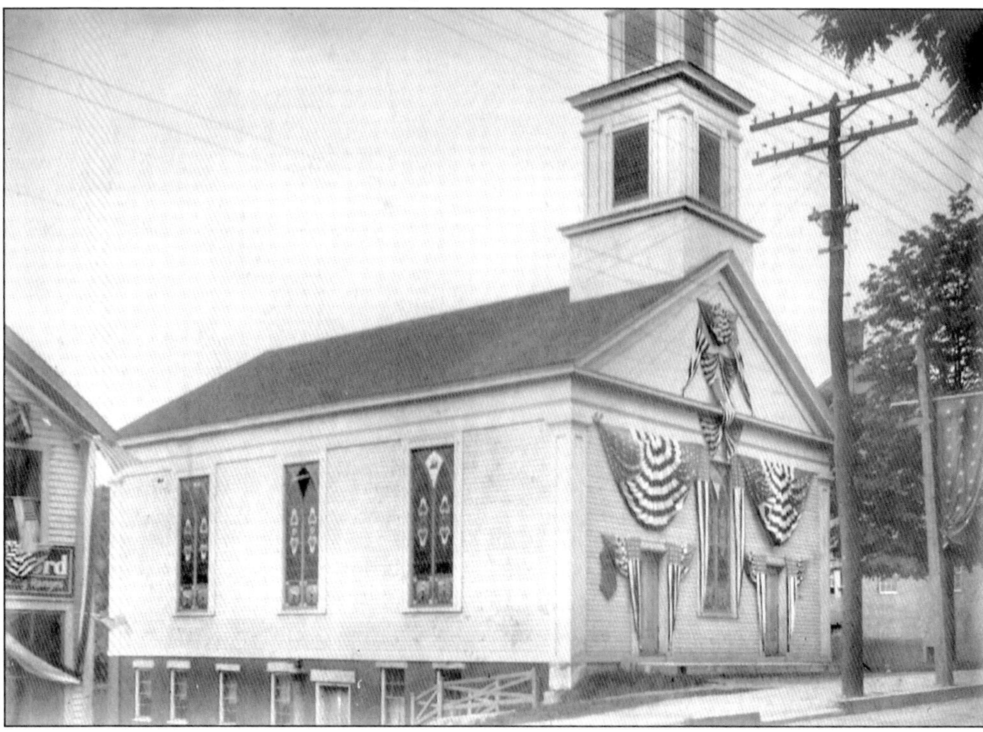

Like many New England towns, Millbury's first churches were Congregational ones, but the town has had many other denominations, including Baptist, Episcopal, and even, at one time, a small group of Shakers. This is the former Methodist Church, which was located on the south side of Elm Street, on the site of what would later be the Elm Draughthouse Cinema. (Courtesy of Millbury Historical Society.)

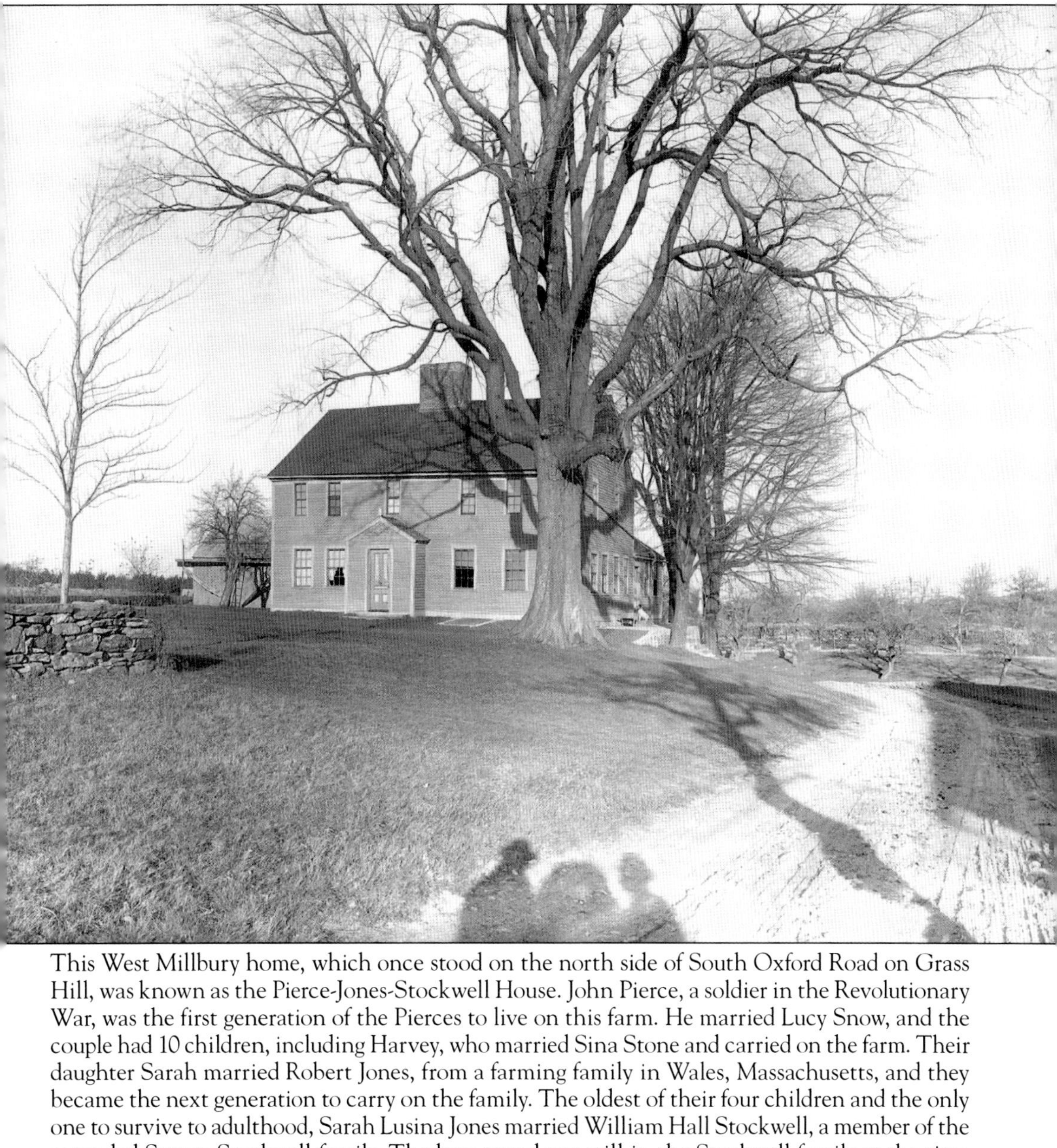

This West Millbury home, which once stood on the north side of South Oxford Road on Grass Hill, was known as the Pierce-Jones-Stockwell House. John Pierce, a soldier in the Revolutionary War, was the first generation of the Pierces to live on this farm. He married Lucy Snow, and the couple had 10 children, including Harvey, who married Sina Stone and carried on the farm. Their daughter Sarah married Robert Jones, from a farming family in Wales, Massachusetts, and they became the next generation to carry on the family. The oldest of their four children and the only one to survive to adulthood, Sarah Lusina Jones married William Hall Stockwell, a member of the extended Sutton Stockwell family. The homestead was still in the Stockwell family at the time this photograph was taken for the town's centennial celebration in 1913. The family dog can be seen waiting patiently by a side door, oblivious to the presence of the photographers, whose ghostly presence is captured in shadow in the foreground. (Courtesy of Millbury Historical Society.)

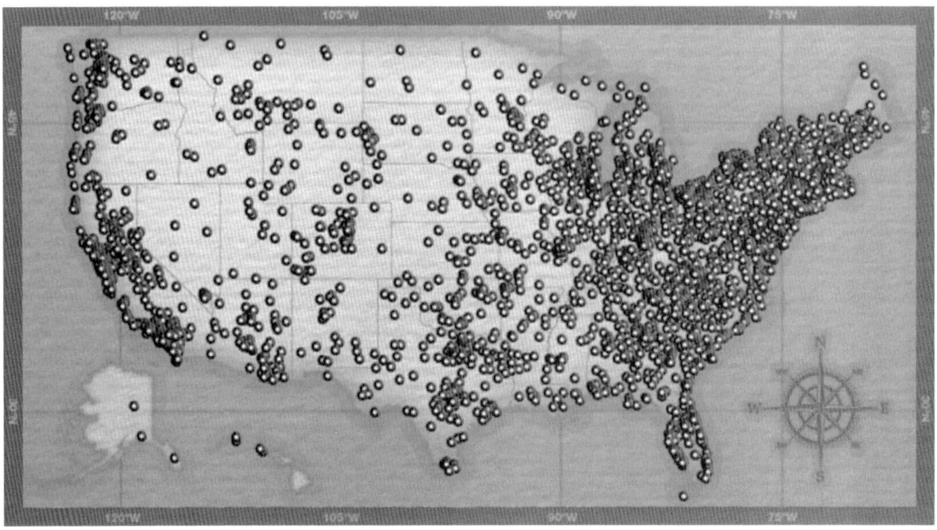